Fifty-Six

Fifty-Six

The Story of the Bradford Fire

Martin Fletcher

BLOOMSBURY

LONDON · NEW DELHI · NEW YORK · SYDNEY

Bloomsbury Sport

An imprint of Bloomsbury Publishing Plc

50 Bedford Square	1385 Broadway
London	New York
WC1B 3DP	NY 10018
UK	USA

www.bloomsbury.com

BLOOMSBURY and the Diana logo are trademarks of Bloomsbury Publishing Plc

First published 2015

British Library Cataloguing-in-Publication Data
A catalogue record for this book is available from the British Library.

Library of Congress Cataloguing-in-Publication data has been applied for.

ISBN: HB: 978-1-4729-2016-4
PB: 978-1-4729-2017-1
ePub: 978-1-4729-2018-8

2 4 6 8 10 9 7 5 3 1

Typeset in 11.25pt Garamond Pro by Deanta Global Publishing Services, Chennai, India
Printed and bound in Great Britain by CPI Group (UK) Ltd, Croydon CR0 4YY

To find out more about our authors and books visit www.bloomsbury.com.
Here you will find extracts, author interviews, details of forthcoming
events and the option to sign up for our newsletters.

To my mum – For showing me the light and making me fight – Still smiling x

Contents

Prologue

It was August 2011 and the opening home match of the 20th season of the English Premier League. Sitting back in my comfortable red padded seat, with legroom aplenty, I was one block off the halfway line at Arsenal's resplendent Emirates Stadium. Two teams full of adored multimillionaires marched out for a once unheard of but now simply untraditional 12.45 Saturday lunchtime kick-off.

The players lined up, but my attention was immediately captured by the banner a few Liverpool fans furled out, before the away end started to demand 'Justice for the 96!' It so struck me that I immediately texted my Tory mum in rural, middle-class middle England: '"Expose the lies, before Thatcher dies" says the banner in the Liverpool end – Indeed.' A few minutes later came her reply: 'I agree!'

Arsenal lost 2–0 that afternoon, undone by the trickery of Liverpool's elusive second-half substitute, Luis Suárez. Afterwards I met two old Warwick University friends and their dads for a beers-and-football chat in the affluent north London streets of Highbury. The night ended, as it so often did, with the last train out of London. As my friends headed back to their families in the Home Counties, I went home to an empty flat on a moonlit Wandsworth Common. Our odd bout of early season pessimism would be borne out the following week when Arsenal lost 8–2 at Old Trafford, their heaviest defeat in a century. Yet though it was a crisis, some of us who'd watched football since before the English Premier League party kicked into gear knew much better than to ever use the word 'disaster'.

Walking home that evening it struck me that it was thirty years since my own dad had started taking me to watch football. I was unsure what such a proud Yorkshireman would have made of his son supporting

Arsenal, but I knew he'd always told me, 'Son, you've got to play whatever cards you're dealt in life as best you can.'

At the Arsenal I'd reforged a bond that I'd been robbed of: there had never been a chance of beers and football with my own dad. As I looked up at the stars on that clear night, I smiled wryly. The moon cast its dark shadow: as with those Liverpool fans earlier, I was also in the shadow of English football's unresolved past – a whole generation on.

Part One

'The blue days of summer when Valley Parade almost became the valley of death are gone for good'

Jim Greenhalf, Bradford *Telegraph & Argus*, 24 December 1984

1

The Fletchers

'What about this one, son?' Dad asked, as I opened the turf-green changing-room curtains in the dimly lit sports-shop basement. Standing there, excited and smiling, he held up a tatty looking white polyester shirt. It had an ugly claret collar and an odd claret-and-amber stripe across its shoulders; there was no badge on this orphan of a shirt. It was no great surprise it lay unclaimed.

I was confused as to why my fashionably rugged, prosperous 30-year-old dad might ever suggest such a shirt. Being just eight it hadn't occurred to me there was anything odd in his insistence on visiting his home city of Bradford that Saturday afternoon to pick out my first football shirt for school PE lessons – and not Mum's home city of Leeds, where we usually shopped and where nobody would have stocked such a shirt. Dad must have cajoled the owner to rescue it from a store cupboard. I laughed when the owner brought it out, wondering what it was. I thought it was a wind-up. I was just waiting for the punchline to some joke.

'That's Bradford City, son,' Dad said, nodding proudly at the shirt. The shirt was actually new stock, delivered from Valley Parade on that morning, the opening day of the 1981–82 season.

'Bradford City? No way. They're rubbish!' I shot back.

Bradford had been trapped in English football's basement fourth division for all but one of the past ten seasons and marooned in its bottom two divisions for 44 years. Their best finishes in that time had been seventh and tenth in Division 3, or 51st and 54th in the Football League. They were shit and they knew they were.

Dad surprised me as, rather than smile, he seemed a little hurt. Mum said later she felt sorry for him as he pointed out to me that they were his team. 'Yeah, well, they're not mine!' I'd replied with the callowness of youth. But he persisted, hoping, no doubt, I'd copy him as I so often did. The thing was, I copied my dad because he was cool – he had the movie-star looks of a young Burt Reynolds, coupled with a Tom Selleck moustache – and this shirt, this club, was anything but cool. 'C'mon,' I thought. 'He must be joking. Not a chance.' I drew the curtain closed, my mind firmly made up.

But people often told me, 'Your dad could sell ice to the Eskimos.' So little did I know my first 'no' was simply his opening gambit, an intelligence-gathering raid to ascertain my objections and protests, before finding a way to overcome them. He was an out and out salesman at heart. Never accept that first 'no' – nor the second, nor the third. Keep on till that 'no' becomes a 'yes'.

I should have known better. On our way to Corinth Canal, a key Second World War battleground, on holiday in Greece that summer, I'd told him, 'I hate the Germans.' Taken aback, he explained the war was over and Germany, indeed Europe, was a very different place now, but I was not for shifting and it seemed Dad had given up trying to talk me round when, the next night, a tall, leggy, beautiful Teutonic blonde came to the table at our beachside hotel to ask me to dance in order to help out Anglo-German relations. As we danced I fell under her beguiling spell, and after a few songs she walked me back to my table, hand in hand, wondering, 'Did you have a good time?' I nodded enthusiastically. She confided that my dad had told her I didn't like Germans, adding, 'Is this true? I am German.' Smiling, I shook my head, assuring her it was all some misunderstanding. After she kissed me goodnight and went back to her table, my dad broke into a broad grin and asked, 'So, you like Germans now, son?' I've never had a problem with Germans since.

Weeks later, I drew the Bradford sports-shop curtain back open, and Dad was smiling again. 'So, you made your mind up, son?' he asked.

'Yeah, this one, Dad,' I told him, as I held up a nifty white cotton shirt, complete with black individual triangular Umbro logos trailing all down the sleeves, a red-and-black stripe running diagonally down the front – like on an Embassy cigarette packet – and a beautiful badge depicting a galleon that had set sail to an unknown destination beneath an azure sky. Below that a red rose lay on a white background, around which bold, black lettering proudly proclaimed: MANCHESTER CITY F.C.

'You're the wrong side of the Pennines for that, you know,' Dad told me.

But he agreed to get it, before picking up the Bradford shirt again. 'OK, but are you sure you won't try this on?' he asked. 'It's the right City shirt for you, it's just you haven't realised it yet . . . and if you like it, I'll get you both. Go on.' He winked at me.

It was a nice try, but he was up against his own son here.

Still, he must have been reasonably happy at my choice. Manchester City had played Tottenham Hotspur in that year's centenary FA Cup final. In an era where the FA Cup final was the only English club match televised live, the afternoon saw red-blooded Englishmen glued to their TV sets across the land. That May Dad had invited friends round and told me I could watch it with them, but only if I supported 'the northern team'.

As the brass band had played the traditional FA Cup final hymn, 'Abide With Me', on the Wembley pitch, Mum brought in some chilled cans of beer. There were several spare, clearly enough to last the half. As they stood on the carpet, by the couch, I adopted Dad's favourite adage: 'If you don't ask, you don't get.' So, pointing at the cans, a cheeky smile on my face, I asked, 'Dad, can I have one?' He almost spat his beer out, and told me, 'No, son, you can't!'

But the laughter that filled the room simply encouraged me further: 'Why not, Dad? Everyone else is having one and it's Cup final day.'

'Your mother wouldn't like it,' was the best he could come up with.

I persisted. 'But if you don't tell her, well, I won't!' I winked.

The young, appreciative crowd were now beside themselves in hysterics, urging Dad to let me have a sip. Playing to the room, I made some comment about him saying he always wanted me to be 'one of the boys'.

So Dad gingerly passed me my first ever beer, and after I'd opened the can and taken my first sip of this mysteriously pungent and overpowering concoction, he asked me what I thought.

It was strong, for sure, but I was not going to lose face now. I told him, 'It's great, Dad, can I keep it?'

'OK, son,' he said, but told me to keep it hidden from view in case Mum came in.

I hid it by the blindside of my chair, taking little sips during a first half that saw Manchester City take the lead with a flying Tommy Hutchison header.

The second half started. I wondered if I could have another beer.

'Are you being serious!' Dad asked in his best John McEnroe voice. 'Are you sure you're feeling OK?' Laughter once more filled the room. Then, incredibly, he handed me a second can. 'Don't drink it too quickly,' he told me, and, thinking back, I'm sure he was weighing up me puking over the carpet (hence trouble with Mum) with a bit of father–son bonding, working up the double act we'd become.

It was certainly a liberal attitude to alcohol, but our young parents must have decided that when we drank for the first time they'd rather we did it safely at home, than with friends on some wasteland. My sips slowed, and though I remember Glenn Hoddle's free-kick with 11 minutes left – which Manchester City goalkeeper Joe Corrigan had covered, till it cruelly deflected off Tommy Hutchison's head into the opposite corner – I fell asleep and woke disappointed to find the Cup final over and all Dad's mates gone.

Little did I know that my first beers watching football with my dad would be my last.

Once I'd chosen the shirt of the team he'd told me to support, Dad must have known he'd soon have me cheering on the right City, his City. So was it any wonder he was grinning as he paid? He knew I was under his, and football's, laddish spell.

Dad had fallen under the spell of Bradford City at Hanson Grammar School where, in the appropriately named Bank Top district, his classrooms offered a fine vista over the bowl of a city in which he'd grown up, enclosed by three, all-encompassing valley slopes. Two miles away, where the opposite valley began to rise, was an odd little three-sided football ground, over which four floodlight pylons towered. It was not long before his own curiosity struck, and Dad visited Valley Parade with some school friends, who included future Yorkshire cricketer David Bairstow, and Dad's younger brother Peter, who'd pestered their mum to go along too.

Dad adored the valley where he was born. Christened in Bradford Cathedral, he saw beyond its imposing post-war planning monstrosities and championed its hidden rugged Victorian sandstone beauty. Today, those monstrosities mostly levelled and its original sightlines restored, Bradford, with 5,000 listed buildings and 59 conservation areas, is an undiscovered gem. It expanded rapidly as the Industrial Revolution took hold and, as such, is perhaps Britain's best monument to Victorian architecture. No expense was spared – in the grandeur of the Wool Exchange, and the ornate Venetian gothic of City Hall, it's possible to see that, like mercantile centres the world over, Bradford was briefly one of the world's wealthiest cities.

Yet its wealth was one of the most unevenly distributed the Western world had ever seen. It belonged to merchants, whose Yorkstone warehouses filled the skyline, and a handful of monopolistic mill owners who made spectacular fortunes from beautiful, gargantuan factories on the sweat, toil and bodily health of the rest of the townsfolk trapped in narrow back-to-back unplumbed slums at the bottom of the valley – into which countless factory chimneys belched poisonous black smoke. Those that could afford to headed to the upper slopes in order to leave the squalor of the spoiled valley behind.

Bradford spawned characters not even Charles Dickens dared dream up. Samuel Lister had built the world's largest factory from the ashes of an 1871 fire – it spanned 109,000 square metres, had a colossal chimney (still in place) and once employed 11,000 workers. Until recent times the huge mill resembled some ornate structure from Detroit, but today Lister's Manningham Mills have been converted into luxury apartments, whose fine, sandstone exterior conceals a darkness at the heart of the mammoth structure. Back in December 1890 Lister told his workforce to accept a 25 per cent pay cut from Christmas Eve, or face a post-Christmas lock-out. A strike followed and the workers organised themselves into the Bradford Labour Union. Although this Scrooge of a man would defeat his workers after five long, bitter months, the members of the Labour Union would go on to form the Independent Labour Party, which, in turn, eventually gave birth to the Labour Party that would do so much to defeat the Samuel Listers of this world.

Today, Bradford's skyline is dominated not only by the nineteenth-century Italianate architecture of Lister's Mill but also a neighbouring monument to Sky's twenty-first-century Premier League riches: the rebuilt Valley Parade.

As for Lister, he is now portrayed as a paternalistic benefactor to the city, immortalised in Sicilian marble in a statue that stands in Lister Park – on land he donated to the townsfolk, for which they are no doubt expected to be grateful, and which for me best explains Bradford. On the one hand Bradford is a city that has a history of organised resistance; but on the other it's a place of doffed flat caps and stiff upper lips, where its pragmatic people would do whatever they could for their fellow man, while simultaneously accepting the injustices that were administered by the few with a resignation that the boat best not be rocked as there's 'now't you can do, lad' or 'past is past, you can't change it'. If you were born there, chances are you'd stay there – 'Tha' were a good mill, son. Good prospects.'

The Fletcher family had been in Bradford since the turn of the twentieth century. My usually guarded granddad, Eddie, told me that we had descended from the great nineteenth-century Birmingham inventor Sir Alfred Bird, son of Eton school astronomy lecturer John Bird who, as a chemist, was the Heston Blumenthal of his day, inventing Bird's Custard Powder to cope with his wife's food allergy, then baking powder, blancmange and jelly powder, which his children commercialised into some of Britain's best known food products.

'So, Granddad,' I asked, 'does that mean we're rich, then?'

'No, son,' he told me with a rueful smile. 'It just means that my granddad was rich.'

His Granddad Bird was a major shareholder in his father's company, Alfred Bird & Sons, but had sold out. So, as one son and grandson of the great inventor went on to become a Conservative MP and Baron of Solihull in the County of Warwick, another son and granddaughter, Nora, my great grandma, born with servants at hand, died, after a life of struggle, in a Bradford council flat in the 1970s. When I asked what had happened to the money, Granddad told me it had simply gone. I was left stunned at how such a world of privilege could simply disappear. Granddad, himself a man of few words, never really elaborated on what had happened to the money. He was someone who refused to have a bank account, thinking his money was safer in an empty house. 'Never trust a banker, son,' I remember him telling me.

My granddad had been left to rebuild his life from the ground up. But then he lost his youth, being just 17 when the Second World War broke out. Like most of his generation, he rarely mentioned the war. My grandma once told me he'd gone missing in the Pacific and was presumed dead. But he miraculously reappeared and they were quickly wed in Grandma's home town of Barnsley in 1942. Not that he ever told her about the war either – but, as with so many Pacific troops, his life was left blighted by illness, his experiences never really leaving him, either physically or mentally.

Growing up with an ill father, my dad was a firm believer in living for the moment, and in the moment, as you never knew when such moments might end. He believed it best to be positive, to take in your stride whatever life threw at you and never allow yourself to be bitter about what you did not have. It was why he'd told me you had to play your hand in life as best you could, as the dealer will never give you another, so you had best find a way to stay in the game and hope your hand improved.

Dad had left Bradford for Leeds in his mid-teens when his parents took on the British Queen pub, in Hunslet, a rough, working-class area of the inner city, within walking distance of Tetley's Brewery and Elland Road. Although he stayed on at Hanson Grammar School, Dad was nothing but a charming underachiever and left at 16 with two O levels and an uncertain future. However, the mid-sixties was a time of plentiful employment, and he quickly found work as an 'office boy' at the Gelderd Road head offices of Leeds-based coach company Wallace Arnold. One afternoon Dad took a call intended for his colleague, Anne. Ever the charmer Dad took the chance to chat to the girl whose voice had immediately smitten him. Once the forwarded call was over, Dad asked Anne who the lovely sounding girl was, to which Anne told him it was her friend, Sue, who she was meeting later.

Ever the opportunist, my dad enquired, 'Do you mind if I come along?'

'Yes, I do,' Anne replied – her plans for a girls' night out did not include having 16-year-old office juniors in tow. 'Forget her, John. She's out of your league.'

So then he suggested meeting Sue first, because he 'only needed half an hour'!

'You're full of it, John Fletcher,' Anne declared. 'I bet you'd never turn up anyway.'

'I bet I would.' And with that, Dad got his half hour (and won the bet).

He spotted the small, pretty 16-year-old brunette outside the Corn Exchange in Leeds city centre and explained he was the John she'd spoken to on the phone earlier: 'I've just come to let you know Anne's running

10

half an hour behind at work. Do you fancy getting a coffee while you wait?' She agreed, and Dad had his window of opportunity. Mum can't remember what they'd talked about, but he'd had an easy manner, and it was pretty much love at first sight. They agreed to meet again.

Sue Reed had had a rough few years, losing her dad, whom she idolised, to an unexpected heart attack a month after her twelfth birthday. With no siblings, she was left with a mother who'd always resented her very presence. With her dad around, tensions were ever present, simmering in the background; in his absence Sue was regularly beaten and browbeaten. She coped by seeking sanctuary from her troubled Harehills home at her grandparents', a mile away, and with friends at the local coffee bar. At weekends she taught Sunday School and got herself a Saturday job on the Boots make-up counter in the city centre. She'd often visit her dad's old print colleagues at the *Yorkshire Post* and watch the papers fly off their giant rollers. She retained a heart of gold and a belief that, one day, she'd find a happy life.

Her dad had called her his 'little scrum-half' but, in the end, like all good scrum-halves, she rebelled. Attractive, though never growing beyond her pre-teen five feet, she was an early developer, nicknamed 'Topsy' by her friends – and, thanks to her Saturday job, was always immaculate. She'd always been a sports fan, having earned the 'scrum-half' sobriquet after giving up on an argument with a bunch of boys who'd not let her join their game of street football, picking up their ball and running – like a good scrum-half. Her dad was a Leeds United fan, though he died a year before they were promoted to the top flight under Don Revie – and a year later Mum walked home from her grandparents' in tears after Leeds lost the 1965 FA Cup final to Liverpool, 2–1 after extra-time. A male admirer once took her to Elland Road where, unable to see from the terraces, she climbed a floodlight pylon, and on being asked by a police officer to come down, she replied, 'No, I can't see from down there!'

Where Anne at Wallace Arnold was sceptical, Mum could see 'potential' in my charming if impudent dad – as well as a fellow kind soul whom she could 'mould'. She soon became part of Dad's large family, centred largely around the British Queen, his mum, Edna, 'more of a mother to me than mine ever was'. Ever the entrepreneur, my grandma found a novel way of clearing slow-moving or out-of-date stock from the pub by placing it on the bottom shelf – all of her customers suddenly keen for the pretty, young barmaid to bend down in her miniskirt and retrieve another bag of Golden Wonder crisps.

John and Sue were engaged after a year. To save the deposit for their first home – a new three-bedroom semi with a long rolling garden in Birstall – they never went out, taking pub shifts in addition to their day jobs. Dad had now started to deploy his persuasive charms in a series of sales roles, ending up with metals stockholders Aalco, while Mum, who'd topped her secretarial college class, worked as a PA. They were so clearly in love that whenever they tried to cuddle on the couch the pub dog, Rif, previously the apple of my dad's eye, would jump jealously in between them.

It took them three years to save their deposit, and once they had they were wed – both aged 20 – on 18 September 1971, on what should have been the bride's father's seventieth birthday. There was no extravagant wedding nor a honeymoon – all that was much less a priority than the house John and Sue hoped would be the foundation of their new happiness – and within six months family life beckoned. They'd never planned to have a family so quickly, but, for Mum's twenty-first birthday, 15 March 1972, Dad bought her a fashionable fur coat and, in the throes of a passionate thank-you, an accident happened and I arrived nine months later, on 12 December. I know there was a time before my brother Andrew was around, it's just I can't remember it, as he arrived when I was 16 months old. Whatever Mum did with him, I wanted to help. Andrew was walking at nine months then climbing my slide at 12 months. We were so close we were often mistaken for twins.

At the age of 27 our parents moved to a brand-new four-bedroom executive detached house. On the upper slopes of the suburban

Spen Valley, in Upper Batley, we could now see our old house at the bottom of the cut, a mile away; and beyond that to the Emley Moor TV mast at the top of the opposite valley. Dad had started out renting a tiny office space in Hull for Aalco, selling steel and other metals to firms along the east coast during the 1970s North Sea oil and gas boom. In no time he was managing director of a successful metals stockholding company with a large warehouse and a seven-figure turnover. A contemporary of David Murray – the former Rangers chairman started at Aalco at the same time as Dad before setting up Murray Steel – Dad also had the former Blackburn Rovers chairman, Jack Walker of Walker Steel, as a customer. Future managing director of the FTSE-listed Amari Plastics, Alex Millar – a former footballer who'd played for Partick Thistle – had backed Dad on his venture in Hull and earmarked him as his long-term successor. Dad also knew the son of the Leeds United chairman who'd appointed Don Revie – and for my ninth birthday I received a signed Mitre 25 Max match ball from that season's Leeds United v Manchester United fixture. At 26, Dad was sporting a moustache (to add a dash of man-of-the-world gravitas), wearing nice suits and smoking King Edward cigars. He was popular with his customers; he'd come a long way from selling coach trips to Mablethorpe. Dad being Dad, he blagged it all like a dream.

We had such active childhoods. Wilton Park was at the bottom of Merlin Court, which was a wooded area that led down to Batley Park a mile away. The park and the Woodlands estate, full of cul-de-sacs and spacious four-bedroom homes, became our childhood playgrounds, me riding about on my gold Raleigh Grifter, Andrew on his blue Raleigh Boxer. At first we shared a bedroom, but I loved life so much I'd wake at dawn then wake my playmate – it wasn't long before Andrew grew tired, and we were given separate rooms. The fourth bedroom was turned into a games room, in which we had a dartboard and pool table, often customised for snooker and Subbuteo. We'd also play Yahtzee, board games like BP Offshore Oil Strike and Monopoly, or on our Atari and

Ingersoll games consoles in the lounge. Dad would spend his weekends playing with us, and we never wanted for hugs. We were all so happy.

Meanwhile, Grandma had left the pub trade. She helped her youngest son, Peter, and son-in-law Mike Moss, build F&M Vendors, an Armley-based business that supplied cigarette vending machines to the Leeds pub trade she knew so well. In school holidays Andrew and I would pack cigarette packets into boxes for customers, and we'd use the giant, noisy coin-counter to bag up money from the machines. F&M Vendors' success led to Uncle Peter buying a furnished holiday caravan let, a house in Pudsey, and a second home in Gildersome. Then he opened a newsagent's famed for its cut-price cigarettes – all by the age of 30.

We should have been poster children for Thatcherism – only we were football fans.

2

Football

I can't pinpoint the precise moment football entered my life. That would be like asking someone who has gone to church every Sunday since they were born when they first became aware of God.

My first memory of football was a scene from my grandparents' house: a lounge door opened, and I saw football lit up on the TV in the corner of a crowded, darkened room. Excited, I ran towards it. My earliest memory of Bradford City had been of Dad leaving me. Standing on Foster Square, in the shadow of Bradford Cathedral, he'd told me he had to go now. When I asked where he was going, he said, 'I'm going to the football.' I demanded that he take me, but he pointed out I'd be too small to see. As Dad walked towards Valley Parade, Mum hugged me. I was inconsolable, somehow convinced I'd never see him again. Bradford City lost an FA Cup quarter-final to Southampton that afternoon. It was 1976, Southampton went on to win it; I was three.

That summer I'd wake to news of a fire. All along Smithies Moor Lane, people stood in their front gardens while smoke billowed hundreds of feet into a clear sky from the textiles factory at the top of our street. As the building became totally consumed in fire I could feel the heat on my face. Some who worked there started to cry – they knew it would never be rebuilt.

It was in the back garden of that house on Smithies Moor Lane that I first played football. I have a distant memory of Dad firing a high shot at me in goal. I was too short to reach it, and as the ball smashed against the kitchen window we both apologised to Mum, who was glaring through the other side. We moved from there when I was five.

At our school, Birstall County, Topps Trading Cards were big. We'd line stake cards up against the bottom of a wall and take turns to skim more cards at them, like Frisbees – whoever knocked down the last card would not only win all the stake cards, but all the thrown cards too. They came five to a pack with Bazooka Joe chewing gum – but one sunny day, as Mum made lunch, I decided her spotless shiny green Renault 12, parked on the drive, would look better with a touch of *Starsky & Hutch* about it. So I took the gum out of my mouth and ran a long, white stripe down the driver's door. As we had lunch it baked on in the heat and wouldn't come off without marking Mum's pride and joy, so she banned me from buying gum until Hubba Bubba invented a non-stick variety. This left me having to hand-pick opponents like a boxing promoter to ensure that I never ran out of cards; cards now so precious I'd lie in bed memorising local lad Frank Worthington's goal-scoring stats, how Bryan Robson had somehow played 23 games and scored 8 goals for West Brom despite breaking his leg three times in a season, and even the height and weight of Jimmy Rimmer – just in case I lost them for ever.

It would have been August 1980, and I remember talking with Andrew in our bunk beds at Uncle Peter's two-bedroom caravan in Primrose Valley, on Yorkshire's east coast, when we heard a loud cheer come from Dad in the lounge. The *News at Ten* headlines had declared Bradford City had beaten league champions Liverpool, 1–0, in the League Cup. The next day Dad walked around the caravan park and its amusement arcade, proud, for once, to tell everyone about his team. Although it was only the first leg, so he knew they'd lose overall (as they did, 4–0, at Anfield), nothing could dim his obvious pride and happiness that day. That was the first Bradford City score I remember.

It was later that season, as I watched Big Daddy wrestle on ITV's *World of Sport* on the TV in Grandma's lounge, that places, followed by numbers, kept appearing under the word 'latest' on the screen. With the men of the family out, my cousin Chris asked what they were, and I suggested results from other bouts, only for Grandma to reveal they were football scores. This inspired me to pick up one of Uncle Peter's blue football bibles, his *Rothmans Football Yearbooks*. I started to thumb its thousand pages – and I'd never really stop, as I learnt about each English and Scottish club, their records, scores, players and their season by season league and Cup performances. Before long I was doing the same for clubs and countries in international competitions. Pretty quickly I became a walking football encyclopaedia, solving playground disputes with my (not so little) blue book.

This absorption of facts and figures led to a new understanding of what Bradford City meant to the world of football – in truth, not a great deal. They'd been the first team to win the newly designed FA Cup in 1911, in the first year it was contested . . . and they'd been West Yorkshire's first Football League side . . . and that was about it.

One Wednesday evening my dad asked me, 'Do you want to go to the football on Saturday?'

Somehow immediately sensing the question was loaded, I replied, 'It depends . . . where?'

Grinning, he said, 'Bradford City, son.'

Full of my new-found love of stats, I told him they'd just drawn their lowest ever crowd in 77 years – 1,249 – to their final home match at the end of the previous season, and that I wasn't up for such rubbish.

'Aha, that might have been so, but it's not the case any more,' he fired back. 'What if I told you they won their last home match 6–2 and won 1–5 away last night? They have a new manager who used to play for England, but who now plays for Bradford.'

This tall tale was getting taller by the second.

'Someone I know you've heard of – Roy McFarland – Derby's old captain.'

I wondered how a man who'd twice won the Football League could ever wash up in a backwater like Bradford.

The answer was that Bradford were apparently 'finally going places'.

Which was odd, because this was a club that had never gone places before. My dad then changed tack, and talked of how going to Valley Parade had been something he'd done with my uncle Peter when they were kids – but it was something they hadn't done with their dad, and so were more than keen to take their own kids.

I agreed to go but remained unconvinced, somehow resisting the lure of having Bradford as my team.

'Look, I'm not asking that you support only one team. You can support whatever other club you like,' was Dad's deal clincher. 'But your local side, you should always support your local side.'

Dad's saving grace was that back then supporting your local team really did mean everything. In 1981 the Football League was still two years from televising its first ever live match, so if you wanted to watch football live, and have a real affinity with a team, you really did have to look on your own doorstep.

To non Sky Sports subscribers it would have been an instantly recognisable world. Saturday lunchtimes kicked off with *Football Focus*, with the added bonus of ITV's *On the Ball* once that finished. Then, on the way to the ground the car radio would be tuned to local stations for news on your team. After the match you'd listen to the local radio reports before tuning into *Sports Report*, which began, as it does today, at 5 p.m., with same theme tune, headlines, classified results (sadly no longer with James Alexander Gordon), reports, news and interviews. Saturday night meant *Match of the Day*, with extended highlights from just two or three pre-selected games, as BBC producers gambled on where the day's best action might be; Sunday afternoon brought a regional ITV highlights show, just after lunch.

This was a world where 92 professional football clubs were divided into four divisions, simply called Divisions 1, 2, 3 and 4, as they had been for nearly a century.

Mum, despite her allegiance to Leeds United, was happy for us to go to Valley Parade. Racism and hooliganism had blighted Leeds' seven-year descent from a European Cup final in 1975 to their eventual relegation in the spring of 1982. School friends had tales of coins, darts, pool balls and seats being thrown by supporters around them. So if we were to watch our football locally, she thought we'd at least be safe doing so at Valley Parade.

Dad, however, was clearly embarrassed by Valley Parade: as the big day dawned, having championed his club's cause, he warned me, 'Don't expect too much tomorrow, son. The football's one thing, but the ground . . . just don't expect it to be like those on TV.'

I wouldn't, I assured him, shutting my eyes to imagine a sparse crowd in the smallest most run-down stadium, something that belonged in the basement of English football's pyramid not its professional Football League.

So Dad's warning meant that, as we parked up on Thorncliffe Road the next day, I was not disappointed by what met us. We climbed on to a large sloping grass bank, where the thousands who'd passed over it each home match had worn out mud pathways that branched off in three separate directions towards the ground. Trees stood behind the Kop, and to reach the Main Stand you passed down a waterlogged dirt track that, with its loose uneven mix of mud and stones, was more like a builder's yard. It was narrow too, no more than a car's width, and bordered on one side by a meshed-wire-topped fence that ran opposite the Kop wall and which seemed to guard nothing but yet more grass. This dirt track led out on to South Parade, a dead-end cobbled Victorian street that ran behind the Main Stand. A programme seller standing in front of a wooden block of turnstiles sold Dad a match programme for 30p, which he then handed to me with its flame-orange cover, a smoky black industrial haze superimposed over the outline of the back of a stand.

We then walked down South Parade, avoiding the puddles between its cobbles. A third of the way down we passed some brick huts, built back from the perimeter wall, which housed four waist-high turnstiles, over which lay loose, rusty sheets of corrugated iron. A little further along South Parade we stopped by a larger set of four brick huts, all with the same loose, rusted corrugated iron roofing. These housed some pretty grim toilets, the club shop, a storeroom and more turnstiles.

The stand had been built into a steep valley slope, so the brick huts sort of squatted on South Parade's pavement, the first one on the corner overlooking the open terrace, the Kop and the pitch below. The others were built into the back of the stand. In the middle of those huts, about opposite the halfway line was a recessed gap where some claret-painted, wooden double doors opened at full time, allowing fans to flood out on to the pavement after the match. There was a similar exit a bit further along, and another right at the end, by the clubhouse. Down the full length of the stand were a bunch of single doors, no longer in use, all boarded up like those you saw in the old Wild West comics. The stand was a bit odd in that you had to sort of climb *down* into it.

Once through the turnstiles of the Main Stand you found yourself in a low, dark concrete corridor. It was as narrow as a pavement, running the length of the stand. It can't have been more than four feet across, bordered on the far side by a claret wooden wall, too high for a kid to see over – which made it all the more exciting when you passed one of the stand's narrow stairwells and caught a flash of the drop and the bright green pitch deep below, beyond the gloomy corridor.

Suspended in coiled steel by each stairwell were large, claret wooden boards with huge amber letters painted over them – 'A' through to 'G' – alphabetically marking out each seating block as you walked down the corridor. G Block was at the top end, near the Kop; A Block down by the clubhouse. We had tickets for C Block, not far from the halfway line. Each block's stairwell cut a path down through the seats into what were effectively partitioned-off boxes. There were only two small gaps, allowing you access further down into the stand; so, unless you were at the bottom of the stairwells between blocks E and F, or blocks B and C, you'd have to come back up each stairwell to get out again. The seats themselves were effectively claret-painted planks of wood, suspended and supported by blocks of wood at either end and divided up by steel markers into individual bench seats. The markers and the end blocks were nailed to some sturdy-looking wooden floorboards that had been laid over wooden sleepers set into the valley. The numbers on the benches were painted in a strangely stylish art deco white Bauhaus script, marking out each of the ten seats on each row – that may have been decorous by 1908 standards, but seventy years later it wasn't what you'd call luxury. It was neat and orderly, though, in an old world kind of a way; but the problem was every seat offered the same severely restricted view, with black metal supports shooting up every five metres or so at the front of the stand, like upturned lines on a NFL field, to support a double-gabled roof – covered piecemeal over the years by several layers of bitumen felt, and sporting a jagged wooden fascia that merely added to the impression of sitting in a rickety old showground stand. Walking along the narrow corridor at the back of the stand was not dissimilar to walking along a non-moving old-fashioned cake walk, albeit one in a high-sided fairground, wood panels painted in a thick amber and claret gloss everywhere – and with a forty-foot drop through the seating down to the paddock and pitch below. The football grounds writer Simon Inglis, writing before the fire, said it was 'like watching football from the cockpit of a Sopwith Camel', and he was right, it was like watching a match sitting in a bi-plane; the Main Stand was truly a museum piece in every way.

You could always pick up the lingering scent of pipe smoke and fags in there too. People had smoked in that stand since it was first built, in 1908. Apart from the 1950s-looking council house (the 'new' clubhouse) that had truncated the far end of the structure, the Main Stand had remained pretty much unchanged for more than 70 years. Certainly this was the case in those elevated boxed-in sections – fans sitting either side of the directors' box and press box, which sat high above the halfway line, surrounded by wooden panels, wooden benches, and timbers supporting a wooden roof. The Main Stand wasn't short of combustible materials, especially to the rear, where the sectioned-off bench seats ran the length of the stand and were separated off from the strip of 1960s plastic seats below by a high, amber-painted wooden wall that had only a couple of gaps, either side of the halfway line. These plastic seats had in turn eaten into the paddock terrace of concrete steps which formed the bottom strip, or layer, as it were, and surrounded the dug-outs before curving back up by G Block, right to the top of the slope. The hard nuts tended to stand at the top of this terrace, but they were divided off from the G Block seats by another painted wooden wall with spiked metal railings on top. It wasn't that easy to get in these rear seats; and it wasn't that easy to get out.

It will be hard for kids growing up today, used to modern, all-seater stadiums, to visualise the ramshackle, hotchpotch nature of a ground like Valley Parade. There we were in its Main Stand, perched precariously on the valley slope, opposite which sat the Midland Road terrace – essentially an elongated bus shelter with a sheer 30-foot drop behind it, over which balls would fly so often that the club employed people to collect them from the scrubland below. The vast, unroofed, crumbling terrace of the Kop sat to our left, and the small cattle shed of the Bradford End was to our right – all of which left the pitch exposed to harsh unpredictable swirling valley winds that caused the rain to bash down so hard that the stand roof sprang leaks all along it.

'C'mon, Colchester,' I sporadically hollered in the first half, and as Colchester went 1–0 up I cheered, before applauding them off at half-time.

During the break a middle-aged man on the row in front of us turned and asked Dad, 'First game with them?'

'Aye, sorry, maybe he'll actually start supporting the right team in the second half.'

'You know what? I think you've got the right idea, son,' the man told me. 'Wish I wasn't a City fan – would have saved me a lot of misery.'

'Aye, maybe, but as I keep telling 'em: you've got to support your local side,' Dad insisted.

'Aye, but have you never considered moving?' he joked.

We laughed, then Dad asked, 'So, who will you be supporting at your next match, son?'

'Not sure, Dad. Who will Bradford be playing?' which prompted more laughter all round.

I must have cottoned on early to the fact that it was the banter that made the football: as the teams came back out for the second half I supported the same team as all those around me, cheering as Bradford fought back to win 2–1. A fortnight later we were back, as Bradford overturned another half-time deficit to beat Aldershot 4–1, a victory that put us top. Dad had suggested I try supporting Bradford, and I loved it – the camaraderie, the banter, the noise, the abrasive language, the adult humour – it was the epitome of a secret little boys' club, something confirmed by Mum proclaiming over roast dinner that night, 'What you hear at the football, stays at the football.'

So, weeks later, I was surprised to find a match programme at my grandparents' from the Port Vale match the previous Wednesday. Grandma told me Dad had gone with Granddad and Uncle Peter, but he'd not mentioned it. Feeling snubbed, as we headed to Valley Parade the next day I asked him why he hadn't take us on Wednesday.

'It was a school-night, Martin. I didn't get home till past your bedtimes – anyway, I didn't think you'd mind.'

'*What!?*' I protested.

So, in little more than a month, Dad had turned me from not wanting to go anywhere near Valley Parade, to having me plead to go to every match with him. His timing couldn't have been better: Bradford were about to make the long trip to Suffolk, for a third-round League Cup tie against UEFA Cup holders Ipswich Town, who'd just finished runners-up in the league and were managed by Bobby Robson. Against the odds, we drew 1–1. This allowed Dad to pitch to Mum an idea first aired after my

Port Vale protest: maybe he'd be best picking up season tickets, as not only would it guarantee us seats for the replay, but in getting regular seats on the back row we could get a better view by standing on the wooden bench. Mum agreed, so we got four season tickets on the back row of C Block. On our first night there, the night of the Ipswich replay, Bradford took a 1–0 lead, before falling behind 1–2, then equalising in the final minutes to take the thrilling tie to extra-time, which we lost 2–3, but left Bobby Robson declaring it to have been as tough as any European match.

In the Main Stand we had our own way of creating a hostile European atmosphere. We'd slap our palms on our wooden bench seats, and stamp our feet on the angled wooden boards beneath us, designed to rest your feet on. This was a practised art, which required slapping those foot boards with just enough force to create an echo but not so much as to kick them in. Dad told me to be careful, but one Saturday, in the excitement I smacked my heel down with such force that the board broke, leaving me with just the wooden banister beside me to slap. Although my board was never replaced, it was the only missing board I can remember on that row. If people took care not to kick them in, they also took more care generally back then. As I discovered one half-time when I screwed up a Kit-Kat wrapper then dropped it through the hole under my seat.

'You idiot. What did you do that for?' Dad scolded me.

Taken aback by Dad's ferocity, I asked, 'What?'

'Dropping litter under a stand like this. Can't you see it's made out of wood?'

'Yeah, so?' I asked.

'So . . . !' I was told, 'It's a fire risk!'

As I looked around for support from those I usually bantered with, it was clear I had none. They all silently nodded their heads in agreement. I was so embarrassed I ended up on my stomach, putting my arm through the void, trying to fish out my Kit-Kat wrapper, but all I could feel were cobwebs. There was nothing to drag out. Dad said, 'Forget it, but make sure you never do that again – OK?' I agreed and sheepishly dragged my cobweb-covered arm out, got back to my feet and padded down my blue parka.

I usually sat on the end of our row, with Andrew on my left, Dad to his left, next to his own brother, Uncle Peter. Most games I'd stand on the bench to leap over the waist-high gated claret wooden banister to my right that separated B and C blocks – the speediest route to the wooden tea hut built over what would have been the three rear rows of B Block. Like the banister, the tea hut was daubed in claret gloss paint; in winter its glass windows misted over as the giant metal urns and pie ovens gave off steam, the smell of pies and Bovril wafting easily as far as my seat on the other side of the stairwell. I'd leap over five or ten minutes before half-time to beat the rush. Sometimes I'd make it back, and be standing on my bench listening to the half-time scores, looking back over the wooden partition while munching on a paper bag full of Sports Mixture (2p each) and drinking from a 15p can of Lockwoods cola, as people jostled down a corridor so narrow only two could pass down it at a time. That always made for entertaining half-time scrums around the snack bar.

During the course of my first season, 1981–82, Bradford City certainly dispelled any notion that they were rubbish. OK, it may have been the old fourth division, but Bradford won the first five league games I saw at Valley Parade and, out of my first twenty league matches there, lost just once, in the final minute of a 3–4 thriller to Mansfield Town on a windswept, waterlogged pitch on a stormy January night. An even wilder, wetter March night saw a gusty wind carry the Stockport County goalkeeper's kick to the opposing penalty area, where Bradford's reliable veteran goalkeeper, Neil Ramsbottom, slipped on coming out to collect the ball and let it bounce over his prone body into an empty net. It was the only goal of the game, until the final fifteen minutes, when Bradford promptly scored five. In my first local derby we beat Halifax Town 5–2, centre-forward Bobby Campbell scoring a hat-trick. His support striker David McNiven then scored four first-half goals in the penultimate home match of the season as we beat Crewe 4–1. In the final home match of that year, against Bournemouth, needing a point to go up, Bobby Campbell gave us a 1–0 lead, before Bournemouth, also seeking promotion, went 1–2 up when, in the final minute, Campbell, midway in his own half, let fly with a stunning shot that rocketed into the bottom right-hand corner. Hundreds swarmed on to the pitch in celebration.

Thousands more followed at full time to celebrate our second promotion in fourteen years. The half of the pitch nearest the clubhouse was packed full of cheering fans as the semi-naked players, many in just their underwear, having been stripped of their kits, came out on to the clubhouse balcony. At right-back, Ces Podd, our all-time-record appearance holder, was too composed a player to ever spend a career in the lower divisions, but a St Kitts-born Leeds lad, he loved a club where there was never any racism. Another denied his chance was powerfully built Dominican-born Joe Cooke, his trademark throw-ins as long and accurate as a corner kick. In midfield, Barry Gallagher averaged a goal every three games with his pile-driving free-kicks. Up front was our leader, Bobby Campbell, a tank of a man who played as if ploughing through the trenches, putting his neck where most feared to put their feet, ably supported by 'Daisy' David McNiven, a silky provider who averaged a goal every three games but struggled with accusations of being too physically lightweight for the fourth division. At centre-back Roy McFarland reminded us why he'd graced the highest level, with his centre-back partner, 20-year-old Bradford-born Peter Jackson, absorbing it all like a sponge. These were my first footballing heroes.

That summer Mum made her first trip to Valley Parade, for a Junior Bantams open day. As we watched a training session from our usual seats, Andrew showed Mum the nail that protruded out of the wooden partition wall that had ripped his coat; and I showed her the hole beneath my seat. Nodding silently, she kept looking around, tutting and shaking her head. Years later she'd tell me the state of the place 'chilled her blood'.

After the training session there were autographs to be had on the pitch. Mum refused to vault my banister, so we headed down the stairwell to search for another way to the front seating section. But there was none; just the two waist-high banisters which separated the various upper seating blocks. Rather than head back out of the stand, Dad urged us over the amber-painted wooden wall, down on to the plastic seats below, but that involved a two-foot climb on one side followed by a surprising four- or five-foot drop down the other. And the only way out of the front seating section was to jump over a claret wooden wall, this one with an eight-foot drop on to the concrete paddock terrace below. This jump scared me so much I wanted to call it off, but Dad went over, then grabbed my legs as I sat on the wall and slid me down. Once on to the paddock terrace, with its bottom step below pitch level, a five-foot white brick wall, taller than me, had to be scaled, and once again with Dad's help I completed this veritable assault course. It had shaken me so much, though, that I had little appetite for any autograph hunting.

Once the players had left the pitch we went to the clubhouse at the corner of the Bradford End and Main Stand. On the walls in there, we looked at faded sepia photographs of a series of failed teams. An old man pointed out the photograph of the 1929 team, which he told us scored a record 128 goals to win Division 3 (North). He spoke fondly of the games and players he'd seen half a century earlier – that championship remained the only piece of silverware the club had won over the previous seventy years. Dad promised us we'd just embarked on a journey that would one day see me speak of our team in the same hushed tones – we were so close to matching the best of what had gone before. I believed him . . .

On the way home Mum challenged Dad about the state of the ground, asking what would happen if it ever caught fire. We laughed – although wooden it had stood the test of time for some 74 years.

Despite promotion to Division 3 our successes continued at Valley Parade. In the season's opener, a 3–2 win over Reading, an energetic, squat 18-year-old ginger terrier called Stuart McCall raced around on his debut at right-back. Valley Parade so unsettled teams that we'd capture

19 points from our first seven home matches there that season. But after winning our first away match of the season, at Orient in the late-August sunshine, it would be November before we picked up anything more than a single point on the road (again in London, beating Brentford 0–2). Having climbed to second by beating Plymouth Argyle 4–0 the day after Dad's 32nd birthday in October – which we all celebrated with a game of football on the school playing fields opposite Grandma's house in Pudsey – the following weekend we all went to Chesterfield, who'd go on to finish bottom that season, only to lose 3–0, and not go top, rather drop to seventh.

A fortnight later came the news Manchester United would visit Valley Parade in the League Cup. We feared nobody at home and that included the mighty United (who'd reach Wembley, win the FA Cup and finish third that season), but on a cold November night United would concede an early goal that was dubiously disallowed, before escaping with a goalless draw. The impact our 34-year-old manager Roy McFarland was having was now being noted elsewhere. Almost immediately rumours started that Derby County wanted him as assistant to Brian Cough's former right-hand man, Peter Taylor. Aside from his happy 14-year stint playing at the Baseball Ground, we felt there was nothing to worry about – what could attract him to a club who, seven years after being English champions, were now fighting relegation to Division 3? We knew we'd lose McFarland to a big club one day, but didn't believe it would be to a struggling one looking for an assistant manager.

But the night before our Old Trafford replay Mum was waiting for me after school. On getting into her silver MG Metro she handed me the afternoon edition of the local paper, the Bradford *Telegraph & Argus*, saying, 'I'm sorry, Martin, but I think you'd better see this.' It declared Roy McFarland and his assistant Mick Jones had resigned with immediate effect. We crossed the Pennines the next night to sit in the Scoreboard End. Trailing 4–0, Bobby Campbell fired a flying header past Gary Bailey into the top corner in the final minute, which was so spectacular it even raised applause from the United's hardcore on the Stretford End. Leaderless, we'd not capitulated, and on getting home I took a black pen, opened my programme on the page of our team photo, and scribbled out both McFarland and Jones.

Although we appointed Leeds United's former England international defender Trevor Cherry as our new player-manager, it seemed our upward march was over. We failed to win in the three matches before Cherry took charge, and then he'd have to wait nine more matches before his first league victory. At best, inconsistency reigned, and during this run the club stopped printing match programmes and started handing out A4 folded white sheets: done nicely in a claret typeface, these were, nevertheless, little more than glorified team sheets. It was a joke of a programme to match our pitch which, permanently waterlogged, was covered in sand and came to resemble an inland beach. The season ended on a high with two derby wins allowing us to finish 12th, but just eight points above relegation, and we knew that only the early-season home form (now a distant memory) had kept us safe.

After the final match of the season, against Huddersfield Town, Dad led us up past decaying metal crush barriers to the top right-hand corner of a weed-covered terrace. The steps of the Kop were crumbling underfoot. When I asked why we were there, he said, 'This is where I used to stand as a boy. I just wanted one last look. Let's be quiet and take it all in, boys.' My emotional Dad stood there for a couple of minutes, as if it might be his last chance. Weeks later *Grandstand* announced Leeds United had issued a winding-up order against Bradford City over an outstanding transfer fee. They were due in the High Court on Monday, and to soften the blow Dad had arranged to take us to Alton Towers, where he warned us as we returned to the car to prepare for the worst.

Only on tuning into the 7 p.m. BBC Radio 2 *Sports Show* the following Friday we learnt of last-minute arrangements that had seen a receiver from Thornton Baker, Peter Flesher, buy time by transferring the assets and liabilities of the old company into a new company. I didn't follow the intricacies of all this that closely back then, but with creditors owed £374,000, it seemed, as Flesher later admitted it had been, 'hard to see a way to save football in Bradford'. Although the original 1908 club had won promotion the year before and seen its crowds increase 65 per cent in just two years, it was wound up that day by an Official Receiver, who later insisted, 'I can't say why the club ran for so long. For a number of years its accounts have shown it to be insolvent.'

Bradford rallied: an appeal raised £55,000, Bobby Campbell was sold for £70,000, and Bradford City Council purchased Valley Parade from the Receiver for £220,000. It was then, on the day the club was due to be closed down, that two local businessmen 'rescued' Bradford. Stafford Heginbotham joined forces with rival bidder Jack Tordoff, who had appointed Flesher weeks earlier, and agreed a deal which saw them each purchase 75,006 £1 shares for just 26.6p a share – meaning that for £40,000, or 10 per cent of the rescue package, they secured 87 per cent of the club's equity, with Flesher subsequently appointed a director. They then raised £40,000 by hiking admission prices up 50p – which doesn't sound a lot today, but was worth £50,000 a season back then. Ultimately terrace prices rose by 66 per cent over a couple of seasons, the price of seats doubling just a year later. Crowds initially fell by a third, yet fans heralded the pair heroes.

The following season, 1983–84, we were so grateful to still have a football club that, shorn of our best player, we weren't too troubled to have won just one of our first fifteen matches. In fact we took a meagre eight points in the first third of the season – relegation form, for sure. Things began to look up as Bobby Campbell, whose move to Derby had not worked out, returned on a month's loan. However, initially it seemed to have little effect, as we collected just a single point from his first handful of games. Then, in the final match of his loan spell, when Millwall took a three-goal lead at Valley Parade and we all began to accept our inevitable relegation back into Division 4, our talisman shook the team by the neck – something clicked, and we stormed back in the final half hour to draw 3–3 and almost win.

The next weekend, Andrew ran in a school cross-country competition, so Dad's friend Colin Butterworth took me to watch Wigan in the FA Cup. Colin was good friends with Trevor Cherry, having been on his testimonial committee at Leeds United, so we were in possession of some post-match players' lounge tickets. After I'd scurried round collecting autographs on my programme, Trevor Cherry popped out of his office and apologised to Colin for not spending time with us.

'Bobby?' Colin asked, aware it was the last weekend of his loan spell.

'Yeah,' said Trevor, a grimace on his face.

'Are we going to sign him?' I asked excitedly.

'I'm afraid it doesn't look like it.'

It was a blow – he'd have made all the difference. Trevor Cherry agreed with me, and said something like, 'Let's just hope and see what happens.'

Bobby Campbell returned. We won our next match 1–4 at Brentford, before we beat Plymouth Argyle 2–0 – which was our first home win of the season, not coming until December. Suddenly a team that had won just once in 15 games couldn't stop winning, as we beat Bournemouth 5–2 a fortnight later, climbed out of the bottom four on Boxing Day with a 1–2 win at Burnley, thrashed Wigan Athletic 6–2 at Valley Parade the next day and ended 1983 with a 2–3 win at Lincoln City on New Year's Eve. 1984 continued in a similar vein: we collected 27 points from 27 and scored 34 goals in nine games to move up to 11th in just seven weeks, victory at Exeter securing a club-record tenth successive win.

The morning after that Friday night match I sat an entrance exam for Batley Grammar School. The hour-long logic exam threw me with questions I'd not seen before; I breezed through the maths exam, before opening the English paper and reading the question, 'Describe a situation where you get lost in a crowd.' I imagined a scenario at Valley Parade where I somehow got separated from my family on exiting the ground, only to stumble, lost, across Manchester United manager Ron Atkinson, who was walking down the rear corridor, took pity on me and escorted me to the players' lounge for a Coke, where we talked about life at Old Trafford. Eventually I was reunited with my family by the clubhouse door.

On leaving the exam hall Dad's car was ticking over in the school car park. I jumped into the back seat and immediately asked, 'We win last night, Dad?'

'Hang on a minute,' Mum protested. 'How'd your exam go?'

'Yes, 2–0,' Dad laughed. 'Now answer your mother!'

We went another six games unbeaten, but the wins stopped, four draws halting progress up the league. By then an offer letter arrived from Batley Grammar School and Dad rang the school and was told my maths paper was 'excellent', the essay showed 'great imagination' and I'd be put in the second set with a view to moving me to the top set, which only my ropey logic paper had prevented. My future seemed set.

But one Saturday morning a few weeks later, as Andrew and I started to play snooker after breakfast, Mum popped in and said, 'Don't get too comfortable, boys.' Thinking we had a free morning, she told us, as she rushed out, 'We're going to Nottingham – in half an hour.' We continued to play as we speculated why. Perplexed, we could see no reason for a mad dash south, not least as we'd need to be back for the three o'clock kick-off at Valley Parade.

Dad had been commuting to Nottingham daily for the past six months and, although his 70-mile journey to work seemed, on the surface, little different to the 60-mile one he'd been making to Hull for years, he was now frequently late, stuck on the congested, urban M1 rather than speeding across the rural, sleepy M62. The miners' strike had started barely a month before, but the movement of flying pickets was already causing the police to routinely stop and search cars heading from Yorkshire to Nottinghamshire. This was the final straw for Dad. As we headed south Mum told us we were going house-hunting as we'd be moving – we might not be happy, she said, but the decision was final and our pay-off would be a bigger house, better bedrooms and, without his three-hour commute, more time with Dad.

It was only after we'd dropped Mum off and we made our way to Valley Parade that I dared raise it with Dad, who assured me I'd be found as good a school in the Midlands and that, although we'd return to watch Bradford, we'd go less often and probably have to give up our C Block season tickets – but he'd compensate for that by taking us to see Brian Clough's Nottingham Forest.

That afternoon we beat Sheffield United 2–1 and then won five games in 18 days, moving us up to seventh. We should have been nailed-on for a play-off place, but in 1984 there were no play-offs, just the top three gaining automatic promotion. A ludicrous refereeing performance against Brentford – five goals disallowed – put paid to our promotion hopes. Wild accusations flew around a normally good-natured crowd, with the referee needing a police escort off the pitch, surrounded by half a dozen riot shields.

But we held on to seventh for the remaining few games of the season. It was our best finish in 26 years. Things looked good for 1984–85.

It took us until the final weekend in June to find a house that we all fell in love with – in the Nottinghamshire village of East Bridgford. Our six-week summer holiday began a fortnight later. To help prepare us for our new rural life we spent a day in Askham Bryan, outside York, visiting a friend of Mum's and spending the day playing with her kids. All of us ended up sitting in a tree watching the sun set. Little did I know that, before long, this was a peace I'd never know again.

3

1984–85 – Our Final Season

It was gloriously sunny the day we left Yorkshire; it was also the opening Saturday of the football season. As Dad's white BMW 323i pulled us up the hill of our cul-de-sac one final time, Mum turned and asked, 'Any regrets?'

'Just that we'll not have our season tickets at Bradford this year,' Dad replied. For once, he thought that we might have a very special season.

As Dad and the removal men put boxes in our new rooms in East Bridgford, I sat on the wide, sand-coloured steps that led up from the fancy driveway – wide enough to fit three cars on – and turned on my small, grey portable radio. I kept everyone updated with scores (Bradford beat Cambridge 2–0) as I basked in the baking August bank holiday sun and took in our new surroundings. A large lawn was fronted by half a dozen apple trees, beyond which sat a mixed array of colourful, imposing plants and flowers that reached up ten feet from the rockery. A conifer hedge, nearly as tall as the house, ran the length of the garden to mark the boundary with our neighbours, and there was a lawn the size of a football field. There were trees everywhere, and a white, single-storey nineteenth-century coach house, which had once served the manor house opposite, was set back and hidden by more mature trees opposite. It was a glorious backdrop to our new lives.

However, our promise of more time with Dad was postponed until he'd made the interior of the house equally glorious. So I spent sunny days with Andrew exploring the village on our Stormer BMXs. Andrew, with his affinity for nature, was enthralled by the wildlife in the fields, the never-ending bird chatter, the nearby riverbank that attracted fishermen from miles around and, most of all, by 'Sam', a squirrel so tame he'd tap on the lounge patio window and wait to be fed nuts by hand.

I was soon bored by all of this, though; by how quiet it all seemed. We were isolated by the fast A roads that encircled the village, and which we were told not to cross. There were few children about. It was not my world.

Dad had decided I should go to our local state school, Toot Hill. He claimed its results would allow me to go to a top university, if I was motivated – and if not, well, that would be the same wherever I went. So a sixteenth-century grammar school where I had several friends was to be replaced by a 1960s low-rise, concrete maze of a comprehensive, where I had none. Worse still, this was a rugby school which, despite a dozen playing fields, banned football from PE for its first and second years.

So, unsurprisingly, when my first day at school arrived, I couldn't even force a smile as my parents, who insisted on taking photos, put it down to first-day nerves. Without my best friend Andrew by my side, my new world so confused me that when I arrived at the school bus stop I was overcome by an uncharacteristic shyness and was practically mute while everyone else, so familiar with one another, caught up on their summers.

An outsider, I soon felt like an intruder. Having missed Toot Hill's induction days, the deputy headmistress took me to my new house, Thoroton, where, in full sight of everybody, I was introduced to my new housemaster, Mr Morgan. Such personal attention got tongues wagging. I looked for somewhere to sit in the packed houseroom, but it was clear I had nowhere to go. Smartly dressed, I also sensed hostility. This was clearly not the like-for-like exchange Dad had promised. I perched on the corner of a wooden ledge and started to cry. I was no longer in the second set of an academically selective school but in a mixed ability comprehensive class.

Worse still, it soon became apparent that the first-year Thoroton house was Toot Hill's dumping ground of a class, where few progressed to A levels. I'd learnt much of what we were taught a year earlier and, keen to contribute, I kept putting my hand up before giving answers beyond what my teachers were looking for. Then in Games and PE I pulled out spanking new kit – Puma Dalglish Gold football boots and Dunlop Green Flash trainers – as most of 1T pulled out their scruffy old kits. It wasn't long before a concerned classmate told me I was becoming seen as a snobby, posh swot.

Affronted, I responded in the worst imaginable way. In a school where there were a few children of working Nottinghamshire miners, I repeatedly referred to the hero of the Yorkshire coalfields, NUM leader Arthur Scargill, as 'Uncle Arthur' and wondered how I could be the one who was posh when it was actually the Nottinghamshire miners who'd sold out their brothers. Although that might have won kudos in Yorkshire, in parts of Nottinghamshire it was social suicide to think, let alone voice such an opinion. And pretty stupid. As what I'd said spread, older lads randomly pulled or violently ruffled my hair, flicked my ears, punched the back of my head or kidney-punched me, some ganging up to push me about, one throwing a coin at the back of my head. That would last for the rest of the strike. In no time I turned from one of the most popular kids at my old school to the most hated in my new.

In total contrast Andrew loved St Peter's Primary School in East Bridgford. A good-looking sporty boy, with a charming and mellow, if fun and mischievous personality, he had an instant collection of female admirers. He was becoming the boy that boys wanted to be; the boy that girls took a shine to. Out of the shadow of the cleverest kid in school – his elder brother! – and finally judged on his own considerable merits, he blossomed. He'd be waiting for me on his BMX at the bus stop outside our house most afternoons. When I saw him I knew my troubles were over for the day, as we'd ride on our bikes, play football or games. With my parents so excited by our new life, I kept my problems to myself and, although I woke each morning in dread, I knew it would soon be over, with evenings and weekends with the family to look forward to.

The one other consolation of our move to Nottinghamshire was my chance to support Brain Clough's Nottingham Forest. Some of my earliest football memories were of Forest's European Cup finals. Although I've no memory of watching the instantly forgettable 1979 final, I do remember, months later, drawing a picture of Trevor Francis's winning header to show to my new teacher, Mrs Taylor. I wasn't allowed to watch the 1980 final, as I was told it would finish past my bedtime. So I lay in bed, unable to sleep, but on hearing my parents get ready for bed, went to the bathroom to ask, 'Did they win again?' to be told by Mum, who saw straight through me, 'Yes, 1–0, sweetheart. Now go get some sleep. It's late!'

Dad was too busy to take us to Forest's first couple of home matches, so the first game we watched was a 3–1 win over Luton Town, which put Forest top of the league. With its riverside setting in leafy, prosperous West Bridgford, and the huge new, futuristic stand built on the back of two European Cup triumphs, the City Ground was a world away from Valley Parade. Only the ends, the open Kop and the cattle-shed-like Trent End, reminded me of Bradford. But as autumn set in, Forest's early season form petered out. The weekend before my 12th birthday saw Andrew and me sitting in the Junior Reds enclosure, convincing the boy next to us that the referee was our Dad and that we'd tell him off after the game for awarding Manchester United a penalty. It was the best game of the season, as Forest came back from 0–2 down at half-time to win 3–2 in the last minute. As fans climbed up the Trent End fence to get a clearer view, policemen used batons like cattle prods to force them back down.

After the match we visited my grandparents in Yorkshire, and they gave me a hardback copy of Simon Inglis's book *The Football Grounds of England & Wales* as a birthday present. As I flicked through it I was startled by a black and white photograph of a packed crowd of supporters being held back by police, who were milling around three dead bodies on the pitch. The photo was from Bolton's Burnden Park, where 33 fans had died in a crush in 1946. It prompted me to thoroughly read the safety chapter and, as we headed home, I asked how a ground like Valley Parade could be safe if it wasn't 'designated'. I was assured that if grounds weren't safe then clubs would not be allowed to open them to the public.

That weekend Mum's mum had returned to Yorkshire after a few tense weeks with us. On her return she discovered her house had been burgled – there was still the smell of the spent matches that littered the floor in the air, suggesting we'd just missed the intruders. It was the final straw for her time in the Harehills terraced house she'd lived in for over fifty years. She came to stay with us that Christmas and my parents began house-hunting for her on Boxing Day – with his decorating over, our promise of more time with Dad was postponed further still.

But on a rainy weekend that Christmas holiday we finally returned to Valley Parade – and it was eye-opening; my first experience of going back to the run-down area you'd grown up in. Bradford beat Bolton Wanderers 2–1 to secure their seventh win in eight games – it was the middle of a fantastic run that saw them capture, by the end of February, 37 out of 42 points. But it was not the football that struck me that afternoon – rather, having become accustomed to Nottingham Forest's modern City Ground, it was striking how badly Bradford's Main Stand roof leaked, how cramped it was, how much the view was obstructed by the roof supports, how narrow and poky and poorly lit the exits were; and how black the darkness on the walk back to the car, through waterlogged muddy pathways, now seemed.

The following afternoon we all watched Nottingham Forest beat Aston Villa 3–2 on ITV's Sunday afternoon football highlights programme in Grandma's lounge. As the table showed Forest had moved back up to fifth I declared, 'Oh, I wish I'd have been there.'

'What do you mean, Martin? You were back watching your own team again yesterday, and we won,' Uncle Peter remarked.

I looked at him. 'But, Uncle Peter, Forest are my team now.'

My dad just raised his eyebrows in a 'you-know-what-kids-are-like' manner.

In the bitterly cold January of 1985 Forest had no home league games till February. They did, however, have two FA Cup ties. On our arrival at the first we found the Junior Reds' section sold out, so Dad bought us three adult tickets in A Block for the third-round tie against Newcastle United. Being together made him realise how much he'd missed sitting with us both – the Junior Reds was strictly kids back then – and we ended up next to three Newcastle supporters. There was no hint of hostility or trouble, as Dad chatted about their season and offered them a swig of whisky from his hip flask. In the last weekend in January Nottingham Forest then welcomed second division Wimbledon to the City Ground, where a dire game finished 0–0. The following Wednesday I listened to the local commentary on the portable radio in my bedroom, and was so disgusted when Forest lost 1–0 at Plough Lane that I went straight to bed, but not before turning over my Nottingham Forest quilt to the plain netting side in shame. I was outraged. About half an hour later Mum came to see how I was, as I'd not said goodnight or told anyone the score.

As Mum turned the light on she asked, 'What on earth have you done to your quilt!'

'They lost 1–0, Mum. To Wimbledon! So I don't want it showing tonight!'

'Oh, grow up, Martin. I'll be telling your Dad, and when he finds out I doubt he'll want to take you to any more games.'

'Yeah, that's fine,' I told Mum, and asked her to turn the light back off on the way out.

I don't know whether it was because of this, or the fact he did not like having to sit apart from his sons at the City Ground – or maybe it was because he felt he was losing us to Forest, or was simply too busy house-hunting for his mother-in-law . . . but Dad never did take us to Forest again.

That spring the year-long miners' strike finally ended. I watched the news programmes with great relief, as it had made my school life a living hell for the previous six months. Although I'd still kept my troubles to myself, my parents noticed mood swings that concerned them, but they blamed my short, volatile temper on puberty. As the Easter holidays ended, Dad took me to the Baseball Ground to watch Bradford play Derby County. After learning there were no seats available for away supporters, we stood behind the goal. Well, Dad stood, guarding me, as I sat on a crush barrier.

'*City Gent*, guys?' asked a fan who worked his way round the away terrace armed with a pile of plain folded white A4 paper stapled into loose-leaf magazines.

'What's that, mate? I've not heard of it before.'

'It's a magazine about City, by the fans, for the fans. We started it earlier this season.'

'Oh, what a great idea,' Dad said, reaching into his sheepskin jacket pocket for some change to buy me one of the first copies of English football's longest-running fanzine.

'Good read, son?' Dad asked me after the goalless draw, as I looked up for the first time since leaving Derby. I was surprised to see we were already nearly back in East Bridgford.

'It's brilliant, Dad. You want to read it when I'm done?'

Dad said he would, but wanted to know just what had been keeping me so quiet. I told him I'd just finished reading an interview with Stafford Heginbotham.

'Aye, and what's he got to say for himself now?' sighed Dad.

'Well, he's talking about how much designation will cost once we're promoted.'

'Aye, and what's he saying?'

'Half a million.'

'Yeah, well, knowing Stafford, it'll end up costing a lot more, especially with our ground.'

'Well, it's a good job he's a rich man, then!'

'He isn't, son,' Dad confided, shaking his head.

'No?' I wondered how he could afford to own a football club if that were the case.

'By coming in at the last minute and stealing it away for peanuts.'

I remember Dad filling me in on how it was actually the vice chairman, Jack Tordoff – and not Stafford – who had all the money. Tordoff owned the JCT600 car dealerships – if you bought a car in Yorkshire, you probably bought it off Jack Tordoff – but, according to Dad, Tordoff wasn't 'a real football man' – his head ruled his heart; he wouldn't just throw money at a problem willy-nilly – 'so I doubt you'll ever see him putting his hands in his pockets. Never has before.'

I wondered what would happen if designation cost more than Stafford said it would, and we couldn't afford it.

Dad said something along the lines of, 'Don't worry, these things always find a way to work themselves out in the end.'

As we drew up on the drive Andrew came running from the house, his face white, with fear written all over it. 'Fire, fire,' he yelled. 'Mum's set fire to the kitchen . . .' Dad and I ran into the house, with Andrew trailing behind us. By the time we reached the kitchen Mum had it under control, but a large thick cloud of black smoke billowed from the chip pan to fill our large kitchen and out the kitchen windows. Not sensing its danger I breathed in the advancing smoke cloud, before I then recoiled, choking.

'Out, out, get out, get out, it's under control, shut that door and get out the back, you two. Whatever you do, don't breathe it in again!' Mum ordered us into the back garden. 'Swill that, then spit it out,' she told me as she quickly brought me a glass of water.

'What were you thinking?' Mum asked as I gulped for breath, leaning against the house, my eyes watering. I had no answer.

Ten days later Dad called us as we got back from school to tell us we were going to Cambridge. Bradford just needed to beat the bottom team to seal promotion back to Division 2. With five games to go it was now simply a question of when rather than if. So, as we headed down the A1, our main concern was when the championship party might take place. I took my *Rothmans Football Yearbook* along to try to calculate from its fixtures section when that might be. I reckoned we'd probably win the league two games later, at home to Reading – on the day Dad was to move Grandma to Nottinghamshire. After a goalless first half at the Abbey Stadium, we won 0–4 to clinch promotion. Bradford fans from the open terrace behind the goal streamed over the fence to celebrate; those of us sitting in the small corner of the away stand followed over a low wall, tearing across the pitch singing, 'We love you, City, we do; oh, City, we love you,' our faces full of wide, beaming, disbelieving smiles.

Eventually Trevor Cherry emerged in the directors' box to cheers. I was too short, really, to see Cherry or his players, but as they sprayed champagne, it hit my arm. I licked it off, getting a taste of our sweet success.

'You want to get on my shoulders, son?' Dad asked, as he crouched down, and he jogged from the halfway line towards the corner flag, with me on his back, Andrew running beside us. It was a moment that I never wanted to end.

The next day, Dad waited for us on our return from school, and took us over to the East Bridgford playing fields. Playing in one goal, as other kids started to use the other goal, Dad suggested we all play a big game together. On Friday nights, on top of a windswept moor at Batley leisure centre, he used to coach Andrew's team – for whom I played in goal or at left-back, while Andrew was a gifted midfielder. This game in East Bridgford was marred by a terrible foul from behind, though, on the eight-year-old son of Nottingham Forest centre-back Paul Hart. The perpetrator was a cowardly lad almost twice his size. As Jamie went down crying, clutching his leg, he was in such pain he couldn't walk. Dad simply hauled him over his shoulder and carried him back to Paul's house, half a mile away. It was hot, the sun shone and he ran back – but on his return Dad's energy for the game had faded none.

The game was Dad's initial recruiting drive for the junior football club he was planning to set up in East Bridgford. He couldn't believe a village with such wonderful sports facilities hadn't established a boys' side. There was, however, an East Bridgford junior cricket team, and it was perhaps the case that football's image was so bad at that point that well-to-do villagers didn't consider it an appropriate pastime for their children. Still, Dad, in looking to overcome people's objections, struck up a friendship with a long-standing villager and together they'd agreed to hold an initial meeting at the cricket pavilion to gauge interest. Three decades on, East Bridgford Junior Football Club fields boys' teams from the ages of 4 to 16; its inaugural meeting was set for Sunday 12 May 1985, the day after the Football League season ended.

The weekend before then, Dad moved Grandma into a new two-bedroom semi-detached bungalow he'd bought her in the village of Cropwell Bishop. On the Friday night, having driven a lorry up from work, he and Uncle Peter rapidly emptied her house. These two fit, strong men – one was used to hauling metal sheets around warehouses; the other spent his time lugging vending machines about – cleared her house of 50 years in no time. By Saturday afternoon I was in the lorry with Dad, as Andrew headed down the motorway behind us in Dad's white BMW 323i with Mum and Grandma. The radio was tuned to a local Yorkshire radio station, then Radio 2, but the news from Valley Parade wasn't great – one, two, then three down. Victory over Reading would have won us the title, as I'd predicted, but my heart sank with each goal flash, and it became clear we'd not win the league that day.

'Cheer up, son.' Dad seemed oddly upbeat. 'This means we can be there next Saturday – for when they *do* do it!'

As Dad and a colleague emptied the lorry in Cropwell Bishop, the classified football results were announced on *Sports Report*: 'Bradford City 2, Reading 5.'

As I relayed this to Dad he smiled and winked, 'Now, not a word, son. OK? I'm supposed to be decorating here, but . . .'

I nodded.

On the bank holiday Monday, Bradford won 0–2 at Burnden Park to secure the title. Uncle Peter was there, but we listened out for updates in East Bridgford, and at full time went over to Cropwell Bishop. As Andrew and Mum took Grandma out to try to find somewhere open to buy a new lawnmower, I sat with Dad in the lounge. He was so happy and proud, a contented man; he looked like he'd finally got everything he ever wanted in place. Sat in silence, I studied each line and contour on his face.

On the Thursday Andrew ran up to me as I got home from school: 'We might be going to Valley Parade on Saturday!' Dad had decorated each evening and long hours over the bank holiday Monday. So when Uncle Peter rang to say he'd bought five of the last tickets going in the stand without first asking, Dad told Mum he now felt obliged to take them.

That Friday we played football in the back garden, using two trees as posts. I could see Dad, in his blue suit and tie, talking with Mum in the kitchen. Mum gave him her blessing and told him with all the work he'd done she'd finish the decorating off the next day. Dad winked and gave me the thumbs-up. Andrew and I celebrated by playing football till the light faded.

4

11 May 1985

The plan was to return to Yorkshire on the final Saturday of the football season to witness our club's greatest day in half a century – such a momentous day that even Yorkshire Television dispatched a camera crew to Valley Parade. It was a day to record for posterity: barely two years after our club had nearly died, an exciting young team had captured Bradford's first piece of silverware in 56 years; we were back in the second division after a 48-year absence. But, unthinkable as it would have been that morning, none of this would matter by the time this day set.

After breakfast we played with a powerful off-road radio-controlled truck Dad had borrowed from a colleague for the weekend. Out on the lawn, Dad showed us how to use and control it; up by the half-landing window Mum stood in her dressing gown, her hair wet. She waved, a wide beaming smile over her face, and we continued taking instruction from Dad. Years later she told me that as she watched us, she had silently counted her blessings at how well her life had turned out. She had found the happy, prosperous home she had always dreamed of.

Then Dad handed Andrew the remote-control unit. He paid little heed to Dad's warnings about the wet grass and, powering the truck forward, shot it impressively across the lawn at great speed. But it had to turn before reaching the line of trees at the end of the garden. Andrew grappled with the handset, but it was too late, the truck was travelling too fast with little traction on the wet grass. Rather than turning, it took off, flying through the air and, once airborne, smashed against a tree trunk with a sickening thud.

'You idiot! You absolute idiot. What the hell did you do that for? What did Dad tell us?' I hollered at him. I was incensed – none of us would get to play with the truck now; it lay nose-down in soil under the tree, its wheels spinning wildly.

'Calm down, Martin, calm down!' Dad admonished me. He went to retrieve the truck, but when he put it back on its tyres it didn't restart, and there was a burning smell coming from its engine.

I'd been so loud Mum came down, alarmed at what might have caused such a commotion. I told her, but she didn't want to know, asking, 'Is that all?' I ranted on, but she told me to, 'Shut up, and grow up, Martin.' As I protested further still she became even angrier, until I was sent to sit in Dad's car. Dad quickly brought me a copy of the *Daily Telegraph*, and I sat there trying to concentrate on that morning's sports pages. Half an hour later, Andrew appeared and handed me my Bradford City scarf and cap, and apologised. I told him to forget about it. Dad reversed round the turning circle and we headed off down the drive. Mum waved from the lounge window, but unlike the others I lodged a final protest by keeping my arm firmly down.

We were passing by the cooling towers on the M1 in Sheffield when Dad spoke about Mum. He explained she was finding it difficult now I'd reached the age she was when her dad died. He talked about the impact this loss had had on her when they met – and how she was still struggling a bit, two decades later – and we agreed how lucky our lot was. He asked me to bear with it, and understand it from her perspective. A remote-controlled truck was just a toy.

Thinking of Mum growing up without her dad, I distinctly remember asking him, 'So, what would you want from me if you were to die?'

'C'mon, Martin, your granddad was 61 when your mum was 12 – I'm 34!'

'I know, but let's just say it did happen. It would be nice to know.'

'Well, obviously I'd want you to both be there for each other and support your mum, and while I hope you'd miss me, I'd not want either of you to be dwelling on that. More than anything else I'd want you to both get on with your lives, so that when people met you for the first time, years later, they'd have no idea of what had happened to you. That's what I'd want – for you both to make something of yourselves and be happy.'

On our arrival in Pudsey Grandma handed me a copy of the *Telegraph & Argus* from the day we were promoted at Cambridge, as well as the promotion supplements published by that paper and by the *Yorkshire Post*. Dad and Andrew left me sprawled over the carpet reading them as they went to get fish and chips. *Football Focus* was about to start as they arrived back, hot bundles of newspaper-wrapped food under each arm. After putting them in the kitchen they joined me and Granddad round the TV. Grandma plated-up the bundles, and for once we hoped Bradford would get some recognition. Yet there was no mention on BBC, nor ITV – we were staggered to see that *On the Ball* were sending cameras to Chesterfield, who'd won the fourth division.

'Anyone got any idea what we have to do to get on national television?' Dad protested. 'It just goes to show, our face never fits,' he concluded sadly.

The chips were good, though. Uncle Peter turned up and Dad settled up with him – £8 for his three tickets; Granddad was upset at not being able pay his £2 as Uncle Peter didn't have change. As we piled into Uncle Peter's blue Ford Cortina Estate, we waved to Grandma, who stood on the doorstep. Dad boomed out, as he jumped into the front passenger seat, 'Now don't forget, Mum: have that kettle on for ten-past five!'

We parked up on our usual spot on Thorncliffe Road, behind the Kop, and headed to the concrete hut called the City Shop. It was overflowing, but Dad was keen to buy me a Bolton programme; it took over ten minutes to reach the counter at the front of the scrum. On leaving, Dad suggested we find a pub to make a celebratory toast. Unsure where the nearest pub was – Manningham was a red-light district, and, with kids now in tow, it'd been a while since he'd had a pre-match drink round those parts – he asked a policeman at the bottom of Valley Parade, who told us it was a ten-minute walk. As we debated if we had the time, the Lincoln City team bus drew down Valley Parade and parked outside the clubhouse. It was 2 p.m., so I suggested we'd be pushing it to get back for the presentation at 2.30 p.m. Dad agreed, and we headed back down South Parade. Outside the turnstile block scraps of plain A4 paper were stuck to the wooden boards that usually had the prices on – blue biro scrawled, 'Sold Out'.

We clicked through the old turnstiles and turned left and walked down the narrow rear corridor to G Block, at the far end of the stand. I asked Uncle Peter if I could have my ticket as a souvenir.

'Can I keep them for now, Martin? In case we need them later. You can have all five after the game. Deal?'

'Deal!' I told him, excited by the prospect of having five instead of one.

Once we'd found our seats – in row O, three rows from the back, in the top left-hand corner of the stand as you looked at the pitch – I devoured the match programme, as usual (a 50p souvenir programme had been issued that day, with eight extra pages justifying the 10p price hike). A brass band full of teenagers in blue uniforms marched round the pitch. The trophy presentation came five minutes early, made in front of A Block, at the opposite clubhouse end of the stand. Even standing on the bench, craning to see, I could glimpse only snatches of the ceremony. Once the squad went on its lap of honour, though, we saw everything: the team joyfully threw the trophy between themselves, and supporters dressed in bantam costumes and 'City Gent' bowler hats climbed on to the pitch to join them, the players shooing the police away. We all stood in proud salute, loudly applauding and cheering before the players disappeared into the clubhouse changing rooms.

They came back out to another standing ovation, lined up in their pre-arranged order on the halfway line, before taking out the claret-coloured lettered boards they'd hidden under their tracksuit tops, to spell out the message 'THANK YOU, FANS', turning in unison to thank each of the four sides of Valley Parade. We should have all left then – the title secured, Lincoln safe from relegation, this was always destined to be a dead rubber of a match. And, true to form, in a scrappy first half the only thing I can remember was an injury to a Lincoln player in the opening minutes. It looked serious, a suspected broken leg. There must have been a five-minute delay before he was stretchered away, to sympathy in the stand.

That day Andrew sat on the end of our row, close to the spiked metal railings separating us from the steep paddock terrace to our left. I was to his right, Dad to mine; Uncle Peter and Granddad in the seats nearest to the aisle. I remember just in front of us that day, there were two good-looking girls about our age, with their younger brother. That prompted a bit of nudge-nudge, wink-wink between Andrew and me. Aged 12 and 11, though, quite what we were going to do about it, I don't know.

Despite the Bradford City scarves Andrew and I both proudly wore round our necks, and the claret and amber Makita cap on my head, we'd mischievously agreed to wear our grey and red pinstriped Nottingham Forest sweatshirts beneath our jackets. Minutes after the Lincoln player was carried away I asked Andrew, 'Can you believe we gave up the chance to see the champions for this?'

'I'd have so loved to have seen Forest beat Everton,' he replied. Andrew sighed, remembering that free king-size Mars bars were being given out in the Junior Reds enclosure that day: 'I've never had one,' he added, wistfully.

'I know, instead of that, we get to sit through this.' I playfully dug Dad in the ribs.

Dad said nothing, before jumping up and heading down the aisle, returning a couple of minutes later. 'Any chance these might keep you quiet?' he asked, taking two Mars bars out of the inside pocket of his brown sheepskin jacket.

Part of the deal was that we had to shut up moaning and I had to swap seats with Dad, so that he could enjoy his moment of triumph in some kind of peace. But still the game didn't improve. About half an hour in, Uncle Peter turned to Dad, 'The boys are right, John. It's getting no better.'

Dad pointed out that the hard work had been done in securing promotion, and that a good game would have been a bonus. 'There'll be plenty of those next season,' he reckoned, before talk turned to Bradford coping in the second division and Dad wondered aloud about getting season tickets for all of us.

'I'd be up for that,' said Uncle Peter. 'It's not really been the same without you lot this year.'

Dad turned to us. 'How about you two?'

Andrew was happy as long as we could still watch Forest too; I was up for it as well, but was also worried about what Mum would think.

'How many more times, Martin?' Dad said. 'You leave your mother to me.' He turned to Uncle Peter: 'Well, that's settled, then. Season tickets it is.'

Keen to beat the half-time rush down the always-congested rear corridor, I headed to the halfway-line huts that housed the toilets. Then, wanting to see the girl in the old snack bar where we used to sit, and to check out whether anyone was in our old seats in C Block, I headed not to the nearest snack bar, but to the far one, where a uniformed off-duty fireman was being served.

'How you been, stranger?' the girl who worked behind the snack bar asked on seeing me.

I remember telling her we were now living in Nottingham, but that we'd be back next year.

'You take care and have a good summer now,' she said.

'You too,' I replied.

Walking back up the corridor with my can of Coke the two pretty girls from the row in front were walking towards me, trying to deal with their brother, who was zigzagging his way down the tight passageway. I remember their pastel suits looking somewhat out of place in the drab, gloomy half-light of the back of that stand. They smiled as I stood in a turnstile to let them pass.

It was the last moment of normality I can remember.

When I reached G Block, I overheard an old man talking to a police officer by the stairwell. 'I can smell something burning under my seat, but I just can't put my finger on it,' he said. Although his words were unusual enough to echo in my ears, I walked on. As I sat back down, Lincoln rifled a speculative 25-yard shot over the crossbar at the Bradford End. There was a break in play, and I remember checking the time on the clock in the corner of the Midland Road terrace and Bradford End. It was 3.40 p.m.

I was just about to open my cola when the tiniest trail of mysterious white smoke began to rise from the front of our seating section. 'What's that?' one supporter asked. Nobody had any idea, and bafflement grew as the smoke did.

'Piss on it, piss on it, piss on it!' those on the paddock on our left started to chant.

'What a pity I've just been – I could have put that out!' I announced, to wry smiles all round.

Over the next minute or so the small white cloud of smoke slowly expanded.

'Bradford's burning, fetch the engines . . . fire, fire, fire. Bradford's burning . . .' sang the paddock.

We could merely watch and wait as the smoke grew. Watch, as the police ordered those on the front rows of this rear seating section up the narrow stairwell, into the one empty area of the packed stand – the narrow rear corridor I'd just strolled down – and wait, as the nine rows in this section started to slowly empty backwards. We kept a cursory eye on the game, but it was the baffling trail of white smoke that had everyone's real attention, with some on the paddock having turned their backs on the game to watch it grow.

'So, where should we go, John?' asked Uncle Peter.

'Same place the police want everyone else, Peter: the corridor. Let them do their jobs and once they've cleared us all out, I'm sure they'll sort that out,' Dad said, pointing to the smoke. 'Where else can we go?' he said, as Bradford City attacked.

'True,' Uncle Peter agreed, as the G Block stairwell ended at a wall halfway down the stand. There was, of course, no exit down into the section of seating below – we'd tried that on the open day. Dad and Uncle Peter agreed that it was a 'wait-in-the-back-of-the-stand job'.

The police cue was clear: yes, there was a problem, but it was manageable, and the best we could do to help them manage it was to clear out. Any attempt to motion us forwards would have simply recongested the area they'd just cleared. And there was no immediate way forwards through this obstacle course of a stand when it was empty, let alone full. So there was only one place to go: backwards. Not that this alarmed anybody unduly: at this point, nobody really expected to have to leave the stand. We half-anticipated a wait in the corridor, before returning to our seats once the fire had been put out; the worst-case scenario was that we'd have to watch the second half from elsewhere in the ground. So one man casually ate a pie as he headed back, and a photographer in the next section, an expensive camera hung round his neck, did not even consider the trail of smoke noteworthy enough to photograph.

The smoke had been rising for two minutes now. It was the contrast of the amber flames against a crack in the claret-painted wooden enclosure wall that hit me. There was a wild and unrestrained movement in their large dancing tips that suggested matters were more serious than anyone had anticipated. I saw a police officer painfully shake his fist after he'd tried to rip the floorboards up, only to burn his leather gloves.

'Bloody hell!' I exclaimed.

'Language!' Dad immediately chided me, rewarding me for my observation with a clipped ear, his attention perhaps on the Bobby Campbell attack that broke down after his poor ball control.

Annoyed at being told off again, I turned to my uncle. 'What's that there, Uncle Peter?' I asked, pointing to the dancing flames.

'John. Get the bloody kids out of here!' he immediately told my Dad.

'Andrew, go with Martin,' said Dad, nodding along the row of vacated bench seats, everyone now stood up, slowly filtering towards the stairwell aisle. 'I'll go with Uncle Peter and help Granddad.'

'No,' Andrew told him, clearly concerned by the suggestion.

So Dad turned to me. 'Martin, you go by yourself, then. We'll follow, but if we get lost go to the car and wait. OK?'

Ordinarily I might well have refused, like Andrew, but, embarrassed by the display of public discipline and angered at having been, to my 12-year-old-mind, unfairly reprimanded for a second time that day, I nodded and told him, 'OK.'

So I jumped on to our now empty row of wooden bench seats, and ran to the end of the plank, past everyone who was filing out. By the time I reached the end of the row my anger had subsided. I turned back to look hesitatingly at my family at the end of the slowly emptying queue. They were starting to move a bit more quickly, but rather than tell me to wait, as I'd secretly hoped he might, Dad shouted in encouragement: 'Go on, Martin. We're following.' So, nodding, I simply jumped from our row on to the row behind, then sneaked through the congestion round the stairwell entry into the rear corridor of the stand, losing sight of the rest of them.

The game wasn't stopped until the flames had emerged in the stand, three minutes after the smoke had started rising. By then I'd been in the corridor for about 30 seconds. Accustomed to its tight conditions and restricted movement I was not overly worried to find my progress halted after a few yards. There was a solid wall of stationary people ahead of me. I'd assumed, as always, it would ease. But the pressure started to tighten from behind as more and more people entered the corridor. By the time the game was stopped the whole of our rear section of G Block was in the corridor.

'*No, no. Leave me alone. Leave me alone. I'm not going, I'm not going,*' one scared woman in the entrance to the G Block stairwell screamed at a policeman, who demanded she go back into the stand. She was blocking the entrance to the stand, so he tried to physically drag her, but gave up. Unable to move I had the first panicky thought: 'We are trapped.' Although the tightening slackened and the woman's screams stopped, their echo made the confines of this already narrow corridor seem even more claustrophobic. Unable to move, and too short to see over the stand partition wall, I was trapped between strangers all taller than me. Where were the police? There seemed to be no effort to alleviate this pressure by marshalling people along the corridor. With each passing second I wanted out.

'Dad . . . Dad . . . Dad!' I eventually shouted, as I began to hit the wall of the stand with my right fist, the slapping breaking the eerie calm in the otherwise silent corridor.

'Martin, Martin. Calm down, calm down. I'm here, just turn around, son. Just turn around and talk to me, I'm here.' Dad was in the corridor too and the pressure had slackened enough that I could turn to look up and over various pairs of heads back to him. I thought I could make out Andrew's head in front of him and with Granddad in front of Uncle Peter on his left.

'I want to come back, Dad. I want to come back,' I told him, as I fought back tears.

'I know, son. I know, but not now, later. It's not possible right now, OK?'

'I know, I know, Dad,' I replied, looking at the dozen or so sad, silent, concerned faces that separated us, knowing that if they could find a way to let me through they would. But they couldn't, as there was no space. This realisation heightened my anxiety further still. By this point the fire behind us would have been a few rows deep, a few seats wide. Enough for the screaming woman to not want to be dragged back into G Block.

'Listen to me. Everything's going to be OK, as long as we all stay calm and don't panic. OK. You can do that for me, can't you?'

'But Dad . . .' I started to say, but broke off as I looked back to watch a narrow channel of white smoke start to funnel through the double-pitched roof above. In seconds all the natural light seemed to drain from the corridor; a daylight perspective was suddenly reduced to a disconcerting, evening one: the smoke was now rapidly funnelling down the roof of the corridor, but with the electric lights still burning it felt like we were suddenly at a night match.

'I know, son. But look at me, look only at me.' As I did so, my gaze started to divert away from him. He must have been about ten or twelve feet away, and he told me again, 'No, Martin. Only at me, son; me and only me, OK? Deep breaths, son; deep breaths. With me, in . . . out . . . in . . . out. Good, now listen to me—' and with my breathing now regulated by Dad's rhythm, as I got large lungfuls of clear air, I nodded. 'I need you to stay calm for me, Martin. If we all stay calm then there's going to be nothing to worry about, OK? I promise you. I just need you to be brave. You can do that for me, can't you, son? I know you can. Just remember, deep breaths, in . . . out . . . in . . . out . . . in . . . out . . .' I kept doing that, getting much calmer with each passing breath. 'Look, Martin. Don't worry. It's OK. Everything's going to be OK – OK?' It was a promise. He'd never lied to me. He was the man who had always made everything OK, all my life, until then.

So I nodded silently, before I turned back round. Embarrassed, I quietly told the man beside me with his two teenage sons in front of him, 'Sorry about that.'

'Don't worry about it,' he told me, as he smiled pensively.

Nobody corrected Dad's impressions. Everybody waited calmly, in silence, perhaps aware that any open expression of fear could likely trigger a stampede. So we waited, united in some kind of conscious desire not to panic, silently praying the fire would stay at bay. Then, it seemed our patience had at last paid off. The gridlock cleared quickly and inexplicably. Having been unable to advance a yard in 90 seconds, we now briskly walked ten yards over the next few seconds.

I couldn't see over the partition wall, but I knew we were no further than the edge of the penalty box, with the nearest exit still a way up the corridor, just past the halfway line. Then those further ahead of me suddenly broke into a gallop, starting to run down the unfathomably emptying corridor ahead of them. I ignored this open space and held back, following those immediately ahead of me who spread out into a recess on our right, the first of the turnstile huts that squatted on South Parade. I stood directly in front of the waist-high metal turnstile and thought its sanctuary might give me a chance to rejoin my family. I glanced at the brass plaque of the original installers engraved on to the claret wooden turnstile desk, then up at the turnstile door. Bolts secured the top and bottom of this door, and padlocks secured these bolts.

'Oh my God! They're locked! They're locked!' the man who'd vaulted the turnstile ahead of me shouted as he began to desperately beat his fists on the claret turnstile door. Two or three others had jumped over the other turnstiles and were doing the same.

I'd been so reassured by Dad that this man's panic seemed to make little sense. Yet somehow it made perfect sense. Not that it had time to spread. I stood there calmly, remembering Dad's instructions from seconds before, taking a deep breath in, a deep breath out, another one in – then in an instant a blackness fell. I thought the lights had failed, but the darkness fell with such speed – it was too black, there was nothing, not even the daylight that should have shone through the turnstile door from the street behind. I struggled for a logical explanation of this total blackness. It was what, 30 seconds since I'd last seen Dad.

Then . . . silence. Seconds earlier I had been braced for the pressure that I'd assumed would follow, as more bodies rammed me towards the turnstile. But after the briefest, momentary surge, none came. There was a loud thumping noise for a second or so, then the silence was total. I was rooted to the spot, disoriented – each second lasted a minute and I failed to make any sense of what was happening all around me. All I did know was not to lose the large lungful of clean air I'd taken in just as the blackness had come down.

In an instant the smoke ahead of me started to swirl, as my feet and hands painlessly clenched up. I gingerly sniffed, but I can't remember dropping the Coke or the Bolton and Lincoln programmes I'd been holding – all sensations must have been subconscious from this moment on, which meant I had no fear. As the swirling became internalised, I felt my consciousness detach from my body – which, in turn, felt as if it were about to shut down. I knew I was about to drop to the floor and that there was nothing I could do to resist it, other than to not take another dose of this lethal concoction in the black smoke. I must have known it was time to die. I had just one image in my mind: of home, and Mum standing there waving, like she'd done when I'd ignored her, just hours earlier.

Then a brightly illuminated silhouette of a person somehow appeared ahead of me. This interrupted my vision of home, and with it my consciousness cleared. Then, just as quickly, the silhouette disappeared, leaving me still holding my breath and praying again that I was still in the real world, and not this hellish, black emptiness.

Utterly confused, I was about to head forwards, towards where the silhouette had appeared from, when I heard a single distant voice from behind me: 'Get everybody on the pitch. Now!'

This voice was muffled by no other noise. There was no shouting, no screaming, no pushing. No sense of alarm nor panic, no fear – just nothing, absolutely nothing. That, I think, is what made me uncertain as to whether I was still alive or not. But this lone voice suggested that maybe I was still alive. So I followed it. It told me where to go. I knew how to get there, and was somehow convinced I'd make it. I felt for the turnstile block wall with my back, then pinned myself against it, and slid along for about five feet. As I did so, I sensed I was not alone, and felt myself push through people, but no pressure came, either with or against me. People still seemed lined up against the opposite partition wall. As the hut wall turned at a right angle back to the stand's main support wall, I turned with it.

It was now that the extent of this blackness finally revealed itself. Although the F Block stairwell was directly opposite me, all I could see was the dark outline of a prone man in front of it, and nothing above or beyond him. Nothing broke the blackness to my left, but to my right a narrow ray of light shone through the E Block stairwell, the next one along. I ran for it. Through the stairwell I could see the pitch, the bus-shelter terrace opposite, its Intasun advertising board, and the industrial valleyscape beyond – it was all oddly monochromatic, orange and black. As I ran to the light in the stairwell I collided with nobody. I looked back through the snack-bar windows, to the familiar terraced housing behind, but again . . . just orange and black.

'Help me. Anybody! Please. God help me . . .' It was the one solitary cry I heard break the silence in the blackness of that corridor, but by the time I'd reached the stairwell it had died away.

I slid my hands beneath my jacket sleeves as I ran through the prickly heat. As I stepped into the E Block stairwell, out of the corridor, I looked right, diagonally across the stand. White smoke now rose from rows of entirely empty bench seats around me, beyond which people moved rapidly forwards in ant-like unison towards the pitch, with those as far away as A Block already down in the front seating section. At last the distant pandemonium of their muffled screams and cries broke the silence.

Free of the blackness, I exhaled, hoping to breathe in clear air. But as I did so, my entire body, inside and out, was devoured by an indescribably painful venomous blast of furnace heat. Stunned, I turned to my left to see an upturned waterfall of fire, with the whole of G Block – its base and parts of F Block – consumed by strips of fire. The advancing wave of fire was racing down the roof to E Block, a narrow strip of flame already lapping the front row of the stairwell I'd have to race down to make it to the amber wall. Something told me this was the only way out – it was certainly preferable to the black graveyard of the corridor behind – but as I looked at the fire, stunned to momentary paralysis, its heat suffocated all rational conscious thought. My mind blacked out – it was now a race against time. I ran for it, down the E Block stairwell, the subterranean fire burning away the toes and heels and the insoles of my black, non-combustible rubber-soled trainers. I made it down the nine rows of E Block seats, and just as I made it over the amber E Block wall, and down through steps of the plastic seating area at the front, the fire which had raged through G and F blocks swept past me, overhead.

Only after I'd made it over the even higher claret-painted wall, down on to the paddock terrace, did my conscious thought process return. That was the terrifying eight-foot drop Dad had helped me over on the open day, but running for my life, my instinct for survival had taken over. But I knew I still wasn't safe; the second double-pitched roof over the lower half of the stand was blazing now too, and I started to feel a burning sensation tear at the back of my head as I watched a man ahead of me struggle to get over the pitchside wall between the two elevated dug-outs. I realised I'd have to try to lift him over before I could scale it. But there was no time, and with no warning I suddenly lost control of my body. It seemed I was having an out-of-body experience. Flying through the air I could see the Kop and Midland Road terraces, my burning head and blurred watery vision the only reminders I was still conscious.

I closed my eyes as I felt myself fall, and was dragged like a rag doll, then rolled over, before I came to rest on the soft, wet grass on my bare, naked stomach, my jacket and top having run up. As I'd made it through the inferno molten tar from the burning roof had dripped on to my jacket, scarf and cap. By the time I'd reached the front paddock I was on the brink of becoming a human torch – then someone had picked me up and literally hurled me over the wall (hence the flying), as another fan ripped his jacket off and smothered me with it, before others dragged me by my jacket away from the burning stand, knocking my burning cap off, then rolling my smouldering body twice over.

These people had all gone to a football match, like we had, to watch their team lift a trophy. But many reacted in that sudden hell, to save lives. They were the heroes of the Bradford fire, unsung.

Sprawled out on the pitch I opened my eyes to savour the smell of the wet green turf. Knowing I'd lost my cap, but not why, I turned to reach it, but my grasp proved just short. As I did so, my outstretched arm was trampled as screams filled the air. I now looked back at the stand to see the cascading waterfall of fire fall from the roof on to the pitch, a white line of smoke exploding like a gunpowder trail, marking out its ever-accelerating advance. It was about to overtake us and those who had rescued people now ran, the terror clearly etched on their faces, as my exposed back began to burn. Stunned, exhausted, I lay prone. As the collection of abandoned police helmets beside me started to smoke, my own flaming cap shrivelled up into blackened ash.

From that point I have no recollection, but somehow I made it across the pitch. The next thing I can remember is pacing up and down like a hurt, bewildered animal. All I could now feel on my face was an inescapable thousand-degree-plus heat that destroyed all the grass by the stand. There was so much screaming, along with the overpowering smell of a mass bonfire – burning timber from the stand fused together with the smell of burnt flesh, and the taste of acrid smoke on my lips.

The far half of the pitch was packed. As I looked away from those gathered around the seriously injured, I caught the stunned horror on people's faces as they created a channel for me – a small, inconsolable, burnt, smoke-smeared child screaming for his dad. Reaching the Bradford End, I saw people fearfully shaking the fences they were trapped behind, the fire advancing towards them. Dehydrated and exhausted, I turned back and reached the halfway line. I tightly clutched on to the cold steel on the top of the Midland Road advertising boards and dug my feet into the pebbly gravel track the ball boys stood on.

'You OK, lad?'

'Yeah, I'm fine, thanks.'

'You sure?' the man asked in disbelief.

I nodded, smiling, relieved to interact with the familiar world once more. 'Do you think the second half will start soon?' I asked, as if we'd stand and watch it together.

He didn't know what to say to that, and after I repeated myself he asked, 'Look, I can see you were in it, but have you actually seen the stand?'

'No, why?'

'I think you should, lad.'

I turned to face it for the first time, properly, since I'd made it out of E Block moments before – but it was gone, totally consumed in an inferno of volcanic fury. Furious deep oranges were interspersed with the angriest blacks; there were several fires within the fire. Then I looked up to see a cloud of smoke as wide as the stand, spewing blackened bile hundreds of feet into the air, dwarfing the floodlights.

'You reckon it'll be on *Crimewatch*?' I asked, little realising the pictures were already being beamed live around the UK.

'Aye, and when it is it'll be bloody murder too,' one supporter said.

'What do you mean?' I wondered.

'Well, I saw people in that stand burst into flames.'

'Really, how many?' I asked, still a bit nonplussed.

'Two,' he said.

As he said this a young boy burst into tears. His mum and elder teenage brother reassured him there was nothing to worry about and that the fire would spread no further. I joined in too, telling him I was OK. His mum managed to calm her son then turned to me: 'We need to get you some water for your burns, love.'

'Nah, I'm fine,' I told her.

Not correcting me, she insisted, 'Come with us to the snack bar, so we can get you some water.'

'I don't need water, but I could do with a cola,' I told her, climbing over the perimeter wall on to the terrace.

'A what?' she asked.

'I dropped my cola and my programmes – I've lost my cap too,' I said, fighting back tears.

'They don't matter, love,' she said. She was kind and reassuring as she told me her name, Margaret, and we headed to the snack bar. But the programmes mattered to me – maybe subconsciously I was clinging to the last scraps of the normal world.

'Can you give him some water for his burns, love?' Margaret asked at the snack bar.

'I can't – we've been told not treat them with water, but to wait and let the hospital treat them,' said the girl working there.

'That's OK, but can you sell me a cola?' I asked, reaching into my jeans for change.

'We've been told to sell no more,' she told Margaret, shocked anyone might want snacks.

Standing on the narrowest terrace in England, I turned to face the stand once more, and unable to believe it was real, I asked Margaret, 'Is there any chance I might wake up soon?'

'That'd be nice, love, but no, I don't think so.'

'My mum's going to be so mad I lost my cap.'

'Trust me love, she isn't.'

I told her again that I couldn't believe I'd lost my programmes, asking again if I could get another one outside. Margaret promised me she'd get me another one if she could, but that I really shouldn't be worrying about that. I think she clocked I was entering into some kind of state of shock, and as I started to shiver, she told me, 'I'm going to let a friend of mine, a policeman, look after you. So we can get a message to your home. Is that OK?'

I nodded. She shouted to her friend, gesturing for him to come over, and I climbed back over the Midland Stand terrace wall. The officer led me a few yards away, to where he was looking after an old man whose face had been reduced to yellow flesh, skin hanging from his jaw and forehead, some of which had glued itself on to his spectacles. The patches of skin that remained were blackened. He'd been smartly dressed, but his suit and overcoat were now meshed into liquefied flesh on the left-hand side of his body. His hands were blobs of yellow flesh too. Yet, although he later died, he lay without complaint. So I did too. I lay on the pitch beside him, a black police overcoat covering me to stop my shivering. Later I learnt this was Eric Hudson, who was 72. He never made it out of Pinderfields' burns unit. On the pitch everyone just knew him as Eric.

An inescapable anger then erupted around me. As I looked up, the television crew seemed to be pointing their lenses at the injured, and fans chanted, 'Turn your fucking cameras off.' Ignored, the supporters climbed on to the roof of the 12-foot high Midland Road terrace, upon which the scaffold gantry stood, and started shaking it. Those on the ground began to pelt the gantry with coins, yet still the cameras rolled. So a few fans climbed the gantry stepladder and wrestled a camera from the crew, throwing it on to the terrace roof. People cheered on the pitch. Once the camera went, the shaking stopped, and the ladder was returned. Bradford had simply decided the world had seen enough.

As I lay there resting, occasionally clutching at the damp grass, my gaze kept wandering back to the stand. The burning structure and plume of black smoke were hypnotic, transfixing – then either a policeman, or a fan, would say, 'Look away, lad.' A policeman reassured me that nobody had died, explaining that all those seen on fire in the stand, like the man beside me, were rescued – and that the rear corridor, after some initial problems, had been cleared. I remember thinking, 'You idiot – you should have just carried on running down that corridor, and got out the back exit on the halfway line, with everyone else.' Dad, Andrew and the others would be back at the car now, wondering where I was. Part of me was also thinking, 'This isn't half going to be a story back at school.' I told the policeman about my dad and the others. Aware of my fears and keen to help, he gave my Nottinghamshire school bus pass to a colleague, who took my photograph and details and said he'd soon be back with my family, as nobody else here would live in Nottinghamshire. But he returned empty-handed.

The policeman offered to arrange an ambulance, but I told him there was no need. He explained that I wasn't in much pain because I was still in shock. I had blistered burns: one, four inches wide, ran across the width of my back, another, across the entire outer ridge of my left ear. The back of my head was burnt by the tar that had seared through my cap and reset. I had three long, narrow cuts on the left-hand side of my face. That I did not realise all this meant I was in shock, and I might also be suffering the effects of smoke inhalation. So we agreed I'd better go to hospital – but only after I went to see if my family were by the car. After shakily making our way down the dreadfully steep terrace embankment stairwell, Margaret, her kids and I walked along an ambulance-filled Midland Road. Burnt fans were everywhere. As we made a left into Thorncliffe Road my heart sank – nobody was by the car. Having been told by Dad to meet here, I told Margaret I'd wait, but as I looked towards our normal route to and from the stand, over the much travelled grass embankment at the back of the Kop, towards the stand and at its blazing roof beyond . . . as much as I wished it, nobody came. After a minute or so Margaret reminded me of the deal I'd made, and when I was resistant to the suggestion we go she pointed out, 'A nice young lad like you wouldn't go lying to a nice policeman now, would he?' Otherwise I'd have stayed there.

By the time we returned to Midland Road, all the ambulances but one were gone. Still, there were plenty of people and cars jamming the road, and drivers were volunteering to ferry people to hospital. The car I got into had a Yorkshire Television pass on its windscreen, but as it tried to pull away, it could barely move. I told the driver about how I'd escaped, and that the turnstiles were the last place I'd seen my family. He looked horrified and, on hearing a siren, jumped out to flag down the last of the ambulances. He pleaded with the driver that he had an injured child on board and asked whether they had room for me. I got out of the car and the paramedic opened the rear doors of the ambulance. A dozen burnt uniformed police officers all sat on bench seats, like soldiers in wartime, each horribly blistered by their bravery. The paramedic said, 'We got room for a little 'un?' As they shuffled across, I jumped aboard.

I told them about my family, and my fellow passengers reassured me as to how they'd successfully evacuated the stand, and especially the rear corridor, 'just in time'. One copper told me it was his mate who'd actually got the doors at the back open, and that people had flooded out – and as soon as we could find him, he'd get me to Dad and the others. The others were all nodding and saying pretty much the same thing: 'Don't worry, it'll be fine.' We sped through the city centre with our sirens blaring, crowds of onlookers standing on pavements, staring in stunned horror at our tinted windows. I was going on about my big toe hurting although, once I'd whipped off my trainer and sock, we all saw there was nothing wrong with it whatsoever – unlike my ear, face and back, as the police pointed out, causing some amusement to the officers with burns far worse than mine. On arriving at the hospital I promptly forgot about my trainer and walked towards the casualty doors one sock on one sock off: a policeman, laughing, handed me back my trainer.

The nurse who treated me on arrival also told me about the safe evacuation from the back of the stand. She'd heard about it on the radio. With no money, no way home and no way of contacting my family, injured policemen, once treated, looked after me and kept me positive with reassuring chats and words of encouragement. They all had the same story, the same answers, the same assurances. People had got out of the back of that stand. Eventually they'd got the doors open. Then a nurse came to tell me I had family at reception. I experienced a surge of joy and ran happily to reception, where I found Margaret with her children. She'd told them she was family in order to bypass reception protocol, so I'd not be alone.

By now a policeman had commandeered a consultant's room. All I could remember was my grandma's address in Pudsey, so he found her number, then let it ring constantly – she'd been out on a shopping trip in Selby, the other side of Leeds. It was twenty minutes or so before she picked up the phone. As the policeman told me my family were on the way Margaret soon left to check on others she knew who'd been burnt.

Back in the waiting area I saw a young, injured police officer, clearly fighting back tears. So I went over to reassure him that the police should all be proud of what they'd done that afternoon.

He clearly struggled to accept my plaudits, and asked, 'Who are you with now?'

'I'm still by myself at the minute.'

'And where was the last place you saw your family?'

'At the turnstiles in the stand.'

'When?'

'Just before the smoke fell.'

His face went red, before he hugged me, in a sort of broken, gentle way, then burst into tears. I remember clutching on to his burnt black overcoat as I hugged him back.

Suddenly there were a lot of charged emotions flying around the waiting room. One man asked, 'Is it true?' Another man tearfully nodded, and they broke down into each other's arms. Then a nurse hugged a tearful, smoke-blackened fireman and poured him a coffee. These were hardened, reserved, Yorkshire folk, so the policeman who'd commandeered the consultant's room soon told me to go and sit in it. Still in something of a daze, and reassured by all the talk about the evacuation from the back of the stand, I wasn't at all aware that I was being moved out of harm's way.

When my aunty Val and uncle Mike came in with my cousin Chris, around 5.15 p.m., they were anxious to learn about where we'd sat, how I escaped, and the last place I'd seen everyone. Aunty Val, Dad's elder sister, wasn't into football, and was the only member of Grandma's family not familiar with Valley Parade, but, on hearing the last place I'd seen everyone was by the turnstiles before the smoke fell, she and Uncle Mike were keener to talk with the emergency workers in reception than to take me home. They left me talking with Chris while Aunty Val kept popping back in to tell us she was waiting for news from other hospitals. I was in that consultant's room for nearly two hours, and I had no idea about the storm that was gathering outside in the waiting room – that amongst talk of an unusual amount of 'debris' by the turnstiles at the back of the stand people's worst fears were slowly coming to the surface; that relatives in the waiting room were slowly, as each list of names came through, being sent up to the wards, or off to another hospital, to be reunited with their injured loved ones. But for those who were still left . . . the nurses could see the dwindling numbers were the ones who were going to be the bereaved.

After a while Aunty Val's updates stopped and so, perplexed by the delay and keen to speak to Mum, around 7 p.m. I ventured back into the reception area, where few now remained.

'Could there have been some sort of mistake in compiling these lists?' my emotional aunt was asking a nurse. 'Are you certain no more lists are going to arrive?'

A policeman I'd recognised from the ambulance earlier nodded in my direction, and told my aunt that he was afraid there was nothing more they could do: 'I think the best thing you can do is to get Martin home and await further news.'

After which Aunty Val quickly recomposed herself while a nurse gave me a red box of painkillers and tube of Flamazine cream. She told Aunty Val that normally they'd look to admit me for overnight observation, but as they had no beds it was best to get me home quickly, let me rest and get me to the GP first thing Monday morning.

As we prepared to leave, Margaret was waiting there with a replacement match programme. She apologised to my aunty Val for saying she'd been family. Aunty Val thanked her for looking after me, and, as they talked in the early evening sunshine, I clutched my new programme and looked out over Bradford, its brownstone buildings, chimneys, warehouses and clumps of green, little realising how this city on this day would define everything about me.

5

Survivor

It was just after 5 p.m. in Cropwell Bishop when the phone rang. Mum was finishing off her afternoon's decorating, precariously balanced in the bath, painting a final corner section.

'It's for you,' her mum told her, as she popped her head into the bathroom.

Mum picked up the phone to hear my dad's mum tell her, 'Sue, it's Martin, he's in hospital.'

'He's in hospital?' my startled Mum repeated. 'What do you mean "Martin's in hospital"? He's at a football match!'

'Have you not seen the news? There's been a fire at Bradford City. A serious one . . . hundreds have been hurt. Now there's reports coming in of deaths, too.'

'*Deaths?* The others – they're with Martin?'

'No, they all got split up on their way out somehow.'

'What!? How's Martin?'

Grandma told her that the police had said I'd burnt my back, my head and my ear, but she reasoned it couldn't have been too bad, as they'd said I could come home, and that Val and Mike had gone to pick me up.

'But the others, where are they?' Mum asked.

'I'm not sure, Sue. Nobody's too sure of anything.' Grandma said she'd ring back when she knew more.

Once Mum put the phone down, she switched on the radio. National radio bulletins were relaying that, in addition to approximately two hundred fans being treated for burns at Valley Parade, another two hundred had been admitted to hospitals throughout West Yorkshire – and that there were as yet unconfirmed reports of deaths at the ground; and the fire brigade had been seen placing white sheets at the back of the stand. On hearing this Mum jumped into her silver MG Metro to hurtle across the country lanes to East Bridgford in case anyone tried to contact her at home. Once there the radio confirmed the coroner had visited Valley Parade and, having identified remains by the turnstiles at the back of the stand, had estimated a death toll of 16.

When I got back from the hospital to Grandma's she ran from the house in tears. Gently cupping my scabbed face in her hands, she said, 'Let me have a look at you,' before giving me a hug. Dad's cousin, Dennis, was there and said he was going to pick Mum up; Aunty Irene, on the phone to a police emergency helpline, called me into the porch and asked for descriptions of what Dad and Andrew were wearing – down to the red graffiti-style American eagle patch on Andrew's jeans. The missing persons reports filed, I finally got to speak to Mum on the phone: 'Sue Fletcher,' said a voice full of tension.

'Hi, Mum.'

'Sweetheart! How are you, honey?' Her tension gave way to utter relief.

'I'm fine, thanks.'

'Come on, Martin, I know you're not fine – you've been in hospital. How are you really?'

'I burnt my back, but I'm fine. I'm in no pain.'

'Are you sure?'

She said she was coming up to check that out for herself. I said I was coming down with Dennis. Mum wasn't too happy about that, but asked to speak to Grandma, who told her I was adamant, and in no apparent pain. By early evening I was heading south with Dennis and Chris.

On the M62 I asked, 'Can you put the radio on?'

'What do you want to listen to?' Dennis asked, perhaps hoping it was a music show.

'BBC Radio 2 news,' I told him, keen to hear what had happened at Valley Parade.

'Are you sure?' Dennis asked, startled, not wanting me to learn of deaths this way.

'Yes, I want to know what's being said on the news. It's nearly eight.'

Dennis said OK, but that we'd just have to wait until we got on the M1 and were heading south – he didn't want to overshoot the exit; he wanted to get me back to Mum as soon as possible, without getting lost.

At the time I wouldn't have been aware that, living in Barnsley, Dennis would have been more than familiar with that exit. It bought him the time he needed, though, and as the exit sign for the M1 appeared, good to his word, Dennis turned on the car radio. He could not have timed it any better: 'In other news, West Midlands Police have confirmed a fifteen-year-old supporter was killed at Birmingham City's St Andrews this afternoon after a wall collapsed following their match with Leeds United,' the newsreader's voice crackled over the static.

'If that's the other news, what's the main news?!' I asked.

Dennis said that Bradford would have been the headline news, but that we'd catch up with it in good time. By now the painkillers were beginning to kick in, and I was constantly yawning. The sun was going down. Sprawled on my stomach across the rear seats of Dennis's Ford Granada Estate I fell asleep, unaware that the death toll had increased to 40 after the rear corridor had been fully searched.

Six hours after the blaze had begun I finally got back to East Bridgford. As I walked into the house, Mum ran to the hallway to hug me: 'Oh, sweetheart. Are you OK? Are you OK?'

I told her I was fine, but wondered if she'd heard from the others.

'No, not yet, honey – so we're going to have to go back to Yorkshire.'

This surprised me, as I'd expected to sleep in my own bed that night, especially with the launch of the East Bridgford Junior Football Club the next day, but Mum told me not to worry as it had been postponed. I was also a bit surprised that we still hadn't heard from Dad. I thought that by now he would have called. But, before I could get too concerned, I remembered the police in the back of the ambulance, and those at the hospital, all reassuring me that the stand had been cleared. The nurses had said the same thing. No matter how sharp you are at 12, you still take what adults say at face value – especially when more than two dozen of them are saying the same thing. I was more surprised to find four neighbours in the lounge, each emotionally asking for gentle hugs before telling me how brave I was. Their red eyes made it clear tears had been shed.

Noticing the time I asked, 'Mum, the ITN news is about to start. Can we watch it?'

'Oh no, Martin, I'd rather we didn't.'

'Why not? I want to see what happened.'

'You were there, sweetheart. You saw everything.'

'I just want to see that it was real.'

'OK, Martin, but I don't want to hear it any more, so how about we watch it on mute?'

The bulletin began. Over a blue background, with a yellow ITN News logo on the bottom, there was the stand, almost half ablaze, and the pitch full of people beneath it. But it was the trail of white smoke, racing fast under and out of the stand roof, which I immediately recognised.

'That's when I got out,' I said to Mum.

'*No!*' Mum exclaimed.

Then G Block was ablaze on the screen, and the fire flashed over.

'That's was when the smoke came down,' I explained, before, sure enough, seconds later, a cloud of black smoke started to funnel out from under the back of the stand roof.

'No, Martin. It can't have been!' Mum said.

'It was,' I told her.

'I don't want you watching any more,' she told me as tears started to roll down her face. 'Be a good boy, go upstairs, get cleaned up and get in the clean clothes I've put on your bed.'

It was walking up the stairs that I felt a searing pain from my burns for the first time. On the half-landing from which Mum had waved to us all that morning, I looked up and thought how empty this big house was without Dad and Andrew home. After wondering why they'd not been able to call, I undressed and then smelt the clothes I took off. Only now did I realise everything was coated in a filthy black smoke. In the bathroom, I saw my wounds in the mirror for the first time. Unable to shower because of the mummy-like bandage dressing around my back, I scrubbed my arms, chest and legs in the sink, then my face, careful to make sure the soap went nowhere near my scabs or hideously red ear. As I washed, the water turned a filthy black. Then, as I put on the fresh clothes Mum had laid out, I thought how wonderfully clean they all smelt.

By the time I headed back downstairs the TV was still muted. With the bulletin now more than five minutes in, it showed the police taking details from people on Midland Road, before cutting back to a shot of the smouldering stand, where firemen were placing white sheets over the turnstile hut I'd run from, and on the floor of the rear corridor beside it.

'Mum, why are they doing that?' I asked, uncertain of what I was seeing for the first time.

'Oh, it's just the firemen wanting to work in private, away from the cameras.'

The TV then showed police officers walking across the pitch, a police officer and fans were interviewed, before pictures of the burnt-out wreckage that littered South Parade. I provided my own commentary to Mum, although I'd not heard newscaster Carol Barnes declare, as the bulletin opened, that, 'Forty soccer fans are now believed to have died in this afternoon's massive blaze which spread, according to one survivor, like a flash through the Main Stand at Bradford City's football ground.' Later, as the white sheets were laid down, the bulletin had revealed, 'Many of the bodies recovered were found by the turnstiles at the rear of the stand, where a crowd had formed as the fans struggled to get out. Most were so badly burned that identification was almost impossible. The recovery operation is expected to last well into this evening.'

Before I knew anything we were out of the door again, on our way back up to Yorkshire. Another dose of painkillers quickly dulled my exhausted mind. While I was asleep in the front passenger seat of Dennis's car, the search of the stand was completed, and the death toll was mounting. I awoke as we headed back into Pudsey and, on reaching Kent Road, Mum was thrilled to see Dad's BMW on the drive.

'Oh, it's John's car! They must be back,' she exclaimed in joy.

'No, Mum. We all went in Uncle Peter's car today,' I explained, knowing it had not moved since late morning.

Tearful hugs greeted us at Grandma's house as it was confirmed there was still no news. Mum gave me some more painkillers, and I headed to bed. That was the first time that I heard mention of deaths. Sharing a room with my cousin Chris, he tried to correct the impression he'd seen everybody feed me, confiding that 'people died today' once our lights were off. I felt woozy and doped up. That sounded like gossip, an isolated view, in direct opposition to everything else I'd seen and been told. But maybe some people with burns had died in hospital. Chris dropped the issue and, heavily sedated, it all washed over me and I quickly fell asleep again. I was only 12, so had no idea, but looking back I wonder if that nurse had given me super-strength tablets because she knew what was coming.

My grandma's next-door neighbour was surprised to find the lights still on as he arrived home, and several cars outside after midnight. So he came to check on those he knew were at the game. A policeman, he promised to return with more conclusive news. When he returned four hours later, Mum was the only one still awake and he knocked on the door to explain that he could not find them – any of them. When Mum asked if they might be unidentified in a hospital bed, he explained he'd checked all the casualty lists, which were complete, and had walked the hospital wards to check on the injured. This was what Val had been told too. When Mum asked if they might be walking around, suffering from some kind of amnesia induced by smoke inhalation – Aunty Irene, Uncle Peter's wife, was a nurse and had mentioned this as a possibility that could arise from inhaling carbon monoxide, and, as implausible as it might seem now, everyone had seized on it as the hours lengthened – he told her the city's streets were empty and there were no such reports. He confided the only place he could get no answers was the temporary morgue set up at Bradford ambulance station, where the last of the visually unidentifiable bodies were still arriving, just before 5 a.m. He reckoned that, as we'd not heard from anybody for twelve hours, we had best prepare ourselves for the worst.

No longer expecting the phone to ring, Mum came to kneel on the carpet by the side of my bed. She held my hand as tears ran down her face. I woke briefly, and she smiled as she cried, telling me, 'Go back to sleep, sweetheart.' I wasn't sure if I was dreaming or not. I remember waking again, briefly, when Grandma and Aunty Val came in to ask Mum to go downstairs 'before Martin wakes', ending Mum's vigil. As I watched them go, exhausted and disoriented, I smiled at how familiar everything seemed, before I fell back to sleep.

Knocked out by the codeine, it was lunchtime before I woke fully. I was told there was no news and that the Sunday newspapers had not been delivered. Nor was I allowed to turn on the radio or television. I was subject to a news blackout. I'd slept for the best part of 16 hours, and although the painkillers had dulled my senses they'd lost their sedative effect – but despite this, my family just wanted me to sleep. Having told them I was not tired, they suggested I go upstairs and rest, to relieve the pressure on my back. But all I wanted to do was be around my family, and I felt very little pain anyway. So in the end Mum promised that if I went upstairs till they called me back down, she'd then let me watch that afternoon's ITV football highlights. Chris kept me company as I lay on my stomach, happy to wait if that meant more football.

I realised later that waiting upstairs was part of a diversionary tactic that allowed nearly everyone to leave. As the police struggled to find a way in that pre-DNA age to collate information that might allow them to identify what was now up to 52 unidentifiable bodies, they asked those they believed to be the bereaved to attend Bradford's Central Police Station to complete forms that not only detailed what the missing had worn, but what they'd eaten for lunch and where their dental records were held. From there they hoped to establish a database to help them start identifying bodies. Mum called me back down 20 minutes before the football highlights began. I lay on my stomach in front of the TV, excited as the 2.30 p.m. start time approached. However, there was no football in Yorkshire that day – what seemed to be a documentary started instead, with the cameras silently zooming in on the white sheets over the burnt-out turnstiles.

'*Turn that off. Now!*' Mum screamed, and I immediately did what I was told.

'But, Mum . . . you promised . . .'

'Martin, I promised to let you watch the football, but that was not football.'

As she tried to hug me, I brushed her aside and lay there for a few minutes, a foot from the TV, sulking at my scarred reflection in the screen and fighting back tears, wanting to know what was being broadcast, what it was that I was not allowed to know. The others, by now back from the police station, looked at each other, wondering what to do next.

Mum eventually bought me off with a trip to the off-licence so she could get me 'some sweets to say sorry' for shouting at me. The off-licence had a wall full of glass sweet jars, and that saw me break into a smile.

As we walked back down Kent Road I asked, 'Mum, where is everyone?'

'I don't know, darling, nobody does,' Mum said.

'You would tell me if you did know, wouldn't you?'

'Yes, I promise, as soon as I know anything, you'll be the first to hear.'

'Do you think they're all OK?'

'I hope so. We've all got to hope so.'

Time seemed to be coming to a standstill. The last twenty-four hours felt so stretched out. Everything still felt stupidly unreal – especially after another dose of painkillers.

I slowly munched at my lemon and strawberry bonbons for the rest of the afternoon. As I did so, I stared at the open porch door, hoping my family would walk through. I also willed the cream phone on the window ledge in the hall to ring, but neither happened. Later, sat on the toilet, my nose started to itch irritably. So I picked it. As I did so straggly black gunk, which looked like snot but had none of its texture or colour, came out and the more I picked, the more this alien black gunk came out. I was horrified as I examined it on my fingers. Then, as I washed out the inside of my nose, the water blackened.

To break the tedium I was packed off to spend the evening at Aunty Val's, where I had dinner and played with my cousins in a house full of toys and computer games.

As I got ready for bed I heard the phone ring. I looked at my aunt expectantly as she answered it. She shook her head and, after putting the phone down, told me it was Mum. 'Believe me, if I had good news at this stage, you'd be the first to know,' she said, her sadness visible.

The next morning was windy, damp and chilly. Mum, Aunty Val and I got to Pudsey Medical Centre pretty much as its doors opened – it had the usual Monday morning hustle and bustle of a doctor's surgery. Having queued to reach the reception desk, I heard Mum tell the receptionist that her son was hurt in the fire on Saturday and that his dad, brother, grandfather and uncle were missing, and that as we lived in Nottinghamshire we weren't registered with them, but that my grandparents were – and that the hospital had said I should see a GP first thing on Monday morning. Stunned, the receptionist looked at my scabbed face and throbbing red ear, and said, 'Yes, of course, right away . . . If I can take your details perhaps we can find a quiet area outside the doctor's room for your son.' So I went with Aunty Val, away from the reception area, where no doubt patients were reading the morning papers . . .

The doctor was a Bradford City fan, but although he was a regular at Valley Parade he'd been unable to go on Saturday due to a family wedding. As he examined my wounds and changed the dressing on my back, he was surprised by the painkillers I'd been prescribed, explaining they were 'knock-out stuff', before prescribing me a new set.

'It was such a dreadful day. I even see the Pope sent a message yesterday,' he told us, as he wrote out his prescription.

'Yes, it was dreadful, but it's so amazing nobody actually died,' I replied.

The startled doctor looked at me in surprise, before agreeing, then adding, 'Before you all go, do you mind waiting outside, Martin, so I can have a quiet word with your mum?'

The doctor strongly suggested to my mum that she tell me everything.

'Well, what do I tell him?' she replied. 'Do I tell him only one of fifty-two bodies has been identified? Or that the missing outnumber the dead by twenty-four?'

'I see,' he said.

'Look, the wait's unbearable for all of us,' Mum had said. 'So how can I tell him his family are dead when we still don't know for certain they are – especially after all he went through on Saturday?'

She promised him that as soon as there was concrete news, she'd tell me, and the doctor gave her his direct line and home numbers.

As that morning's painkillers began to wear off, the pain, for the first time, began to tear at my back. It was excruciating and, unable to sit, I went upstairs to lie on the bed. The weaker painkillers weren't as strong – and I began to feel more normal again. I'd been there an hour when I heard the phone ring, and made my way downstairs. But as I opened the lounge door I saw four of Dad's senior business colleagues, who lived as far apart as Hull, Nottingham and Surrey, in a tearful huddle near the door. Then I saw my relatives, in tears, all doing the same. As Mum caught sight of me standing by the staircase door, she blurted out, 'Oh God, no!' and fled the lounge in floods of tears. She slid the porch door shut behind her.

'Go back upstairs, honey. Someone will be with you in a minute,' my aunty Val told me.

I was happy to beat a hasty retreat to try to cast these confusing and troubling scenes from my mind. Lying back on the bed fear, doubt, questions about what I'd been clinging to, what I'd been told for the last

36 hours, darkened my mind. At last I sensed something was seriously wrong. I stared at my watch. It was half past twelve. Fearful of what the next few minutes might now reveal I begged for its second hand to stop, but, of course, it did not. Then I heard footsteps on the stairs.

By the time I got out to the landing, Mum was at the top of the stairs. 'Martin, I'm afraid I've got some bad news to tell you. I think you'd best sit down,' she said, leading me into Grandma's bedroom, where we sat on the bed. 'That was the police. They've found them, and I'm afraid it's not good news,' she explained, as she put her arm gently round me.

'Where are they?' I asked, still hoping we'd see them soon.

'They're dead.'

'Who's dead?'

'They all are.'

'What! But nobody died. So how can they all be dead?' I protested.

'There's been a mistake. Lots of people died, Martin,' Mum finally confessed.

As I looked into her bloodshot eyes, she started to shake, powerless to find the words to convince me, but that in itself revealed a truth words alone could not. Seconds later, knowing what I'd seen in the stand, I collapsed into my mum's arms and began to cry, harder than I ever had before, longer than I ever will again. As Mum cradled my limp body, people came upstairs to try to comfort me but, wrapped in my mum's arms, I was truly inconsolable.

An hour or so later Mum told me she had to go to the police station. I wanted to go with her, but she was adamant – 'No, Martin, it's no place for you' – so, bewildered, I spend the rest of that afternoon in a daze. My grandma kept a close eye on me, insisting I sat in her armchair, rather than lie on my bed, as she feared my being alone. Wearing Dad's grey Wrangler sweatshirt I kept glancing at the match programme and promotion supplements on the cabinet beside me which, although just two days old, clearly belonged to an altogether different world – one I could not believe had gone for ever. I stared silently into a tear-blurred space, striving to imagine our new world, before trying to sleep, hoping I'd wake to a different reality.

At Bradford Central police station burnt possessions were laid out on trestle tables. The police led Mum to a table where she instantly recognised Dad's watch, its face burnt out and gold strap blackened, then saw his gold engagement ring, also coated in black, before she was shown his wallet, which looked like it'd had a good soaking from the water jets that had put the fire out. She then saw a fragment of Andrew's blue jacket, a white mesh and a yellow hoop on its elbow, unburnt and undamaged as if it had been found locked in what we'd always joked was Granddad's death-grip. As Janice McLean, the officer assigned to Andrew's body, saw his photo she said to Mum, 'Oh, what a beautiful boy he was,' before going to the window to wipe her own tears. She urged Mum to 'Remember him how he was.' Dental records were needed to verify all their identities.

In Pudsey my news blackout ended as I awoke to the headlines of the *ITN News at 5.45* then watched the *BBC Six O'Clock News*, followed by Yorkshire Television's local *Calendar*. I reeled as an array of stark pictures and emotion-laden reports now confirmed the enormity of what I'd witnessed two days earlier. There was also Leon Brittan, the home secretary, announcing to parliament there would be a full inquiry into crowd safety and control after the events of Saturday, both at Bradford and Birmingham, where the one fan had died. Mr Justice Popplewell was coming to Bradford the next day.

Mum returned from the police station just as the *Coronation Street* ad break started. 'We need to talk,' she told me, as she led me to the bedroom, off limits all afternoon. She confirmed that they were all dead – but that didn't stop me breaking down again.

'Martin, we did this earlier. I need you to stay strong now; we all need you to stay strong. You know how your dad always made you the man of the house when he went away on business? Well, that's what he'd want from you now, isn't it?'

I nodded tearfully.

Fifty-Six

'That's what they'd all want from you now,' Mum continued, 'and that's what we all need from you. It's so hard, I know, but I'll be there to support you. So you can do that for me, for your dad, can't you?'

I battled to regain my composure, and for the first time, really, the sheer numbers of people caught up in this hell began to hit home. It's impossible to comprehend the loss of three generations. We went downstairs to a lounge that night of six adults and five children. Four of the six adults had lost parents, husbands, or children; three of the five children were fatherless – and the other two children had lost their granddad and both uncles. Ten of the eleven had suffered multiple bereavements, that was 40 close relationships ended, 30 of them involving people below the age of 35. One man remained, there were three widows, two mums with sons to bury, and two grandmas with a grandson to bury. Of the five children, two were so young they never really knew their dad, and one was left an only child. Heartbreaking scenarios like this were being played out in homes all over Bradford, or Yorkshire, even Lincolnshire. But for our family, not one of the youngsters in that lounge that night – today, in their thirties and forties – has gone on to have children of their own.

After lights out, Mum speculated what Dad might have made of it all: 'I know how much you loved them and I know how much you'll miss them, sweetheart, but try to remember what a great fatalist your dad always was.'

'What do you mean?'

'Well, he always believed that when his number was up, his number was up, and for some reason it seems all their numbers were up on Saturday.'

'I know, but why Valley Parade? Why all of them?'

'What your dad would have told you is, had it not been Valley Parade it would have been somewhere else, for all of them; but at least they died together, happy, in a place they all loved.'

'Do you believe that, Mum?'

'Ah, we're not talking about what I believe, Martin, but I know how you always looked to your dad. And I know now, at this point, that the only thing I can find any comfort in is what your dad believed.'

'But, why did I get out? I should have died, like everyone else around me.'

'Perhaps, but you didn't, and your dad would have told you that's because it wasn't your time.'

'Why not?'

'I'm not sure, sweetheart, I'm really not; maybe we'll find the answer to that one day.' Mum speculated that maybe there was a reason, something we'd all understand one day, and said, 'If there is a reason you're still here we can only find it by living our lives in the way you know Dad would have wanted. And that means not giving up, but somehow finding a way to fight through this terrible mess together. You know that, don't you?'

As Mum spoke I thought back to what Dad had told me on the M1 in the shadow of the Tinsley cooling towers – it was as if he knew that was a conversation we were always destined to have.

6

Mourner

By the time Mum woke me the next morning a police guard was patrolling Kent Road. Overnight the media had learnt three generations and four members of the Fletcher family were 'missing', which with all the missing now accounted for could mean only one thing. With the eldest Fletcher traced to Kent Road at a property owned by one of his missing sons, a little digging soon revealed a fifth family member, a child from the same small Nottinghamshire village where the father was listed as 'missing presumed dead', and the son was on the hospital list as being treated for burns. It was the ultimate human interest story.

Guarded in West Yorkshire, the press descended on East Bridgford. When strangers bought drinks in Dad's local, the Reindeer, and started to ask if they knew John Fletcher or the Fletcher family, the landlord, Tony White, told them journalists were not welcome and asked them to leave. When they refused, Tony and some burly lunchtime regulars hurled them out on to Kneeton Road. So they turned their attention to the school's playing fields. Andrew's classmates had bravely decided to go ahead with a cricket match that afternoon. But as the 9-, 10- and 11-year-olds who made up the away team arrived, they were accosted by journalists and cameramen wanting to know if they knew us. Horrified parents ran to the adjacent school, where the home side changed, and, led by the headmaster, village policeman and vicar, chased the press through the village and out into the open countryside beyond, telling them to never come back.

As we heard this on the phone, from friends in East Bridgford, we had a knock on our door.

'Yes?' Uncle Mike said, opening the door to a paperboy, a yellow bag over his shoulder.

'This the Fletcher house?' he asked.

'Go on, get lost, you little . . .' Uncle Mike replied, slamming the door in his face.

The young, engaging PC, Janice McLean, who was only 20 and lived in Pudsey with her parents, was soon round. She'd built an instant rapport with Mum and soon became our unofficial police liaison officer. She explained journalists had bribed the paperboy to wait till our guard switched shifts and, when they did, he pounced to confirm which house we actually lived in.

'Have you given any thought to releasing a public statement to the press?' Janice asked.

'Funnily enough, we've had other things to worry about today,' Mum replied.

'I know, I know, I'm sorry. But I'm just trying to tell you what they've told us they want.'

'What "they want"! After what they've done today, do you think we care what "they want"?'

'How can I put this?' Janice pondered, struggling to find the words she was asked to relay: 'We've been told unless you make a statement they'll make your lives very uncomfortable.'

'Ha!' scorned Mum. 'More uncomfortable! Our lives? Any idea how they might do that?'

Janice said she didn't, but was worried that unless we gave them something to publish, they'd publish whatever they wanted, and we 'may not like it'. That was what she'd heard anyway.

'Let them. Frankly, we're not rewarding this sort of behaviour – it's nothing short of blackmail!' Mum said, to nodding heads all around.

The house spent the rest of the day each taking turns to make phone calls to a wider circle of relatives and friends from Grandma's single landline. Most were shocked, some thankful for personal confirmations, and others had heard rumours they simply hoped were not true. Mum wanted everyone to learn the terrible news directly from us rather than through the media – as the coroner was set to release the names of the dead at 9 a.m. the next morning, there was a very limited window to operate in. Everyone agreed – we felt we owed it to our loved ones to tell those they were close to ourselves – and the grown-ups were on the phone till late in the evening.

On Wednesday morning, 15 May, Mum woke me with anxiety written all over her face, her eyes bloodshot. 'Martin, the papers – you're really not going to like what's been written about you.'

Once downstairs, Mum handed me a copy of that morning's *Yorkshire Post*, assuring me, 'Remember, we all know it's a lie.'

Reports suggest Mr [Eddie] Fletcher tried to keep the family together, but Martin ran off in panic. He managed to escape on to the pitch while the rest of the family were caught in the inferno as they tried to make for an exit.

I looked up at Grandma, who said, 'Don't worry, Martin, I know it's not true.' Mum then handed me a copy of that morning's *Telegraph & Argus* with the same lie in it:

Eddie Fletcher, a lifelong City fan, tried to keep his family together as they fought to flee the blazing stand. But Martin broke away from the group and managed to scramble to safety. Shocked relatives were too upset to talk about the incident and neighbours stayed silent as a mark of respect.

Rereading this three decades later, I find my anger, if anything, has deepened over the years – this was little short of a vicious, cowardly and libellous attack on a child, which stated I'd panicked and in the confusion that followed survived while the others didn't, implying I was somehow culpable. Aged 12, though, I just shook my head. I knew everyone in the room knew it was an absolute joke, so it seemed best to respond in kind: 'So, Granddad's a lifelong City fan now, is he? He'd not be happy about that.'

Granddad had been a lifelong Bradford Park Avenue fan till their demise, a decade earlier. We all laughed, then mocked how they said Granddad had invited us to the match, not us him, and how it must have been his health – so good that it had necessitated his early retirement – that qualified him to lead the escape party.

As a response Mum decided to release a statement that night. She argued that that wasn't going back on her principles, nor giving in – it was just a case of putting the record straight. She also decided I needed to be out of the line of fire. So that afternoon Dad's friend Colin Butterworth picked me up so I could spend the evening with his family. I was bought off fairly easily: the Cup Winners' Cup final was going to be on, live from Rotterdam: Everton v Rapid Vienna.

Colin picked me up a little before 4 p.m. As we drove into Gildersome, the local news started, with that morning's list of the dead re-broadcast in full – Sarah Elizabeth Turner, 16; Gordon McPherson, 39, who'd died with his wife Irene, 28; Adrian Wright, 11 and Christopher Bulmer, 11, who'd both died with their grandfathers; Jayne Sampson, 18, had been the girlfriend of our young striker Don Goodman, and had celebrated his 19th birthday with him, just two days before she'd died with her friend, Elizabeth Muhl, 21, at their first ever football match. It went on. We fell silent as we listened; it finally came to an end in Birstall.

We headed to a windswept Princess Mary Athletics Stadium in Cleckheaton for a schools' athletics meeting. Standing at the edge of its track, we watched teenagers run, jump and throw, all in a hive of healthy, noisy, teenage activity. I backed Batley Grammar School, for obvious reasons – not least because, if I had gone there we would have kept our C Block season tickets, and Dad, Andrew, Granddad and Uncle Peter would still be alive.

The athletics over, Colin's eldest son, Andy, who was 13, came over with a couple of friends. He greeted me like an old friend, as if nothing had changed or happened – which, indeed, it hadn't between us – but when Colin asked one of Andy's friends, 'How's your Dad?' I realised that

85

was something I'd never be asked again. Although part of me envied them their world – a world I sensed I'd never belong to again – I was glad to be let back in, to be normal once more, listening to music on the car radio and talking about sport and football.

But as we queued at the traffic lights at the crossroads of Huddersfield Road and Bradford Road, the names of Bradford's dead were broadcast again. I turned to stare at the still burnt-out shell of the factory on my left – the Smithies, which I'd watched burn as a three-year-old. An uneasy silence began to fill the car, and I was reminded how my world would never be normal again. However, wanting to focus on something else and just be one of the boys for the evening, I switched the radio off after the fourth Fletcher name was read out.

After playing computer games we settled down to watch Everton beat Rapid Vienna 3–1. The unmistakable drawl of the co-commentator was that of Brian Clough, welcoming me back to the world of football, to something like the normal world other people inhabited – but just for one night.

After the match the phone rang. Colin answered it, then stuck his head back in the door: 'I've got Trevor on the phone, he'd like to speak to you.'

At first I was unsure who he meant, and certainly didn't want to speak to a journalist.

'Trevor . . . You know, Martin?! *Trevor Cherry!*' Colin had a glint in his eye: 'He clearly knows you and would really like to speak with you, but if you don't want to I could tell him no . . .'

I rushed to the phone and spent a quarter of an hour talking to Bradford City's manager about the match, my family, how he and the players were, and the upcoming FA Cup final – which he said I could watch with him and his family if I fancied it. Colin later told me that, having seen Mum's statement on TV, he rang for a chat, only to find me hiding there.

There was no hiding after that night, as the truth gave the media a much better story. Mum publicly applauded me for following Dad's instructions to go alone, described how I'd seen my family seconds before the smoke fell and, having first gone to the turnstiles, had somehow escaped on to the pitch. She praised how 'unbelievably well' I'd coped, declaring me 'a very old and very wise 12-year-old', her 'little hero'. The next morning, in the doctor's waiting room, our photos stared back from the front pages of people's newspapers. That was pretty weird, especially as strangers, lost for words, pointed, or silently nodded, wherever we went. Some even started crying on seeing us. We were in danger of becoming the public faces of this disaster.

That night we returned to Valley Parade for the first time, just our family. The forensic search over, Janice McLean arranged for us to go in darkness so as to avoid any prying lenses. As she chatted in my grandmother's lounge, she went silent, her horrified face going white as I walked into the room wearing a matching blue jacket to the one Andrew was found in, with the white mesh and yellow hoop armband on its elbow, the fragment of which was found locked in my grandfather's palm.

It was nearly 10 p.m. by the time we reached the ground. Back on the rear corridor, I looked out on an exposed crater of a bombsite. Under the moonlight, down where the front of the stand had once stood, odd looking metal stakes pointed high into the night sky, the roof they'd supported now gone. A loose, shallow ocean of pebbly black charcoal pungently snaked up the valley. We stood on this newly raised concrete platform that ran to the rear of this bombsite, along which metal columns jutted up, with the wooden partition it once supported gone too. In its absence the encasing corridor now encased nothing. You could now walk through the open black-edged cuttings of its brick support wall at will. It was too dark to see everything clearly, but in the same way I'd known the layout of the stand as the smoke fell, I still saw it all now – I always would.

To try to help my family better understand what had happened I retraced our steps. I knew we were only three rows from the back, and it was difficult to find your footing, but we clambered down on to the beach of charcoaled wood, where Grandma lay a red rose on what had been Granddad's seat; Mum did the same for Andrew; Dad's elder sister Val lay a rose where he'd been sitting, and Uncle Peter's wife Irene put one by the side of theirs. By mine I placed a wreath to remember them all.

The only problem was, in all this twisted metal, charcoal, filth and darkness it was impossible for those looking at this crater for the first time to ever see what I saw. They couldn't visualise the long queues of people on the rows above us, the narrow stairwell, the gridlocked corridor . . .

'Why couldn't they have just jumped down there?' asked Aunty Irene, pointing down to what had been F Block.

'There was a wooden wall there, taller than me,' I told her.

But Mum remembered how difficult it had been to make our way forwards – the wooden partition that tore our jackets, the hole beneath my seat, the stairwells that led nowhere but to the front of each seated section, the high wooden walls with serious drops the other side – and that had been when the stand was empty. Now, under calm starlit skies, this open structure belied its true nature: enclosed, cramped and dangerously laid out. There had been too few, irregularly spaced exits – and many of those had been boarded up. Now they just looked forlorn, blackened open cuttings, lining the brick wall behind us. It had been Mum who once asked us what would happen if the Main Stand ever caught fire; it had been Mum who sensed a death trap.

That Friday I read the previous week's newspapers Mum had got me from the leftovers pile at the local newsagent's. As I sifted through them it was clear the devastation across the lives of people in Bradford was just appalling. Such was the nature of community life in Bradford and its terrible generational loss, everybody in the city was said to know someone, or of someone, who'd died. Ours was one of several families shattered: the headmaster of a local deaf school, Peter Greenwood, 46, had died alongside his two sons, Felix, 13, and Rupert, 11; electrician Gerald Ormondroyd, 40, had died with his 12-year-old twin sons Richard and Robert; and Trevor Stockman, 38, had perished alongside his 16-year-old daughter, Jane, and 14-year-old son, Craig. It was also clear that, as teenagers and younger men generally stood 'on spec' on the terraces, a lot of the victims in the stand had been the old – after years on the Kop, they'd no doubt fancied the comparative comfort of a seat to rest their legs – or the very young, out at the match with their parents or grandparents. A hardy, robust bunch of no fewer than 25 aged 63 and above, who'd all survived the Second World War but had failed to survive a local third division football match. Amongst them were Jack Coxon, 76, who died with his son Leo, 44, who had a pregnant wife at home. Fred Hindle, 76, also died with his wife Edith, 79. And Roy Mason, 74, who'd been seen on national television calmly walking across the pitch in flames, took two days to die in hospital, but I was told he suffered little pain as his nerve ends had been burnt off.

And in there were some I'd had direct contact with. On seeing his picture, I knew it was Mr Greenwood who I'd apologised to after Dad had calmed me in the rear corridor.

Reading through the papers I was also struck by the comments of Mr Justice Oliver Popplewell on his trip to Bradford. Even to a 12-year-old it seemed odd he wasn't going to 'apportion blame'. My family assured me such issues would be dealt with later, by the police and the courts, if we let them do their jobs – it was the job of the Popplewell Inquiry to ensure football grounds were safe for me, and other football fans across the country, when we returned in August.

The next day was the FA Cup final. It was a hot afternoon, T-shirt weather. But the only T-shirt I had up in Yorkshire – having been away a week now – was a red one picked up at an old promotional printing firm Mum had worked for. It had 'Tetley Bittermen' written across the front; 'If you can't beat 'em, join 'em' on the back. Thus attired, I turned up at Trevor Cherry's house which, although nice, was a typical four-bedroom modern executive detached house in a cul-de-sac in Huddersfield. Cherry had played for Don Revie's legendary Leeds United side, captained England and won 27 caps, so I'd expected him to live in some kind of palace, or at least somewhere bigger than our house – whereas his smart, suburban pad merely reflected the rewards then on offer in English football. I didn't really understand any of this at the time, and despite his successes Cherry was an understated, unassuming man. A local newspaper once said he could have been mistaken for the accountant he planned to be before he became a professional footballer at his local club, Huddersfield Town. Dressed in grey trousers, and a tank top over a polo shirt, he looked like he'd just got back from the golf course. He was softly spoken and clearly cared, asking again about my family and mentioning how keen Paul Hart, his old room-mate at Leeds, was to see me.

I spent the match sat between Trevor and Colin on his three-seater couch. Trevor warned me beforehand that the much anticipated final – Everton were going for the treble – would be a poor game and that Manchester United would win narrowly. He turned out to be spot on – it took a stupendous Norman Whiteside strike eventually to break the extra-time deadlock of a dour final. Little more than two years into management, Cherry seemed to be one of football's great new thinkers, which given he'd beaten George Graham's Millwall to the third division title, he probably was. Graham went on to greater things, but Trevor Cherry paid the price for staying loyal to Bradford.

Just a week ago he'd been unable to find his family in the directors' box – happily they'd made it out – and, knowing that he had only seconds and couldn't outrun the fire, he ventured up into the smoke-filled rear corridor. (Later he said the real disaster occurred out of sight.) As we watched the final I noticed the time on the green digital display on the video recorder below the TV turn to 15:40. I fell silent as I stared at the clock. Precisely a week after smoke had started to rise at Valley Parade I was sat there joking with the Bradford City manager. As I watched each minute turn till half-time, I pondered if I should feel guilty, sitting here smiling, but I thought about how Dad would have told me to live for the moment. So I guess I did just that.

After the game Trevor showed me the glass-fronted mahogany cabinet in his dining room. I picked up his 1973 FA Cup final runners-up medal and he joked about how he was still trying to work out how Sunderland's inspired Jim Montgomery foiled him with his famous double save. He also spoke of Leeds' record unbeaten run at the start of the following season – he had his 1974 league championship medal in that cabinet too, alongside his 1975 European Cup runners-up medal. He spoke in awed tones of facing Barcelona's Johan Cruyff in the semi-final – a great player, but they'd kept him quiet! – and joked that he'd better not start talking about the referee in the final as he didn't like swearing in front of children. As I put on an England cap, Colin took a photograph in Trevor's front garden: me smiling, wearing that and holding his third division-winners' medal that he'd auctioned on breakfast TV just a few days before for the disaster appeal.

The next week was dominated by preparations for the family funeral, to be held on Friday 24 May. A talented local florist made tributes: a claret and amber football rattle, a Bradford City bar scarf, a panelled claret and amber football and, for each coffin, an oversized match programme and football shirt. We could each request one hymn for the funeral, so I went for the FA Cup final hymn, 'Abide With Me'.

We returned to Valley Parade the afternoon before the funeral. As we got there torrential rain fell, and Mum suggested, 'The heavens must be crying for them all.' That evening we visited the four sealed beech-wood coffins in a chapel of rest on the Leeds ring road, which was the closest we'd get to seeing our dead – the only way to tell who was in which coffin was to read the brass name plaques. My family left me there, alone in this coffin-filled room, so we could be a fivesome one final time and say the farewells I'd been unable to twelve days earlier.

The next morning I woke in utter dread. I couldn't face the day ahead, and lay in bed staring at the walls, hoping it might pass me by. Mum eventually got me up and in the bath, where I lay for about an hour, thinking about how I should have been among the dead, not the mourners downstairs. Mum hammered on the door, but lying in dirty, cold bathwater seemed preferable to what lay ahead. I took an equal eternity to get dressed.

As our funeral cortège crawled through the streets of Pudsey it became clear why we needed a police escort. There were four hearses, half a dozen cars full of mourners, and dozens of private cars following the route. Bands of people, some in tears, stood on pavements with their children. As the hearses left Kent Road, a policeman stood in proud salute, which reduced Grandma to tears. As we drew up to the church, hundreds were packed on to the pavement, massed behind police barriers. With the church full to capacity the service was broadcast on loudspeakers outside. The media demanded they have access – cameras and journalists in the church – but Mum refused, adamant it was our private ceremony. So Mum and the family compromised: the deal was that if no reporters approached mourners for interviews then we'd allocate areas opposite the church, and in the churchyard, to take unobstructed pictures.

As we arrived at the church there was a gauntlet to face. Sitting in the lead hearse – me, Mum, Grandma and Aunty Irene – it seemed that nobody wanted to leave. As the women tried to control their emotions and wipe away tears, unsuccessfully, I was determined to face down the media scrum. As the pall-bearers got each coffin out of the four hearses and waited on the pavement, the four football-flower-topped coffins on their shoulders, I took my mum's hand and smiled at Grandma, and the rest of the car nodded before opening the door.

Stepping out of the car I looked at the flowers in the four hearses beside us, then at the army of cameramen beyond. I straightened myself out, held my head up high and fixed my eyes on the coffins, almost dragging Mum by the hand. As I followed the coffins into the church all I could hear was the sound of scores of clicking cameras, but I kept focused on the coffins – nothing else. I can't really remember much else about the funeral, it was just a tearful blur.

The following day the *Daily Mirror* headline declared 'THE BRAVEST BOY IN BRITAIN is just 12 [and] the only man left.' The article explained, 'Ashen faced, the 12-year-old stood ramrod straight and comforted his weeping mother Susan. He held on to her as they walked behind the coffins.'

I allowed myself to cry just twice that day, in the hearse and the church. Once in the church I was in a terrible state, sitting on a front-row pew a few feet from the four coffins, but once the service had finished I managed to control my emotions and wipe away my tears, before heading back out to face the media scrum. The rest was a public show.

The next day we took our claret and amber floral football tributes back to Valley Parade to place them all at the turnstiles, one for each person found there, and they stayed there until the stand was cleared two months later.

The *Daily Express* wrote, 'The courage of Martin Fletcher was plain to see yesterday. He stood firm, comforting his mother, while all around people wept . . . It was the same courage that took the 12-year-old boy through the flames and smoke of the Valley Parade stand to safety.'

More horror stories were coming out in the local and national press all the time. And I wasn't the only survivor who had lost people in that stand. Of those I read of (and later learned of), Mandy Roberts, 20, had been at the back of a large family group making their way towards the pitch when she and her mum were told to go to the back of the stand, where they were assured the doors had been opened, only to be met by a blanket of choking smoke – Mandy died and her mum was overcome and suffered bad burns before being somehow dragged clear. Nine-year-old Karl Hepton had been on his way with his grandma, Nellie Forster, 64, to his dad in A Block, when the smoke overtook them too. Before it engulfed them, Nellie passed Karl through a broken window in the back of the B Block snack bar, down into the stand, and told him to 'Run! Run!' Maurice Bamford (who'd go on to spend months in Pinderfields burns unit) had lost his dad, Herbert, 72; Muriel Firth, 56, suffered terrible burns along with her husband, Sam, who'd also lost his uncle, a former president of Bradford City. Muriel would shortly lose her battle, leaving Sam a widower.

Sunday saw me back at my first football match – a charity game played for the Bradford disaster appeal in Huddersfield. Mum told the press, 'He's trying so hard to be brave, but he is fighting a continual battle inside.' Which was true: on the surface there I was, autograph book in hand, meeting the likes of Mike Summerbee, Frazer Hines and David Hamilton and others who'd agreed to play – like Leeds United and Wales legend John Charles – then touring the changing rooms with Jeremy Beadle and Cannon & Ball, before watching the game from the dug-out with the trainers (the organisers understandably not wanting us to be seated in the wooden stand).

A few days later, back in Pudsey, a fortnight on from the fire, my burns had healed enough for me to play football again – for the first time since that beautiful, sunny Friday evening with Andrew. Hurling myself around Grandma's back garden, my cousins took shots at me.

After the May Bank Holiday weekend we got our ashes back on the Tuesday. Aunty Irene decided she wanted Uncle Peter's scattered at Valley Parade, and Grandma, not wanting her youngest son to be alone, followed suit; but Mum decided to put Dad's and Andrew's in a wooden box in the newly established garden of remembrance at East Bridgford village church, ahead of a memorial service scheduled for the following Sunday. As Grandma could not face returning to Valley Parade she asked me to scatter Granddad's ashes.

So that afternoon we were back at the ground again, this time walking out of the players' tunnel – which was something I'd always dreamed about, but not under these circumstances, not in this living nightmare. As we reached the centre circle, I unscrewed my black jar and started to scatter the ashes. As I did so a gust of wind unexpectedly blew across the pitch, causing the ashes to fly back towards me. I looked up at that mocking, burnt frame of a stand, then lowered the jar and carried on walking around the centre circle, letting the wind carry Granddad.

The following evening, keen for our final night in Yorkshire to be more light-hearted and spent in good company, Mum arranged for us to have dinner at Colin's ahead of the 1985 European Cup final. As we switched on we were greeted with scenes of chaos at the Heysel Stadium in Brussels – crumbling, empty terracing littered with people's possessions, a collapsed wall, people fighting, running – and disbelief as it became clear another football disaster was unfolding in which, this time, 39 people died. We decided to watch the final, but there was an air of unreality in the room: there could only ever be one winner, not that it mattered. In fact, nothing mattered. Having come to Yorkshire eighteen days earlier for a celebration that turned into a catastrophe, I'd leave Yorkshire that next morning having witnessed yet another football disaster.

The aching emptiness of the large house we returned to swallowed you whole. I looked out of the front window and saw the road I'd never cycle up with Andrew again; out of the back windows lay an empty garden in which we used to play football. As I switched on my Commodore 64 computer I selected one- not two-player games. In the utility room I found the broken radio-controlled truck lying on a 10 May newspaper, the wet grass of the morning of the fire dried on its tyres and undercarriage. All life had been drained from the house. I sat with Mum in the lounge that evening listening to music – and looking at their photographs I fully realised they'd gone for ever. Only one of Mum's 'three boys' had made it back from the football alive. With that realisation I turned to Mum, who cradled me as I broke down and cried.

7

'Moving On'

I'd been back at school four days when the boy sitting next to me at the back of the school bus asked, 'Why do Bradford City need a new striker?'

Confused, I told him, 'We don't, we've got Bobby Campbell.'

'No, they do, trust me. Don't you want to know?' he persisted.

'Er, they don't, but OK, why?' Perhaps he had some transfer gossip.

'For the match!'

His *boom-boom!* was followed by my left–right as the bus came to a sudden halt. As the other boys dragged me off him I heard the driver shout, 'Stop – Off!' Then, much like a player who knew the red card was to come, I turned to make a lone walk down the aisle of the silent bottom deck. As I prepared to get off I heard the driver tell the whimpering boy, 'You too!' So I waited for him on the grass bank by the bus door. As he reached it, he hesitated, the fear clear in his face.

'I'm sorry, Fletch,' he stammered, the tears streaming down his face.

I knew his own words had shamed and humiliated him enough, and said, 'OK.' We jogged back into the village for the bus that followed ours. It was forgotten about till the following Monday when it got back to Mum. Where Dad would have been proud of me, Mum was appalled. It reduced her to tears and shaking, and she made me promise to never respond to such words with violence again.

East Bridgford rallied to our support. A succession of villagers with baked goods visited our house. On our first morning back I drew my curtains to see the steel goalposts Dad had not found time to erect in the garden, now up. The Reindeer's landlord Tony White made clear we were to treat his pub and living quarters as a second home. The Hunts, next door, told Mum they were her parents now. The memorial service in the village church on our first Sunday back was full to capacity. Paul Hart and his family often invited us to dinner or met us in the Reindeer's beer garden. So it was hardly a surprise Mum did not consider brawling the best way to repay all this, in a village where reputation meant everything.

Nottingham Forest also rallied to our support. Chairman, Maurice Roworth, who lived in neighbouring Lowdham, was at the village memorial service, and the club arranged several fund-raising events. The biggest, at the Commodore International, was attended by several Forest players, including Steve Hodge, Chris Fairclough, Steve Wigley and Paul Hart; Nottinghamshire cricketers Sir Richard Hadlee and Clive Rice were also present and, with Maurice, I thanked everyone individually from the podium. As that night closed the six hundred present linked arms, and I ended up in a duet with Gerry Marsden, leading the packed room in a rendition of 'You'll Never Walk Alone'. There was barely a dry eye in the house.

In retrospect it seems almost beyond belief, but the day after that, just three days after we'd laid our family to rest, the Popplewell Inquiry opened.

Forest set up the Martin Fletcher Family Appeal that summer. And on a Sunday in August, a day after the first match of the season, hundreds of rubber ducks were thrown from Trent Bridge, followed by a flotilla of boats full of players. The person whose duck made it first to the City Ground was deemed the winner. This kind of thing made Mum happy for me to return to football. The fans and Forest, through the club's appeal, raised nearly £10,000 to help support us financially.

Mum had so fallen in love with the village and her dream house that she saw East Bridgford as her adopted home – a place she never planned to leave. However, for me, it was a place I had never wanted to be: in my head I should have been at Batley Grammar School with all my friends; we should have still been C Block season-ticket holders. Just four days after the fire, Mum had turned down her old job back in Leeds and made it clear she'd never return to Yorkshire – it held too many haunting memories. She wanted a fresh start, a new place, but one where she felt close to Dad and Andrew. For Mum East Bridgford was perfect – and although I can see it was a lovely place full of lovely people, for me it was a personal hell.

Mainly this was because of school. I loathed Toot Hill. On my first day back after our memorial service, I was struck by the forced smiles and fake niceness. These kids who had previously hated me soon made it clear they were only being nice because their parents had told them to be. One lad, who'd written a lovely message in a get-well card my tutor group had sent me in Yorkshire, pointed out, 'What was I meant to put – "Wish you were dead"?'

'*Help me, help me. I'm on fire, I'm on fire,*' were the random screams I'd unexpectedly hear from school windows. A few pupils came up to me and talked normally, but called me 'Bernard', as in 'Burn 'Ed'. 'All right, Burn 'Ed?' they'd say, as I walked around school, my hair yet to lie down properly. I couldn't help getting into a few scrapes; my teachers would resort to the 'sticks and stones' analogy, warning that by physically responding I'd just make matters worse – but as far as I could see they didn't punish the bullies. There were plenty of kids with reputations, or protective elder brothers from untouchable, thuggish families. It was clear who had the run of the school.

Worse, I had to keep this all to myself. I daren't tell Mum who, despite life in our idyllic village, was having her own problems. Unable to sleep, I'd hear her cry at night. She'd also stopped eating – the weight of an already slim, tiny woman dropping to an extremely worrying level. I'd end up spending all my pocket money on boxes of her favourite Black Magic chocolates to try to get her to eat. She needed my support, not stories from Toot Hill that could tip her over the edge.

So, told by my teachers the taunts would disappear if I ignored them, I withdrew. I'd spend breaks and lunchtimes on my own, finding refuge in the library or just walking the school's empty playing fields alone. Once home, Mum was happy for me to stay in during the evenings. Retreating into a kind of survival mode, I counted down the weeks until the six-week summer break.

The start of the summer holidays: a time full of glorious sunshine and unfulfilled promise – unless you happened to be at Valley Parade that last weekend of July 1985. There, rows of chairs had been laid out on the pitch, facing the charred, tangled remains of the Main Stand, which was to be demolished the next day, the forensic search already finished. In the centre of the burnt-out structure, a defiant giant crucifix, made from two huge charred planks of wood, stood as tall as the stand had been. The black ocean of charcoal still stank, but at least flowers and scarves from across the country adorned what was once the front seating section. In front of the charred crucifix was a cardboard heart, behind a platform on which 56 posies of white flowers were placed. Local schoolchildren separated out the flowers of the posies before giving them to the crowd as the service ended.

A 6,000 capacity crowd, larger than that season's average gate, was in place on a hot, cloudless afternoon to bid the stand farewell. We were sent front-row tickets by Bradford City Council, who organised the service. However, I remember it was odd there was no parking at the ground – Uncle Mike and Dennis had to drop us off then walk back twenty minutes from the city centre – and nothing laid on at the clubhouse. Well, nothing for the families, that was; it was the VIPs who gathered there. The seated families then had to wait for the 'dignitaries' and club officials, who appeared to march triumphantly down a specially constructed 'VIP' corridor at the side of G Block. Finally, our service could begin.

Many tough Yorkshiremen wept unashamedly through the next hour as they bid farewell to what once seemed their happy, indestructible home and pondered again the terrible loss of life. I stared blankly, often through a blurred tearful vision, before finally sinking into Mum's arms. Some folk were so heartbroken they left early, but that wasn't really an option for us trapped on the front row, the lenses trained on us – we would have to see it through to the bitter end. By the time the service ended, all the emotion was drained from me and I stood there feeling like a weak, frail old man.

One of the young schoolchildren smiled sympathetically as she handed me a white flower from her posy. It was the only beautiful part of the service.

With Colin Butterworth (Dad's friend and Trevor Cherry's mate), I then climbed through the rubble of the stand one final time. As we retraced my steps from May we stood in silence at the turnstiles, before skidding down the stand to the pitch. I looked around at the four empty sides of Valley Parade, ringed by a rare clear sky, and took in one final memory – once it was cleared I had no plans to be back.

On leaving Bradford we waited at the traffic lights outside the glass-fronted offices of the *Telegraph & Argus*. Suddenly we heard a sound we'd not heard all day – laughter. Perhaps hoping to share a brief moment of someone else's happiness, we turned to the car alongside us and saw its occupants – including Bradford City chairman Stafford Heginbotham – all laughing away. Grandma, Uncle Mike and Aunty Val yelled through the open windows, wondering exactly what it was that he had to be so happy about. A guilty look fell over Heginbotham's face, like a boy caught with his hand in the cookie jar.

That evening the interim findings of the Popplewell Inquiry were leaked to the press. The hearing had opened in Bradford, on Wednesday 5 June, and wound up just over a week later, on the following Thursday. Seventy-seven witnesses had been called, but, on the basis of just five and a half days of hearings – processing the testimony of anywhere between twelve and eighteen witnessess a day (the 2014–15 reopened Hillsborough inquest heard from one to three people per day) – Popplewell announced that the fire was caused by 'the accidental lighting of debris below the floorboards of the stand' by a smoker, in what he declared to be 'nothing more than a tragic accident'. I have never understood how he reached this conclusion – people had smoked freely in this stand for eight decades without incident. Popplewell kept to his assurance that it was not his job to apportion blame. He declared 'it would be grossly unfair to point the finger at any one person', thereby making it seem to me that everyone was blameless.

On that summer night of the Valley Parade memorial service, it was what everybody wanted – if not needed – to believe. The next day the inquests opened and would conclude three days later – Coroner James Turnbull advising his jury (possibly due to the remit of the Popplewell Inquiry) they must not 'imply criticism suggesting that any particular person should be criminally liable or liable to civil proceedings'. I remember playing pool with a bunch of kids at a friend's house in Birstall the day after the service, and Mum brought that evening's *Telegraph & Argus* in when she came to pick me up. She slapped it on the table. There was a photo of the smoke rising from G Block on the day, and headlines about the Popplewell Inquiry's crowd safety recommendations, for example that there be no new wooden stands. We had all expected more. 'It's crap,' said Trevor Wass, a friend of Dad's. Mum agreed with him that the inquiry's remit was too narrow and that more investigation was needed, but when he asked her later, in the lounge, what she was going to do, she just said, 'Well, what can I do?'

'That's true,' he said, resignedly. Yorkshire fatalism was coming in to play again.

Mum was not happy, though. The haste of it all, the lack of any culpability, and the absence of any real new safety standards worried her deeply. We needed someone to be held legally accountable for this tragic loss of life and, as my mum would later say, 'for justice to be seen to be done'. A month later, on the day before the new football season started, she decided she'd bring a civil test case with West Yorkshire police, so liability would be apportioned. At a national press conference in Nottingham she warned that despite the findings of Popplewell's Interim Report, football grounds, with the new season about to start, remained unsafe. A duty of care needed to be established between football clubs and their supporters. As it happened two parallel cases would run in November of the following year: Susan and Martin Lee Fletcher v Bradford City, the Health and Safety Executive and West Yorkshire County Council; and PC David Britton v the same parties. Mum's warning about a duty of care needed to avoid any future disasters at football grounds was something she'd repeat periodically over the next two years, but her warnings were ignored.

Fifty-Six

The test case wouldn't be heard for nearly 18 months. For now, ironically, the dawn of the new football season filled me with hope. Nottingham Forest chairman Maurice Roworth invited me and Mum to the opening home game of the season, against Howard Wilkinson's Sheffield Wednesday. We were handed car-park passes, shown the trophy room, entertained in the directors' suite, and given seats next to the chairman in the directors' box. Maurice conducted me on a personal tour of the warren of rooms under Nottingham Forest's Main Stand before the match, taking me into the changing rooms and on to the pitch. Then, finally, we approached the door with 'Manager' on it.

'Mr Chairman,' Brian Clough enquired, as he looked up from his mahogany desk. Well, I assumed he looked up – I wasn't certain because I was hiding behind the door, not knowing how he'd react to being interrupted in his lair.

'Hi, Brian . . . I've got Martin Fletcher with me. Martin lost—'

'Now, Mr Chairman,' came the unmistakable nasal drawl, 'I know full well who Martin is. Won't you come in, my lovely, and stop hiding?' he asked. By the time I'd walked into his office, he'd come from behind his desk to shake my hand and gently ruffle my hair.

He then handed me the team sheet he'd completed at his desk: 'Now, young man, I'm just about to give this to the referee. Is there anything I should change?'

I looked at the small piece of paper. Still nervous, I couldn't really concentrate on the blur of blue biro scribbled all over it – but it felt like if I'd suggested a switch at right-back I'd have got it. Ultimately, although there were many things I wished he could change, his team sheet was never one of them, so I looked up and told him, 'No, sir.'

'OK, Martin, so long as you're happy. Now, tell me, how are you and your lovely mother?'

'We're OK,' I said, not wanting to complain.

'Now, would you like a job, young man?' Clough asked.

I nodded.

'Mind you, the job I've got in mind for you is an extra special, big one. But, you being such a lovely young man, you can do it for me,' Clough assured me. 'I want you to make sure you take extra special care of your lovely mother for me. OK, young man?'

'Yes, sir.'

'And remember: be good, Martin.' And with those very words, he signed my autograph book before heading off to find the ref. Unfortunately Forest lost 0–1, but a few days later I was back for a Junior Reds open day at the training ground along the River Trent. After a training session we were all queuing for photos with our heroes, when a familiar voice boomed, 'Martin, come here, young man. Are you looking after your mother for me?'

'Yes, he is!' Mum told him as we jumped the queue and all smiled for the camerawoman.

'Good boy,' said Clough, patting me on the head. 'Come with me, young man.' The squad, just about in position for a team photo, parted as Clough positioned me in the middle of the team line-up. After the photo was taken he reminded me, 'Now don't go forgetting about that job I gave you, Martin. I'll see you later, lovely. Be good.'

Summer over, my second year at Toot Hill started the following week. Sitting in French on my first day back I waited as our teacher told us who'd go into the top set. As I'd topped the class in my first year, I listened for my name as our teacher read out names in no apparent order. But it never came. I questioned the decision as soon as the lesson finished, only to be told 'in light of events' it was felt it would be best not to have the 'pressure' of the top set. I was outraged. All I wanted to be was normal, but now not only my peers but also the teachers made it clear I was anything but.

I withdrew completely into myself from this point, cutting off all relationships with everyone but Mum. I knew I had to find my own solutions. I punched a new first year who told me a joke about Bradford. As he burst into tears I told him that if he didn't like it he should tell our housemaster, which he did, only to find himself in trouble as I got off scot free! That taught me a valuable lesson: I had a good punch, and it was no bad thing to be known to throw it if provoked. So comments I'd have once let pass I now responded to with a punch, and if somebody complained I'd tell the teacher they said something about the fire. It was double dealing, but it meant that pretty soon I too became an untouchable, albeit one who was a surly, moody loner.

I'm not sure when the taunts stopped for good, but I remember that as Mum's weight returned to normal, I felt I could stop buying her chocolates and was able to save up for a Walkman, which I'd listen to whenever I could, on the school bus, or during breaks and lunchtimes. To cut myself off, all I now had to do was plug in my earphones and crank up the volume. Pretty soon an element of cool was added to the menace and, ironically, I slowly started making a few friends.

But it was at the football that I felt I belonged most. Only at the City Ground did I feel able to blend into the background and pass as an unnoticed face in the crowd. Some fans would nod or smile in recognition, but they were looks of respect. And then there were my new friends in high places: a week or so after I turned 13 Brian Clough's assistant, Ronnie Fenton, on seeing me with Mum one morning in the Christmas holidays, asked if I wanted to go training with the first team, in which Des Walker, Stuart Pearce, Nigel Clough and Neil Webb were becoming established. Unfortunately though, I was now so withdrawn that I turned Ron's kind offer down.

Every other Saturday provided the one oasis in my troubled life. In the Junior Reds' section I got sitting and chatting with other lads at school. Never short of an opinion or fact, I'd put on a half-time floor show revolving around the only way to shut me up: stuffing ever-increasing amounts of Polo mints into my mouth, all at once. By the time five or six packs were in there, everyone waited to see if Forest could provide the punchline by scoring at the start of the second half. If they did the kids in front of us would get showered by the warm melting Polos that flew out of my mouth. The City Ground was my new home.

'Moving On'

Although Stuart McCall sent me his match shirt signed by the whole squad, together with a signed ball and pennant, a trip to Elland Road, Leeds Road or Odsal Stadium, Bradford's temporary homes, was not on the agenda. Bradford City were my family club – but my family were now gone.

I did return, with Mum, to a wet Valley Parade on Christmas morning, 1985. We parked up on a deserted South Parade, the pavement now free of flowers, the stand support wall bricked up. There were puddles everywhere among the cobbles and, as the rain poured down, it had never seemed so desolate. We placed flowers on the pavement where the turnstiles once squatted, and I broke down, no longer sensing my family there. I told Mum I never wanted to return. Then, an hour later, as I busily tore open my presents, I opened a Bradford City promotion book from Aunty Irene, the side holding the trophy, presented an hour or so before the fire, on its cover. I recoiled.

Incredibly, nine months later, as I listened to local commentary from Nottingham Forest's 2–6 win at Chelsea, news of another fire at Bradford broke. I could not believe my ears and switched stations in search of more news. This time Leeds United hooligans had set fire to a fish and chip van at Odsal Stadium before trying, unsuccessfully, to tip it down grass terracing on to Bradford City supporters below. I was horrified at the reports of tearful fans fleeing in terror. It violated the memories of my loved ones, belittling them in a way that declared they did not matter. To this day, Leeds United and their supporters have never been forgiven in Bradford.

This attempted re-enactment of what was at that point English football's biggest disaster, dug a knife through my heart. I went through my promotion supplements, cutting out articles and photographs to put in a scrapbook. Then I did the same to my 13 May 1985 *Telegraph & Argus* 'Day of Disaster' newspaper, stuffing some photos behind my school bus pass. The following Monday, as I listened to my Walkman in the houseroom, my housemaster, Mr Morgan, found me staring at pictures of the fire, battling to make sense of the senseless. He was so horrified he immediately rang Mum.

Mum and I saw matters very differently, though. As I vented my anger and hatred of Leeds and Leeds United, she reminded me that she was proud to be from Leeds, supported Leeds United as a girl and that Dad had spent his teenage years in a pub within walking distance of Elland Road; my family ties to Leeds were as strong as those to Bradford. She assured me every right-minded person in Leeds was ashamed of what happened. Of course, she was right. (Two years later a young girl at our old hairdressers on Chapeltown Road in Shadwell told me, as she washed my hair, that she'd been at school with the 15-year-old responsible for the fire and how nobody ever spoke to him again.) But it left me so disorientated that I looked to reconnect with Bradford City. And now I wanted to return to Valley Parade when it reopened at Christmas 1986, a feeling that was heightened still further when Forest drew Bradford City at Odsal Stadium in the League Cup that autumn. Boys at school told me I could only support one club. I chose the family club of memory over the club where I had a season ticket. Sadly, I didn't make it to the game – we were in Leeds for the civil case that week. But it wasn't the end of the world when Forest won 0–5.

After the Odsal fire my troubles at school got worse still. Now, early in my third year, I'd given up on schoolwork altogether. I'd do no homework, making some flippant remark if a teacher asked to see it. My results suffered dramatically, and I fell to the bottom of a class I should have topped. A couple of teachers threatened to put me on report and to alert Mum. But with the civil case upcoming, I'd retort, 'Don't you think she's got enough to deal with without this too?'

In the end my own sloppiness rumbled me. We were watching the TV one Sunday night when Mum asked, 'Martin, I haven't seen your homework diary for some weeks.'

'Oh, you have, Mum,' I tried to reassure her. 'You must have forgotten about it.'

'No, I haven't, Martin. I've actually kept a track of it these last two weeks and I've definitely not seen it – or before that even – so stop trying to insult my intelligence!'

Unfortunately I'd been forging Mum's signature for several weeks. As she flicked through the pages of the diary she looked at me with real disappointment for the first time. A huge row followed, one thing led to another, Mum contacted Toot Hill, then threatened me with a new school – possibly Nottingham High School – if things didn't improve.

With all this going on, the civil case started at Leeds High Court. Mum's test case spanned two weeks in November 1986, with the police case running parallel. But it was just Mum fighting for the rights of the bereaved and the survivors, 110 people in all (PC David Britton was fighting for 44 injured official personnel). Her legal advisors told her it was a cast-iron case and Justice Cantley found the football club, who had been warned their stand was a fire risk, two-thirds liable, with West Yorkshire County Council, who'd warned them but whose fire authority didn't follow it up, one third liable. Justice Cantley stressed that football clubs did indeed have a duty of care, and that this duty was to ensure fans could escape quickly and conveniently should the worst occur, regardless of security concerns. Although civil courts could not consider issues of criminal liability, this was a landmark civil judgment that should have made football grounds safe for supporters throughout the country, by placing clubs and councils on alert to their responsibilities. That thought satisfied Mum, but the county council reserved a right to appeal, and that dragged to its conclusion in February 1987, when they finally accepted they had no defence.

Mum had set up a fighting fund that other families contributed to in order to receive damages. And, of course, we won. We received the equivalent of 12 years' salary for Dad, as a 34-year-old in 1985. The main aim in taking the case on was to prove the club and the local authority were liable, and therefore responsible for their fans; but as far as we were aware, Dad had no plans to retire at 46. In fact, Dad's employers produced salary projections that forecast he'd have been the managing director of a FTSE250 company by his mid-forties, so the financial aspect of the case rumbled on for a few years. But in the end, from a financial point of view – particularly after Hillsborough – we began to wonder why we'd started this in the first place – wanting to get on with life, we chose to accept this meagre offer rather than go back to court. West Yorkshire County Council had long gone, but their insurers paid up.

But back in that winter of 1986–87, with the legal and moral responsibility for the disaster established as much as Mum felt it ever would be, it seemed a cloud had finally lifted from our troubled lives. My school work had improved dramatically after the case had finished in the November, and Mum agreed, in a decision that ripped her apart, to let me return to Valley Parade when it reopened in December. She made it clear I'd only be allowed to continue going to football matches in Bradford if I got the results we agreed on. I was a very precocious teenager, some might say old before my time, but Mum did everything possible to give me control back over my life, and to treat me like the adult she demanded I be.

Valley Parade reopened on Sunday 14 December 1986, two days after my fourteenth birthday. As a birthday treat I'd gone along with Pennine Radio commentator Tony Delahunty to the newly rebuilt stadium on the Friday afternoon – Mum had bonded with Tony during the fortnight of the civil case. I walked around the stand and on the pitch, confronting my demons, before spending that evening at Odsal watching Bradford lose 1–3 to West Brom. I remember standing around in silence in the bar at half-time while Stafford Heginbotham came up to talk to Tony. I returned to Valley Parade with Tony on the Sunday for the unveiling of a memorial sculpture, donated by a private benefactor, which was scheduled to take place a couple of hours before a charity match kicked off. But the press instantly recognised me. Unbowed and with nowhere else to go I went to my seat in A Block, but with the stadium largely empty I was spotted then approached by some journalists, until police officers intervened and advised me to wait in the back of the stand until nearer kick-off. I did, buying a new scarf, two badges and pencil portraits of Bobby Campbell and Stuart McCall, before having a pie. But when I returned an hour later the lenses were waiting. After a minute's silence, where all you could hear was a clicking turnstile and what sounded like a pushbike's pedals turning outside, Bradford beat a Bobby Robson-managed England XI 2–1 – with a telephoto lens trained on me pretty much all the game. My moment of joy when Bradford scored would feature in the next day's newspapers.

I was only 14, but I landed my first job through the civil case, as a sports assistant at Bradford's Pennine Radio, through Tony. Tony Delahunty had famously broadcast live from the stand on the day of the fire, leaving only as the flames headed towards him. He'd taken us to watch Halifax Town v Leyton Orient at the Shay on the Friday night after the civil case finished – the idea being to let me practise some off-air radio commentary with him. Having watched too many football games, I was a natural, so he asked for on-air comments that night, and had me in the studio the following day. I watched my first Bradford City match after the fire from the press box with him. He soon had me filing reports, acting as his head researcher and attending yet more Bradford City home matches as his assistant. It all filled me with confidence once more.

Life was slightly happier. I'd still not go out after school, preferring to spend a lot of time completing football scrapbooks, reading football books and researching for Tony – helping prepare his crib sheets for Saturday; making notes on the form of our players and the opposition; working out a few stats – or just watching TV with Mum. Mum booked us dinner once a week, invariably at the newly opened, delightful Tom Browns, in neighbouring Gunthorpe, where girls from Toot Hill worked as waitresses. Saturdays would either mean a drive north with Mum to work on the radio, or we'd go to her mum's in Cropwell Bishop in the morning before I'd head over to the City Ground, where I'd kept my season ticket.

Forest would go on to finish third in the 1987–88 season, but still 17 points behind champions Liverpool. I loved Forest, but I was being slowly drawn back north too: Bradford City had their own good season, narrowly missing out on promotion to the top flight for the first time in 66 years, on the last day of the campaign. Enthused and energised by their challenge, I spent most Saturdays watching them in their first full season back at Valley Parade. Unfortunately Mum had a falling out with Tony, who'd actually moved to Radio Trent in Nottingham around that time, and that was the end of my budding radio career. Bradford's charge up the table was accomplished by what had been largely Trevor Cherry's team, but chairman Jack Tordoff failed to add to a small squad before the transfer deadline day in March, and we lost our final two matches of the season having gone on an 11-match unbeaten run and lost only once since 2 January. We missed out by a single point. But standing on the Kop that season with Colin and his son Andy, on the part where Dad had told me he'd stood, new, happy memories of Valley Parade were formed, and trumpeted the possibility of new beginnings.

Now in my fourth year at Toot Hill, the headphones were ditched, as I played football and touch American football at break and lunchtime, joking with new-found mates about sport, TV and girls. In class I was disruptive, playing the fool and enjoying being the centre of attention – but teachers smiled and shook their heads rather than chided. I remember two holidays that year offered me a first glimpse of a future untouched by my past. At 15 I'd fully matured and looked several years older. In Orlando, in April 1988, as I went to meet Mum for dinner, I was confused as an elegant, beautiful Asian woman in her early twenties started to chat suggestively and flirt with me in the hotel lift, asking how long I was in town for and what my plans were, and that she hoped to see me again. Then that summer in the Sheraton Sand Key in Clearwater, Florida, I had two beautiful sisters in their late teens, one blonde, one brunette, vie for my attention in their skimpy bikinis round the pool. And late one night, as we chatted by the pool, a beautiful girl sat nearby and looked over longingly in my direction, prompting Mum's departure so we could be alone. I now realised people could see me for me, and not the damaged goods I always assumed people saw.

My confidence grew, and by and large I managed to transport the cooler, confident teenager by the pool in Florida back to Toot Hill for my GCSE year. I also graduated from the Junior Reds' enclosure at the City Ground to the Trent End. And in Nottingham city centre I found pretty girls to flirt with who knew nothing of my past. At last I felt free, and living such new beginnings meant that I had less need to visit Bradford. I trusted and believed in life again, happy, it seemed, in being the master of my own destiny.

Then Nottingham Forest drew Liverpool in that year's FA Cup semi-final at Hillsborough, Sheffield.

By April 1989 football's future had already dawned. The success of CCTV, the anti-hooligan intelligence unit and stiffer sentencing had seen the worst excesses of hooliganism largely pass. English crowds had increased for three successive seasons for the first time in 40 years – even women and teenage girls were no longer that unusual a sight at football. There was a growing sense that football could be a valuable media property. British Satellite Broadcasting (BSB) were looking to break up the cosy cartel formed by the BBC and ITV. As far as any concerns for the fans, though, the powers-that-be failed to see why anything should change.

For the second consecutive year the Hillsborough semi-final would have been a fitting Cup final. Between them Forest and Liverpool had lost only two apiece of their previous 42 games, and the previous Sunday Forest had won the League Cup, their first major trophy in nine years. So we headed into Hillsborough three-quarters of an hour ahead of kick-off in great anticipation and hope that our team would come of age against the defining team of the era. For the second year running Forest had been allocated the large Kop – and although it was full, we found a spot a third of the way up at its far edge, nearest the North stand to our right.

Fifty-Six

As we cheered our side out none of the 21,000 on the Kop saw the initial surge on the Leppings Lane terrace. Our attention was on the Forest players as they warmed up, then on the match itself, which apart from a couple of corners in the opening minute, was mostly played out in front of us. When we did break out of our third of the field I was momentarily distracted by the large number of police officers massed in tight formation in front of the North stand. Inexplicably, a few Liverpool fans were walking around the edge of the pitch. Then, seconds after Liverpool hit the crossbar, Forest looked to cross into the penalty area at the Leppings Lane end and a police officer ran on to the pitch to stop the game. Fans, now massed behind that goal, walked on. As the numbers of fans spilling on to the pitch increased, beginning to almost fill the penalty area, so did our confusion. Then I noticed people in the stand above the Leppings Lane terrace starting to grab hold of the arms of desperate fans below, dragging them up to safety. As ominous sirens filled the air I perched over the fence beside me and caught sight of a road full of waiting ambulances.

Eventually one Liverpool supporter ran towards the Kop, and others followed. As they stood there, arms flailing, frantically trying to explain the unexplainable, the catcalls ended and Forest supporters climbed over the Kop fences to help them tear down advertising boards for makeshift stretchers. What those in earshot learnt rang round the Forest end in seconds. People were dying. I'd returned to hell.

An endless tide of fans started heading that way – prone figures carried in fireman's lifts, arms draped around pairs of supporters; or seemingly lifeless on advertising boards. I quickly stopped my initial count of the injured, as the numbers were too great, and started to count those beneath me on stretchers, several with their faces covered. It became a relief to see people struggling to stand, or in pain – as at least that meant there was life. I reached a death count of 40, before I could count no more.

Supporters everywhere had their heads in their hands, grown men were slumped on the pitch, openly weeping, others were frantically trying to revive crushed supporters. There was a cheer as life briefly flickered in one boy, only to be extinguished just as quickly – many burst into tears as he died before us.

An ambulance trundled back from the far end, just as another ambulance headed in through the narrow gap between the stand and the Kop – so narrow, you'd only get one ambulance through at a time – and both had to brake sharply to avoid a head-on collision.

By this point nobody expected the game to resume, but we knew we had to wait and bear helpless witness. I looked across the Kop end; plenty of Forest fans were just staring at the ground or straight ahead. By 3.30 p.m. the occasional person started drifting away. I knew Mum would fear the worst, so I turned to Mick beside me, one of the lads from Mum's garage who I'd gone with, and said I needed to find a phone. Twenty minutes after that, once most of the injured Liverpool fans immediately beneath us had been ferried to ambulances, Kenny Dalglish made an announcement. He explained over the tannoy that there'd obviously been one or two problems, before asking us to remain patient and stay where we were to await further announcements. He then asked that we put our hands together for the efforts of the emergency services. We left a stadium in muted applause.

I went to a Charlie Browns motorist discount centre across the road and they let me use their phone. Mum's line was engaged and every two minutes I tried again, only to find it inexplicably engaged again. My frustrations grew with each failed attempt. Finally, after six or seven failed attempts I phoned next door and spoke with Gavin, a friend a year above me at school, who told me that his mum was with mine, and that Mum knew of the disaster and had taken it badly. Although he told me he'd pass my message on, he didn't think she'd accept it from him so he urged me to keep trying.

There was one of those display boards of car radios in the garage, where you could fiddle about with the knobs on any model you might fancy buying. Between attempts to get through on the phone, I listened to various stations. A death toll that began at 25, grew every minute or two, till it reached 40. As I listened my anger grew at the death toll. Yet another disaster at a football ground, and more fans needlessly dying – it was too much to take in. All my suppressed emotions welled over and I burst into tears. Mick hugged me and tried to calm me down in the service area. He went to get me a drink. I slumped to the floor and began to bang the back of my head on the wall behind me. I did this a few times, but luckily Mick reappeared with a coffee, and put his hands behind my head.

Finally, I got through at home. On hearing me speak Mum sounded as much heartbroken as relieved. She'd been cleaning and had put on BBC Radio 1, who reported news of an 'updated death toll from the Hillsborough terraces'. As Mum had bought me a terrace ticket, she believed fate had come to reclaim me and that I was dead. Despite later assurances that Leppings Lane was the Liverpool end, she'd only believe this on hearing my voice. (Strangely, all these years on, the perpetually engaged phone remains a mystery. Mum was sitting by it all the time, waiting for me to call.)

We headed back to our coach past sad Forest fans starting to leave the stadium and loose bands of distraught Liverpool fans – there were rows of ambulances filling Penistone Road. The memory of ambulances lined up along Midland Road four years earlier rushed up at me and my knees buckled. A couple of school friends helped me up and on to the bus. I became an inconsolable sobbing wreck on the back seat of our bus in the depot. Once the ambulances cleared, we were allowed to leave. The suburban houses we passed were full of people standing by their windows, some shaking their heads. As I looked back down at Hillsborough from the hill, I noticed a programme on the pavement, its pages flapping in the wind, abandoned like so many lives below.

Getting back home it was dusk. After a day of beautiful spring sunshine, East Bridgford had never seemed so serene, the sun setting, birds chirping. Mum was standing by the lounge window, red-eyed. As Mick's car drew up – the bus had dropped us in Arnold – she ran from the house to hug me. Similar scenes that were now happening across Merseyside had been played out in Bradford four years earlier.

Inside, I filled Mum in on the horrific moments of the day: the bodies on the pitch in front of me; the radio stations' reports of the metal gate being kicked down. It was all too much. I began to hyperventilate, and Mum rushed to get me a paper bag to breathe into. Later that night the chief constable of South Yorkshire claimed that, although the fans had not smashed the gates down they had rushed them, thus leaving the police with little option but to open the gates . . . Eventually I calmed down and talked through it all with Mum, who mentioned she'd heard on the radio the capacity of Hillsborough was 54,000. Being the sad sort of teenager who knew this kind of thing, I was pretty sure it was 51,000. I checked in my *Rothmans* – and, yes, that season had seen an 'increased capacity' but this must have been the first time it had been seriously tested.

The next morning, we looked out of the lounge window to see a small band of people carrying notebooks walk up our drive. We stared at each other in disbelief. 'Bradford boy now a season-ticket holder at Forest' had been the gist of a couple of articles in the *Nottingham Evening Post*, and even in the national press – complete with photos of me smiling in a Forest kit. They knew I would have been at Hillsborough.

'Don't worry, sweetheart. I'll get rid of them,' Mum assured me.

I hid away from the window. Several minutes later she returned.

'What took so long?'

'They wanted to hear it from you,' she replied, angrily shaking her head. The boy who had been at two major football disasters in the space of four years.

More journalists turned up at Toot Hill the next morning, but I wasn't there. Mum took me for a drive round the countryside, and we had lunch out. As we drove back into the village, I asked, 'Mum, why didn't the fences come down after Bradford?' To me that was the one obvious lesson of 11 May – Bradford's Main Stand had as many standing spaces as it did seats, with a third of the Kop able to escape only through a random gap in its fence.

'I don't know, sweetie, I really don't.'

I knew something just stank.

'So, really, Thatcher let our family die in vain,' I said.

Mum just drove on in silence.

Part Two

'The new Bradford City, which had risen from the ashes of the 1908 club in the summer, seemed doomed to nosedive back into the flames'

Jim Greenhalf, Bradford *Telegraph & Argus*, 24 December 1984

8

Rebuilt

As I came to, I could feel the warm sun beating down on my face; I could hear the sound of people playing on Richmond's Thames riverbank. Groggy, I opened my eyes slowly, fearing it might not be real – but the sight of a dozen friends playing an impromptu game of cricket, with tipped-over champagne bottles and water-filled ice buckets lying all around, made me smile. It *was* real. A decade had passed, and Bradford City had just been promoted to the Premier League.

To say there had been plenty of ups and downs along the way would be to make something of an understatement – and that's before we get on to Bradford City.

After Hillsborough, I'd planned to start my GCSE revision. That didn't happen until a week before the exams. I just scraped through, but I was so full of hate and anger that year that I scared many, including Mum, who was more concerned about me after Hillsborough – having lived through everything after Bradford – than back in the summer of 1985. I'd withdrawn into myself once more; any sense of humour was replaced with an air of menace. People gave me a wide berth. The first year of sixth form wasn't particularly easy, or pleasant.

But then that summer Mum gave me a good talking to. On holiday at the Bali Hyatt, she left me sitting on a pagoda overlooking the Indian Ocean, having told me it was time to have a good hard look at myself; I was too young to let anger and hate consume me, to isolate myself like I had. As the palm trees swayed on a hot tropical night, I cried for what I'd lost, what I'd seen, and the uncertain future I faced. But, as the tears fell, I smiled too; I came to see that while the fun and happiness of the world that I missed so much was now gone – that, in itself, didn't meant life shouldn't be lived 'in the moment, for the moment'. After all, you never know when such moments might end – as Dad always said – so life was there for the living.

The easy solution would have been to leave Toot Hill to start afresh. First, though, I had to learn to be Martin Fletcher, in a place where everybody knew who Martin Fletcher was. It was the focus of my final year at Toot Hill, as I became one of 'the lads', playing poker in the common room all day, clubbing in Nottingham or drinking in Bingham by night. Life was rolling: I remember going down to Twickenham to watch England win the Five Nations Grand Slam against France, then catching bar-diving topless girls in an excited crowd in the Orange Tree pub down the road; Forest reached the FA Cup final; I zoomed around the pit lane on a quad bike at Silverstone, before sunbathing on the roof of a motorhome at that year's Grand Prix. I'd missed out on the post-exam celebrations after Hillsborough; two years on six of us celebrated our A levels in Corfu, drinking until the last club in town closed, or at least until we found a girl to go home with. It was the life I should have always had, the life I'd been denied, but the life I was now determined to claim back.

Something of a shame then – if not a surprise – that I left Toot Hill with two Ds.

I got through two new A levels in nine months and resat English in a string of three-hour Saturday morning exams, and won places at both LSE and Warwick University. After attending an open day at Warwick, I fell in love with its green campus and union – everything was centred around the students, rather than lost in a bustling metropolis – so I accepted a place there to study Politics with International Studies.

After getting an A and two Bs, Mum suggested I no longer watch Bradford, as life should be about my future, not my past – and knowing how it pained her, I agreed. Warwick seemed to offer a fresh start. Only there was no avoiding the obvious fresher's week starters for ten: 'What does your dad do?' and 'Do you have any brothers or sisters?' I'd clam up, not wanting to deny Andrew's and Dad's existence, but willing to reveal only that they'd died in a fire. To those with happy privileged pasts, mine no doubt seemed evasive, shifty even. Clearly hiding something, I was, again, immediately different, a mystery man with something of an edge. A severe gastric illness, which laid me up for a term, didn't exactly help matters either. I once again became withdrawn and irritable, resentful of those with their perfect lives.

But the thing about patterns is that they tend to repeat themselves. I knew I needed to forge a new identity and meet new people. I threw myself into several societies: I joined the W963 radio station sports department, headed by future CNN sports anchor Alex Thomas, and befriended an easygoing affable gent called Ben Livermore. I wasn't bad at pool; I drank a shitload of beer; I remember watching Oasis, Radiohead, Shed Seven and Skunk Anansie, all of whom stopped by the student union in my time there. However, although I could have a laugh, I'd also have unexpected outbursts of irritability and anger. Some people remained wary.

Mum was happy too, though: she'd met someone and was embarking on a new journey.

I was 21 on the ninth anniversary of the fire. Geoffrey Richmond had just bought Bradford City and made a good first impression on the families at the 1994 memorial service, making clear his wish to put 11 May at the heart of the club. After the service, having laid our flowers where the turnstiles once were, I was sitting in Mum's car in the Valley Parade car park, making some bland observation about it being nice to see the flags at half mast for a change. I reassured Mum I had no plans to be back there week in week out, but wondered if by now there was any chance she'd stop hating the club.

'No,' she replied, clearly with no wish to elaborate.

'Why not?' I pressed. The fire had had nothing to do with Geoffrey, or Dave Simpson before him, and both had tried to do the right thing. I reminded her that 'doing the right thing' was the one thing she'd always said she wanted from the club.

'I know, Martin, I know. It's not them, it really isn't . . . I'll just never forgive Bradford City for as long as I live.'

Something in her tone really jarred, so I carried on, partly buoyed by the service, but also trying to get at what she really meant. Eventually, she'd had enough and interrupted me.

'Martin, you're an adult now, so I'll tell you. But I'm warning you, you may not want to know.'

I looked at her. 'Yes? And . . .'

'Well, you know it wasn't Stafford Heginbotham's first fire, don't you?'

I nodded. I was only a kid but I dimly remembered there were a lot of fires when I was growing up in Bradford. There was even the one at the top of our road.

'So, it was all rather convenient, don't you think, that the stand burnt down on that of all days?' she said.

I digested this for a second or two. 'Er, what are you saying?' I half laughed. 'That it wasn't an accident?'

'No, Martin, I never believed it was an accident and I never will. I don't think Stafford intended for people to die . . . but people did. All because he went back to the one thing he knew best that would get him out of trouble.'

'*What?*' For a second or two I didn't really know what to think. 'Ah, c'mon, what have you got to support that?' I asked, incredulous.

'Oh, nothing concrete,' she said, breezily all of a sudden. 'You know, just intuition . . .'

'*Your intuition!*' I scoffed.

Mum became angry again. 'Yes, Martin, my intuition. Look, I'm not going to sit here and debate it with you. You wanted to know why I'll always hate Bradford City, and now you do. OK?'

Mum never really spoke about it again, and I didn't ask her. On some subconscious level, I didn't want to go there. I became wrapped up in my own life. I got through my final year, then my exams.

But like plenty of new graduates, I didn't really know what to do next. A year of quiet self-reflection followed in Nottinghamshire. The quieter it became, the more I tried to understand my demons, and started researching post-traumatic stress disorder. It dawned on me that the distortions in my personality were not, really, my own. Withdrawal, irritability, anger, no sense of a normal future – all were symptoms of post-traumatic stress disorder. It was liberating to know that if I could control these I could control my demons. I realised I did not see what others saw in me; rather, just a damaged reflection, frozen in time. If that could be changed, perhaps I could be set free.

But fuck all that – there was a football tournament on. Euro '96 was the perfect excuse to ignore the calling of real life. I had tickets for 17 of the 31 games. A bit of serious, logistical thought, and if it was a day when games were being played, I was there, watching at least one.

Just ahead of the tournament I'd been in Cologne for Ben's twenty-first birthday. He was an exchange student, and had warned his mates – and his beautiful girlfriend, Danielle, a member of the Cologne Philharmonic Orchestra – of my troublesome reputation. But the weekend went well. I was determined to grasp and share life, and I hit it off with everyone, including Danielle's equally beautiful best friend. I hadn't felt this free in years.

We spent the next three weeks approaching stadiums with the sunroof of my red Golf GTI open, Ben madly waving the flag of whichever nation we'd adopted, me honking football tunes on my horn – well, at least that was the case when the car stereo wasn't blaring out tournament anthems such as 'Three Lions', 'The Life Of Riley' by the Lightning Seeds, 'Walkaway' by Cast and 'Don't Look Back In Anger' by Oasis. Everyone was wrapped up in it – even Mum came to a few matches with me, openly weeping in happiness in the stands after England's penalty shootout win over Spain in the quarter-finals. Euro '96 made me believe in the unconditional beauty of life once more. One of our own, Forest hero Stuart Pearce, exorcised his personal demons from Italia '90 by scoring his penalty against Spain, and we returned to Wembley the following Wednesday for the semi-final against Germany, half a dozen rows back, level with the penalty area from which Alan Shearer headed England's opener, Paul Gascoigne lunged millimetres short of a winner and Darren Anderton hit the post – all before the penalty shootout. Afterwards, as the defeated England team walked towards us, remembering what Stuart Pearce went through, I stood on my seat and, with my Ray-Bans hiding my tears, started to sing like a lunatic, 'There's only one Gareth Southgate.' Initially, fans looked at me, puzzled, but I raised my arms to rouse them, and they soon joined in, the rousing chorus spreading through our block – until the German players did their customary collective celebratory dive, to boos from the home crowd.

It was time to let go and move on. Mum had sold the house in East Bridgford and was now living in the Cotswolds; I returned to Warwick to do an MA in International Political Economy. I'd written a paper on 'the globalisation of football' – I was ahead of my time! – and I'd end up writing a dissertation entitled 'The Business of Sport: Processes of Marketisation and Denationalisation'. But before heading back to Warwick, I took my extensive Bradford City programme collection, pruned it down to just the games I'd attended, and chucked the rest in a recycling skip in Bingham; then spent the next year revelling in student life. Drinking, hanging around the student union, and occasionally battling with research models for my grand sports marketing thesis – in the parlance of the day, I worked hard and I played hard. I was now simply 'Fletch'. Nobody knew me as 'Martin', with all the baggage that entailed; but I remember a northern girl once enticed my Christian name out of me, and looked crestfallen when she realised who I was.

After graduation our campus life moved to London. Always half a dozen strong, sometimes over 50 of us worked our way through a series of West End and south-west London bars and clubs. Big football games tended to morph into raucous house parties that lasted all weekend; and I could be out five or six nights a week. I got a job with a firm as a trainee independent financial advisor (IFA), started earning a half-decent salary, and had no real worries. But, like most, I lived for the weekends. Ben was working as a contracts negotiator in the travel industry. His firm, keen to cut flight costs, asked him to stay over in various Scandinavian and East European capitals. I'd fly out for long weekends, and twice a year he'd organise a huge get-together. Ben is one of those blokes just happy for everyone else to be having a great time. I remember dancing to Destiny's Child's 'Bootylicious' in a Reykjavik nightclub with female fashion models, but not a great deal about the post-show party; another time we convinced a Russian baker in St Petersburg to sell us beer at 7 a.m. and, while we danced with his pretty bakery girls, confused Russians queued for Monday morning bread and pastries. This was life in the moment, and for the moment.

Amidst this Bradford City had been promoted in May 1999. As their promotion got nearer, so did my urge to return to Valley Parade. I finally succumbed and tried to get last-minute tickets for the final match of the season, at Molineux, but Bradford's commercial manager, Christine Gilliver, couldn't help out. So a dozen friends came over to the Racing Page in Richmond after Bradford had beaten Wolves 2–3, and we ended up on the riverbank where, after consuming several bottles of champagne, I'd fallen asleep in the sunshine, never happier. That night, on crashing on my mate Will's couch in Battersea, a friend asked, 'Is Fletch asleep? He's still smiling!' Will told him that I'd been smiling like that when asleep earlier – in fact, I hadn't 'stopped smiling since Bradford got promoted'!

Thirty-six hours later I was back in Centenary Square in Bradford for the 14th annual memorial service, a gathering that ended in spontaneous applause for the team. In the years I'd been away Geoffrey Richmond had been good as his word and begun to send a full representative party to the service, a tradition maintained to this day. He'd also instigated a minute's silence before the last home match of each season, and was planning a memorial to the victims at the ground. After the service, I badgered Christine once again, at a time when the scramble for Premier League season tickets was on, and got her to save me two in the newly opened Bantams Bar, an executive-style bar at the back of the new Kop. Framed photographs and match programmes lined three walls, while tinted glass windows overlooked the pitch. It seemed the perfect way to be back – for one, long extended goodbye. Mum was OK with it.

As I returned for the 1999–2000 season's home opener against Sheffield Wednesday I looked out over the tiny Bradford End towards Bradford city centre, then behind the Main Stand, pretty much unchanged from when it reopened in 1986. I thought, 'I'm back home.'

In fact, despite a 400-mile round trip I'd return to almost every home match that season. I was living for the weekend again – so much so that my IFA job in Surrey became a hindrance, and I packed it in. Seeing I was troubled, my boss, who knew nothing of my past, told me, 'Just go away, find a hillside somewhere and work out what it is you want to do – you'll be great at it, whatever it is.'

A few weeks of soul-searching in wet, wintry Guildford followed, before I finally arrived at what it was that troubled me so: my past.

9

Reclaimed/Central Failure

The Bradford Fire. Everyone knows it involved a carelessly discarded cigarette end or match that set light to rubbish beneath the stand. It was 'a tragic accident'. I grew up believing this – and I was there. I was Martin Fletcher, 'Kid Courage, the Bradford Fire Survivor', whose family perished in the flames.

I'd known Ben six years now – although we'd never talked about the fire. Or, rather, he knew what had happened, but through student days and drunken nights in Reykjavik or Berlin, the actual events of 11 May 1985 had been off limits.

Then, on a cold February afternoon in early 2000, Ben came up to Yorkshire with me to see Dean Windass and Dean Saunders get the better of Thierry Henry's Arsenal, Bradford somehow winning 2–1. After the match we were having a pint at the back of the Kop, watching a groundsman tending the pitch. The floodlights were still on, but the deserted neon-lit stadium felt ghostly. I talked Ben through, moment by moment, the events of 11 May 1985.

He was pretty stunned, but pleased it seemed relatively easy for me to talk about it at last. 'Tell me what caused it again?' he asked.

'A cigarette, or a match setting light to rubbish beneath the stand.'

'And you're happy with that?'

'*Happy?* Mate, I'll never be happy about anything that happened that day, will I?'

Ben apologised, alarmed he'd disrupted our relative calm. 'No, sorry. I meant, are you happy with that as an explanation?'

'Of course. Why not? That's what the Popplewell Inquiry thought.'

'Oh, I was just wondering . . .' He shot me a look that unnerved me. It was a look I'd seen before in a Warwick seminar: 'C'mon, you're smarter than that.'

I'd lived through Bradford, I'd been at Hillsborough; and I'd started writing about May 1985 as a therapeutic release. Now, armed with the degrees I had, and the vague notion I might try to write a book – I didn't have a great deal else on, after all – I decided to start researching the fire properly. Maybe I'd come up with those answers Ben was so surprised I didn't have.

As far back as our first day at Warwick I remembered Professor Iain McLean telling us that, as we didn't live in a world preordained by God, there could be no such thing as an 'act of God'. It had struck an instant chord. Where an event such as Bradford, say, could be termed 'an act of God', my Warwick training suggested a moral imperative to look beyond any superficial analysis of what brought the accident to pass, and to focus on the goverment policy-making decisions from which everything else flowed. The only place to start was by analysing the history of UK sports-ground safety legislation. I knew my Simon Inglis (I never really stopped digesting *The Football Grounds of England and Wales*, and subsequent editions), but I also headed to the British newspaper library at Colindale, north London, to see what had contemporaneously been said in response to Britain's various football disasters. I couldn't really understand why their lessons seemed to have never been learnt.

'A mass audience at a football match deserves as much and as rigorous protection as a small one in a theatre,' declared a *Guardian* editorial, before going on to warn, 'the name of the game will suffer if it is seen as unsafe to watch.' The same day a *Financial Times* editorial criticised 'a long record of government inaction' and criticised the state of UK grounds compared with those in the rest of Europe. These weren't opinion pieces published in the wake of Hillsborough, however; they were leaders written after the Ibrox disaster, eighteen years earlier, in 1971. Back then hooliganism was rearing its head and crowds were beginning to plummet accordingly (crowds would fall by 45 per cent over the next 15 years – and take 30 years to recover). But Ibrox had come on the back of decades of disaster after near-disaster at Scottish and English Football League grounds. Looking back, 1971 was the moment when football's madness should have been stopped.

Astonishingly, 1971 hadn't even been the first disaster at Ibrox. In 1902, before the annual Scotland v England match, the wooden West End terrace, on which 33,000 stood, became so overloaded that it trembled, then swayed, as its timber steps, supported only by small wooden joists, splintered and shattered, leaving a gaping thousand-square-foot hole. Those unable to escape fell some 50 feet through to the ground below – 26 died and 300 were injured. There were indications of similar pressure elsewhere across the terrace. In the inquiry that followed, wooden terraces were banned but, despite a similar incident at Blackburn, this ban was not applied to stands for another 83 years. Bradford City were founded a year after the first Ibrox disaster, and five years later they built their wooden Main Stand – the centrepiece of an impressive ground – in 1908.

Most schoolchildren have heard of the White Horse final, at Wembley 15 years later, but it was only a miracle that disaster was averted that day. The ground's owners, so confident they could meet demand, declared that games at the new national stadium need not be all-ticket. But for the first big match, the 1923 FA Cup final, up to 300,000 descended on Wembley – the turnstiles were forced to close over an hour before kick-off. Inside the stadium, supporters who wanted to be close to the pitch became crushed around the lower tier, despite the terraces of the upper tier being relatively empty. Outside, the throng continued to build, and half an hour before kick-off the gates were somehow breached. Fans inside only escaped the human tidal wave by spilling on to the pitch – relatively easy in those days of low perimeter walls – and did so in such numbers that only the crossbars remained visible in the penalty areas. Upon the arrival of King George V, mounted police – including, famously,

PC George Scorey on his white steed, Billie – and some of the players at last managed to coax people back on to the large greyhound track surrounding the pitch. Following the delayed kick-off, the excitement of an early Bolton goal resulted in crushed fans encroaching back on to the turf. By this point they'd managed 11 minutes of football. There was a further delay, and at half-time the players had to remain on the pitch for their team talk, as there was simply no way back to the changing rooms.

What the media described at the time as an 'ugly day' is now fondly recalled as the 'White Horse final'. A thousand injuries were considered a lucky escape, and one report stated, 'Everybody realised it is all important that nothing of the kind ever be allowed to occur again.' Andrew Bonar Law's home secretary Viscount Bridgeman convened a government departmental committee on crowds, to be headed by his predecessor Edward Shortt. A month later the Shortt Inquiry recommended big games be all-ticket and terraces be fed from the top – with separate entrances to each section and staggered crush barriers. A further set of recommendations divvied up responsibility for crowd control: outside the ground was the prerogative of the police; inside responsibility lay with the club stewards; with regular communication between them (via telephone) encouraged. Adequate signage around generous gangways, and limits on the numbers through each turnstile, and the dividing up of terracing into smaller, more manageable pens – as well as the provision of ambulance facilities – were also established. Critically, to enforce this, the committee report recommended the government introduce a local authority licensing system for grounds. The recommendations, however, were never implemented into law – it was suggested clubs would follow them on a voluntary basis.

Two decades later, on 9 March 1946, the Burnden Park Railway End terrace at Bolton was full to bursting, 25 minutes before kick-off. Club officials had failed to monitor this, however, and despite reports of crushing it took a further 15 minutes to close the turnstiles at that end; the communication between club stewards and the police, inside and outside the ground, was also found wanting. By the time the turnstiles were finally closed 2,000 more spectators had crammed on to a terrace where over 28,000 were already struggling for room. It later became clear that a further 1,500 fans had also climbed over the turnstiles from the railway, or flooded through an emergency gate (the lock of which had been picked by a father desperate to get his son out of the crush). Two improperly placed, corroded crush barriers collapsed as the players came out, and many of the 33 fans who died were sucked to their deaths, asphyxiated and trampled upon. Over 300 were injured, a figure that, again, would have been higher had so many fans not been free to escape on to the pitch over a low wall at the bottom of the terrace.

In those pre-hooligan days it wouldn't have been for the subsequent Hughes Inquiry, established by home secretary James Chuter Ede, to speculate what might have happened had there been fencing around Bolton's Railway Enclosure. Justice Hughes did recommend the capacities of terrace enclosures be scientifically calculated, though, with mechanical apparatus installed to record when such limits were reached – a situation that was to be monitored by the police. Concerned by the state of grounds in 1948, Hughes also made the wider observation that, 'By law a stand must be approved as safe for the number of people it is intended to accommodate, but there is no subsequent periodic inspection, nor statutory duty, to maintain the stand in a safe condition. Legislation,' he recommended, 'should close that gap.' He also recommended that grounds be closed until such a time when they were examined by local authorities, who would issue safety licences once satisfied – a process that would be repeated by annual inspection. Justice Hughes also felt that, 'The insurance for greater safety of the public demands a premium. The payment will be willingly made.' The cost of this left the home secretary to opt for a voluntary licensing system. As Simon Inglis pointed out in *The Football Grounds of Great Britain*, the system in place after Hughes 'was still inadequate because all it depended on was proof that an inspection had taken place. It did not lay down specific standards, gave no guidelines, and the FA accepted each report without question.' Clubs were essentially allowed to keep ground-safety matters 'in house': the FA didn't specify the criteria of the 'qualified personnel' carrying out the inspections. As Inglis noted, it could have been the club chairman carrying out the annual inspection.

All of which simply goes part of the way to illustrating how the culture of institutional neglect around football has such deep roots – a recurring tale of successive governments ignoring the recommendations of the bodies they've created. Even after the Bradford fire, and still alarmingly so after Hillsborough, it was clear that both grounds did not meet many of the recommendations of even the 1923 government report – but at that time Bradford were still not compelled by goverment legislation to do so. In the case of Bradford, if the guidelines to provide sufficiently wide gangways, adequate stewarding and ambulance provision had been made compulsory . . . then, four years later, after Hillsborough, there was still much talk of visible signage, set numbers on turnstiles, police control outside of grounds and safely staggered crush barriers. None of these concepts was new; all came to light in the aftermath of the 1923 FA Cup final. It was only the people's game, after all – the goverment and the football authorities did not care enough about ordinary people.

But back in the early 1960s, fire authorities – not football clubs themselves – campaigned for greater safety at sports grounds. One senior fire officer warned that if fire did break out, in most grounds narrow gangways and locked gates would prevent supporters escaping and result in a major tragedy. Then, as Nottingham Forest played Leeds United in a Division 1 match in August 1968, a blaze did break out in the City Ground's Main Stand. Thankfully, the structure was only four years old, and had contemporary design features, with wooden seats the only combustible material. There were no casualties and those who headed to the back of the stand found a wide gangway, off which open doors ran down wide external staircases to a large open car park. Looking at photographs taken on that sunny Saturday afternoon in 1968 – from the car park, where many gathered as big clouds of black smoke billowed out the back exits of the stand – the similarities with and crucial differences from Bradford 17 years later are striking. The charred timbers and rubble of the morning-after photographs initially look similar too, but at the City Ground there is plenty of brickwork and a wide corridor visible; at Valley Parade there is nothing but a sea of black debris – practically the whole internal structure and everything in the stand has been consumed – and it's disturbingly clear from the remaining poles still standing just how narrow the rear passageway was. At the City Ground the fire brigade immediately searched the rear gangway for casualties. And those who headed down through the stand to the pitch found wide stairwells that all led directly to an easily surmountable wall. Still, there was no loss of life or serious injury; the only inconvenience being Forest having to relocate across the Trent, to Notts County's Meadow Lane, until the Main Stand was rebuilt.

Although the Lang Report of 1969 echoed the political mood of the day – its primary brief was to tackle 'crowd behaviour' – it sought to reconnect with a few of football's long unaddressed issues, pointing out that seating was a useful deterrent in the battle against hooliganism, and again recommending legislation to introduce a local authority licensing system that would issue annually renewable safety certificates for grounds. But it stopped short of making this compulsory, and for the third time in four decades the government failed to enact recommendations.

Two years after the publication of the Lang Report, Rangers fans headed down Ibrox Stadium's steeply banked, notorious Stairway 13. In 1961 two people had died when a wooden barrier had collapsed, and no fewer than 32 been injured on leaving the East Terrace down this stairway in three separate crushes during the course of the sixties. Squint at an old photograph of the stairway today, and you could mistake it for an out-of-season ski slope. One supporter would later say, 'I've come down there many a time, my feet touching one step in a dozen. You're just carried like the wind.'

It was a cold Glasgow night on 2 January 1971, but home fans leaving an Old Firm derby were jubilant after Colin Stein's last-minute equaliser had saved the day. Hats, scarves and programmes had been tossed in the air, and it seems two boys bent down to pick something up, causing those behind them to stumble and fall. Those heading out of the East Terrace could feel the crowd around them get tighter, but they were still forced down the stairway by pressure building behind. Within minutes Stairway 13's steel barriers collapsed causing yet more to fall. Those that could, climbed or were pushed over the stairway's side fences, on to the vertiginous grassy embankment. While a police cordon cut off further people from reaching the top of the stairway, movement for those already trapped further down it proved impossible – 66 would die and 145 were injured.

Ibrox was the first disaster of the television age, and offered a modern-day opportunity for contemplation and change. Dr Harrington, a Birmingham-based academic, told the BBC the next day that, while only 16 per cent of club directors had concerns over ground safety, the vast majority of supporters were unhappy – he 'felt that such a further disaster was more or less inevitable'. The shadow sports minister, Denis Howell, declared, 'Unless new safeguards are enforced by law the risk of another Ibrox will remain.' In the not too distant future, certainly ahead of Hillsborough and the Taylor Report, Rangers would investigate all-seater stadiums, with a sectioned-off standing area; an idea borrowed from the Bundesliga in Germany. But following the Ibrox disaster the subsequent Wheatley Inquiry and its 1972 recommendations were immediately accepted by Edward Heath's Conservative government. Lord Justice Wheatley made clear that the 'present law falls far short of providing proper or effective control [because] there are no requirements as to the competence of a person chosen by the club who carries out the annual inspection of a ground'. There were local authority licensing systems in place for other public entertainment venues – cinemas, concert halls, etc. – and for Wheatley there was 'no good reason why football grounds should not be similarly dealt with'. It was the fourth time in five decades that such a call had been made.

Lord Justice Wheatley's technical appendix provided the safety laws still in use today. To ease the local authority burden Wheatley recommended a licensing process staggered over four phases, with larger stadiums (first and second division grounds; international stadiums) covered in the first phase; third and fourth division clubs to be 'designated' – issued with a safety certificate – in phase two (and on through grounds with capacities of more than 10,000, phase three; and less than 10,000, phase four). As to cost, Wheatley insisted, 'Clubs which charge the public for admission have a duty to see that their grounds are reasonably safe for spectators. That is a primary consideration.' A *Times* editorial added, 'No club has the right to regard safety precautions for its supporters as an optional extra.'

The Safety of Sports Grounds Act, which implemented Lord Justice Wheatley's recommendations, began its parliamentary passage a year later, but was immediately held up when a January 1974 snap General Election was called, and so it didn't come into force until September 1975. The Act worked through what is known as the Green Guide. It recommended that gangways, lighting, walls and railings should be well maintained, and that the crowd capacity of specific terraces should be decided by their condition, crush barriers, exits and stairways. A stand of non-combustible material should be evacuated in under eight minutes – but for a wooden structure that was reduced to two and a half minutes, with all combustible material removed from beneath such stands and any cracks or gaps in the wood, through which litter could fall, sealed. Stewards in these stands should be trained in emergency fire measures; all exits should open outwards and be manned so they could be opened in an emergency, and all spectators should also be within 30 metres of an exit. If a designated ground failed to comply with these laws the local authority would not issue a safety certificate, and if on annual reinspection the certificate was found to be breached the licence holder could be fined and even jailed. The undesignated Main Stand at Valley Parade, ten years later, did not meet any of these recommendations; Simon Inglis, called to the subsequent civil case as an expert witness, had his own eyewitness account of how such recommendations were ignored at non-designated grounds – visiting the ground on a routine research trip one midweek morning, he'd seen a member of the groundstaff lift up a flap in the wooden flooring of the stand and sweep the rubbish underneath. As he wrote in *The Football Grounds of Great Britain*, this individual told Inglis that it was common for litter to be swept underneath the stand 'but that rubbish was cleared out at the end of each season when repair work was done'.

Progress of the Bill through Parliament was slow. Sports minister Denis Howell and the minister for health and social security, Dr David Owen, both warned of the dangers of delay, pointing out that until designation was complete disasters were likely to occur at any time, at any ground. He went as far as to suggest that the greatest danger lay at a football ground where a normal crowd was easily containable, but a special event, such as a championship parade, meant a full house . . .

First and second division grounds were designated by 1979; under the steam of the Labour government, phase one was complete – and at that slow pace third division clubs should have been designated by 1981 (phase 2 by 1983). But there was a change of government, and new home secretary Willie Whitelaw then played politics with public safety, while lower division clubs became involved in what Simon Inglis called, in 1983, a 'considerable lobbying' of government. While they were worried about the excessive financial outlay designation required, there was no organised counter-lobby; no Football Supporters' Association back then – in fact, the Football League itself were far more interested in lobbying for the interests of their hard-up members than seeking designation. Third and fourth division chairmen certainly weren't unduly concerned by the slow progress of the extension of the Green Guide.

Then came the Bradford fire and Leon Brittan's universal designation – an immediate extension from phase one to phase four of Lord Justice Wheatley's original plan. For a club like Halifax Town, for example, the consequences were huge. Their ground, the Shay, nestled in a picturesque Pennine setting, had originally been fashioned from a council rubbish tip and held a capacity of 16,000. Overnight that was effectively slashed to 3,000. 'In total 27 league clubs plus three in Scotland kicked off the 1985–86 season with stands or terraces either closed or severely reduced,' wrote Simon Inglis in *The Football Grounds of Great Britain*. 'At least 15 clubs played for most of the season with at least one side of their ground closed, with all the loss of atmosphere that entails.' Included in those clubs were the likes of Preston, Bury and Brentford, but also Chelsea. Inglis also considered Barnsley's case. They had risen from the fourth division to the second, spending £250,000 on ground improvements following designation but, as Inglis wrote in the second edition of *The Football Grounds of Great Britain,* when they realised 'it would cost £80,000 to add a further 2,000 to their capacity [it] was hardly worthwhile.' In the first edition of his book Inglis invented a fictional club, Borchester United, who on reaching the second division realised that, for a club with such a poorly maintained ground – and a tough local authority insisting on ground improvements *before* the next season begins – promotion is nothing short of a financial disaster. That was written in 1983, and reflected the climate of the times. In some aspects he may as well have been writing about Bradford City.

After the Thatcher government had first come to power there were no further sports ground designation orders. Venues like Ascot, and various cricket and rugby grounds were also reluctant to be caught up in 'red tape'. That the Football Grounds Licensing Authority – the current incarnation of which was formed after Hillsborough – didn't extend its remit and accordingly mutate into the renamed Sports Grounds Licensing Authority until November 2011 gives some indication of the forces of inertia at play. Up until the Bradford fire, and then again until Hillsborough, it wasn't too difficult for those in power to turn a blind eye to dangerous conditions. A decade after Ibrox, the concept that clubs might voluntarily comply with the Green Guide was still a given – rather than a fallacy proved to have failed disastrously time and again over seven decades. Then, by the eighties, the era of laissez-faire government was well under way; the Thatcher regime was more interested in deregulating free enterprise, looking to lift restrictions not impose further regulations or obligatory costs, even in the name of safety.

The debate had been won as the Safety of Sports Grounds Act had passed through Parliament; the first attempt to derail it had come in the House of Lords. On 5 December 1973 the Labour peer Baron Stow Hill of Newport had put it to the Lords that designation could be optional for struggling lower division clubs, and that the home secretary should be free to consider what resources might be available in choosing to extend designation. 'Designation shouldn't mean bankruptcy,' he stated. But another Labour peer, Lord Wigg, intervened, warning the public shouldn't be put at risk: 'We are going to get another Ibrox should this Bill not go far enough.' Thankfully Stow Hill's amendment was rejected by the House of Lords. Yet, after 1979, Margaret Thatcher and her government would ignore the legislation on the Parliamentary Roll that stated designation should be applied to sports grounds holding more than 10,000, by simply using the home secretary's discretionary power to deem a ground did not hold 10,000 fans – even when the official publicly stated capacities of all Football League grounds did so. Deregulation by any other name, for sure; but where, in theory, that should have ultimately guaranteed a more rigorous system of inspection and checks, in practice it merely delayed matters – there were no more designation orders passed for a further six years. And at that time Valley Parade had a capacity of 18,000.

It's not as if financial help hadn't been available to assist clubs with up to 60 per cent of the cost of making all lower-division football grounds safe. In 1985 it was estimated £18 million would be required to bring all remaining 36 undesignated Football League clubs up to scratch. Over the previous decade the Football Grounds Improvement Trust (FGIT) had distributed £29 million from 'spot the ball' competitions, yet only £19 million of this had been designated for safety work, the remaining £10 million being used for 'cosmetic improvements' – a bit of pitch drainage here, a new bar for the clubhouse there. Then, in early 1985, with a £3.3 million reserve and no demand for safety grants, the FGIT retrospectively increased all previous grant applications by 15 per cent. As the Trust effectively provided 75 per cent of all grants to clubs, by 1985 the £13.5 million needed to have made all Football League grounds safe was in the kitty (as third and fourth division 'undesignated' clubs had to find 40 per cent of the finance for ground improvements, demand was limited, the FGIT were not exactly rushed off their feet with requests). But still the home secretary failed to pass a designation order.

Until, of course, Monday 13 May 1985, when Leon Brittan finally announced to Parliament, 'The time for selective action has passed . . . the public should be given all the protection that the existing laws allow.'

But by then it was too late: over fifty more football fans were dead.

10

Reclaimed/Local Failure

If there'd been inertia, institutional neglect and prevarication at the level of central government, then that was matched by the local licensing authority, West Yorkshire. While a sensible step forward, which had been called for from as far back as Edward Shortt's day after the problems at the 1923 FA Cup final, local authority licensing in itself didn't mean an answer to safety concerns, per se. In Thatcher's Britain, where some grounds were beneficiaries of rigorous inspection – Highbury and Upton Park, for example – Simon Inglis describes a 1980s landscape of what could be politely termed regional variation. In West Yorkshire, though, it was definitely a case of inconsistency.

A West Yorkshire health and safety inspector had visited Valley Parade in 1980 and wrote to the club instructing it to remove litter from beneath its Main Stand. After a second inspection, a few months later in the summer of 1981, the same officer then wrote to ask the club to consider how it could evacuate the Main Stand in under two and a half minutes. The West Yorkshire County Council fire authority had twice held meetings with the health and safety executive to discuss safety at Valley Parade, and had twice classified the ground's fire risk as 'substantial'.

But nothing was done. West Yorkshire's chief fire officer, Graham Karran, would claim that although he considered the stand a death trap, 'There was nothing I could do to make the club listen.' Only there was. The Safety at Sports Grounds Act and Fire Services Act provided the fire authority with the power to inspect undesignated sports grounds. If, after such inspections, their requests for safety improvements were not met, they could use emergency powers under Section 10 of the Safety at Sports Grounds Act, or Section 9 of the Fire Precautions Act of 1971 where a ground was not designated, to close stands. This had actually happened in Bradford, of all places, at the undesignated Park Avenue ground, where Yorkshire County Cricket Club had taken residence from the now defunct Bradford Park Avenue. The rickety double-decker stand, with its intricate lattice-work and arches, resembled the Raffles hotel in Singapore or the Victorian seafront at Brighton. It offered fine, elevated views of the crease, but was condemned as a fire hazard, much to the consternation of cricket lovers. That was in June 1977; for some reason this never happened a few miles north across the city, with the equivalent structure at Valley Parade, despite inspections during the club's 1976 Cup run.

It wasn't as if Bradford City themselves were unaware of such local authority powers. The Midland Road stands had twice been condemned by Bradford Council, in 1948 and in 1960, after inspections had highlighted dangers in the structural foundations. Valley Parade had had several brushes with disaster: on two occasions floodlight pylons had collapsed, in 1962 and 1983. In 1977 a large section of the Kop boundary wall collapsed and, after they won promotion that spring, a ten-foot-high Main Stand wall collapsed, resulting in several injuries, including two broken legs. In 1980 a health and safety inspector wrote of the Midland Road terrace exit: 'One person missing their footing on these stairs would result in a situation similar to that in Ibrox.' Then, in 1982, a crush barrier collapsed in the Bradford End, forcing Manchester United supporters to climb fencing to escape. Yet although all but one of these incidents was prominently publicised in the *Telegraph & Argus* – always as front-page news – none ever prompted a direct response from West Yorkshire County Council in the form of an inspection.

In fact, Bradford City did nothing to encourage any local inspecting body to visit Valley Parade – perhaps no surprise from a club who'd already had two stands on the same site closed. Bradford made no contact with the local authority working party responsible for sports grounds safety after 1976, and failed to reply to a 1982 letter that offered goodwill fire prevention and crowd safety advice, but which also warned, 'The authority has emergency powers in relation to any sports ground in the county.' In 1984, after wood fell from the roof of the Main Stand during a match, an initial repair-grant application was rejected by the Football Grounds Improvement Trust, who told Bradford that supporting documentation must come from the local authority – something vice-chairman Jack Tordoff should have known (given previous grant applications at the club, such as to repair the floodlight damaged in a gale in 1983). But instead he obtained a letter from the local police force supporting the application. This in turn led to a second rejection, the FGIT reiterating that such letters, by law, needed to come from the local authority. Tordoff's next move was to appeal in the *Telegraph & Argus* to any companies who fancied taking out an advert on the stand's roof – any fees obtained from the advertising would pay for the roof's repair in return. The Main Stand roof, nestling in the valley, was visible for miles, and Tordoff was quick to see the opportunity – a bit like Brentford daubing KLM over the roof of their old New Road terrace, which lay directly beneath the Heathrow flight path. But having told the *Telegraph & Argus* that 'We don't qualify for a grant,' the vice-chairman eventually approached the local authority once it seemed there were no takers, and West Yorkshire County Council's structural engineer visited the ground on 4 July 1984. A week later he wrote a letter to support the club's grant application. A week after that the engineer, Andrew Shaw, felt compelled to write another letter, this time to the West Yorkshire deputy fire prevention officer, enclosing the findings of the first letter, and copying Bradford City in.

18 July 1984
Dear Sir,
Safety in Sports Grounds,
Bradford City AFC.

Further to my Engineer's visit to your ground, of 4th July 1984, I am
pleased to enclose a letter which may assist you in obtaining a grant from
the Sports Grounds Trust, towards the cost of re-covering the main stand
roof. Nothing in that letter should be construed as implied approval of
the condition or structural adequacy of the stand.

As the West Yorkshire Metropolitan County Council is the Licensing
Authority under the Safety of Sports Grounds Act, 1975, it may assist
you to know what some of the council's other considerations would
be should at some time in the future the provisions of the Act apply to
Bradford City AFC ground.

These are: -

1. *Main Grandstand*

The unusual construction of this stand makes an appraisal of structural
adequacy desirable.

The timber construction is a fire hazard and in particular there is a build
up of combustible materials in the voids beneath the seats. A carelessly
discarded cigarette could give rise to a fire risk.

Egress from the grandstand should be in 2.5 minutes.

2. *Other stands*

Appraise for structural adequacy and maintain to adequate corrosion
protection standards.

Repair defective roof sheets.

3. *Perimeter and crowd control fences*

Repair and strengthen to acceptable standard.

4. *Crush barriers*

Test, strengthen and repair to acceptable standard.

Lack of barriers reduces safe spectator density on terraces.

5. *Terracing*

Overhaul terracing to provide acceptable surfacing from slope.

Provide adequate exits from terracing.

These considerations are contained within the publication 'Guide to Safety at Sports Grounds – Football' published by the H.M.S.O.

In concluding may I point out that the above considerations would form part of the statutory consultation process required under the provisions of the Act. The County Council is obliged by law to have regard to other considerations e.g. Fire Safety/Precautions (Chief Fire Officer); crowd control/supervision (Chief Constable); and local building control requirements (Bradford Metropolitan District Council).

Yours Faithfully

Executive Director of Engineering

Andrew Shaw later told Mum's civil case this letter 'haunted' him. Justice Cantley, presiding over matters in Leeds High Court, would conclude that any competent fire prevention officer who received that letter would have taken immediate action, but stressed, 'I have no evidence he did anything apart from file it.' The said fire prevention officer, Neville Byrom, also a member of the local authority working party on sports ground safety, had already told the Popplewell Inquiry the letter 'must have come across my desk', but claimed he considered it a 'housekeeping' matter that did not warrant further action, despite the fact that Byrom knew full well the state of Valley Parade, as he attended matches there with his son.

The West Yorkshire fire authority had significant resources to inspect premises such as Valley Parade. In the early eighties, a 38-strong fire prevention team made 28,000 annual inspections, and chief fire officer Graham Karran told the inquiry he could think of no other premises that held such numbers which would not be inspected. He claimed it was 'inexplicable' that the Main Stand was not inspected. In West Yorkshire, only Elland Road, Headlingley, Leeds Road and the Odsal Stadium would have had greater or equivalent capacities to Valley Parade – it seemed that in carrying out their 28,000 annual inspections the fire prevention team had neglected to inspect an old wooden stand in the fourth or fifth biggest venue in the county. When you consider that the fire service did inspect the clubhouse beside the stand before granting it a licence in 1984, and that the fire brigade watered the pitch and held fire drill exercises there, and that the links between the fire authority and club were so strong that a charity match was scheduled to take place between a brigade team and former players' team, in support of a firemen's charity, on 12 May 1985 – subsequently postponed, for obvious reasons – that sense of inexplicableness felt by Graham Karran only deepens. So it wasn't the case that the West Yorkshire fire authority hadn't been aware of the dangers of the Main Stand, rather it seems – for whatever reason – they had neglected to address them. As Lord Justice Wheatley had warned, the danger of an undesignated system lay in 'the possibility that standards of judgment may be influenced by the knowledge that a club's finances are poor'.

It was October 2000, and I found myself in the West Yorkshire broadcast archive in Bradford, studying their collection of TV interviews. The archives were housed in a gothic shell of a building, with towering ceilings and draughty rooms. I was booked in to see what they had in relation to the fire. As I sifted through their materials I came across Betamax videos of live footage shot from the day, as well recordings of the news reports that followed. I worked my way through the Betamax videos, the VCR attached to a tiny portable black and white TV, pausing then playing them again for a few more seconds, pausing and rewinding again, until I'd transcribed everything correctly. As I listened in such fractured, microscopic detail I was struck by how strange things seemed compared to what we'd all accepted over the years.

Fifty-Six

From there, now hooked on this research project, I was making the daily half-hour drive from Mum's in the Cotswolds to the Fire Service College at Moreton-in-Marsh, where I'd learnt, stored in their library, were the full transcripts of the Popplewell Inquiry. I dissected the week's worth of testimony, line by line, day by day – about a hundred pages of dialogue a day. Before long I'd painstakingly picked through the full Popplewell Inquiry transcript.

Little did I know I'd never use my season ticket again.

11

The Popplewell Inquiry

One of the first things I came across in the Bradford box files at the Fire Service College library was Lord Justice Salmon's 1966 Royal Commission Report on Tribunals of Inquiry. Salmon stated, 'We do not agree with a suggestion that has been made to us that the powers [of establishing an inquiry] should be vested in some high officer of state.' But on 13 May 1985, it was Leon Brittan, the home secretary, who announced to Parliament that he would hold a joint inquiry into the events of two days previously – both at Bradford, where 56 died, and Birmingham City, where one fan died after a wall collapsed following crowd trouble. Brittan stated that the new inquiry would examine 'the operation of the Safety of Sports Grounds Act 1975 and recommend what if any further steps should be taken, including any that may be necessary under additional powers needed to improve both crowd safety and crowd control at sports grounds'. The deep irony was that it was precisely his government's failure to fully implement the recommendations of the original 1975 Act that had laid the groundwork for the Bradford fire. And, unusually, Brittan did not appoint a Lord Justice to the inquiry – as had happened after Ibrox (Lord Chief Justice Wheatley might have been an idea here) and would do so again after Hillsborough – but a High Court judge with less seniority than those who had overseen previous inquiries of a similar nature.

Lord Justice Salmon also stressed in 1966 that inquiries could be justified only if Parliament had 'clearly considered whether or not civil or criminal proceedings would resolve the matter and decided they would not'. This was because 'the publicity that surrounds [any inquiry] would make it impossible for anyone against whom an adverse judgment was made to obtain a fair trial thereafter'. No one has been privy to how Leon Brittan could have determined within 48 hours of the fire being put out that no such civil or criminal proceedings would be necessary at Valley Parade. So, that Monday afternoon in Westminster, it was hardly surprising the announcement of an immediate inquiry was met with a parliamentary ruction, as shadow home secretary Gerald Kaufman stated, 'We need to know what happened, why it happened, whether there was any criminal involvement and whether it could have been prevented.' Time was required, he believed, 'to get to the bottom of allegations that arson may have caused the fire'. The morning after the fire, the *Sunday Mirror* had run with a headline WHO DID IT? And at the Yorkshire television archive I'd come across several interviews recorded on the pitch on the afternoon of the fire. Ben Ford, the former Bradford North MP, had stated, 'It's almost obvious that somebody has deliberately set fire to the stand.' On the Monday morning, Chief Constable Colin Sampson had been quoted in *The Times*: 'There was a great deal of gossip last night about whether it was deliberate and if it was who could have done such an horrendous thing. There are stories from both sides – stories which show no evidence of a deliberate act and other stories that may lead us to a different conclusion. The stories conflict and therefore my mind and the minds of the investigating officers must be kept open.'

Gerald Kaufman also told the House he was concerned about the dual nature of the inquiry: 'The opposition believe that the government have made a serious mistake in linking in one statement and in one inquiry the Bradford fire with the violence at Birmingham. The nature of those two events is different, even though some matters are relevant to both. To begin with, it is unfitting that questions on the disaster and on an outbreak of mob violence should be mingled. . . . The opposition believe that the government should have ordered a separate public inquiry . . . into the circumstances of the Bradford fire.'

There was talk of 'astonishment and disbelief' at the joint nature of the inquiry; both Max Madden and Thomas Torney, Labour MPs in Bradford, talked of people in the city wanting their own, separate public inquiry. Leon Brittan reassured Max Madden that there was 'no question of there being anything other than the fullest examination of what occurred at Bradford', and he hoped that that would be appreciated by the people of the town. But, nonetheless, the home secretary wasn't for hanging about. He told Parliament, 'I shall ask that the inquiry proceed with all possible speed.' This directly contradicted Lord Justice Salmon, who had stressed in his 1966 report that 'time in preparing the material for arriving at the truth is a small price to pay in order to avoid injustice . . . if more time is given to collating the material evidence before the public hearing begins, the tribunal should have an ample opportunity of defining the allegations and pinpointing the relevant matters to be investigated.' The inquiry into Bradford would open just 13 working days after the forensic search of the site was completed. As I read more of Salmon it seemed like the home secretary had loaded the dice that day.

The inquiry transcripts I read also made the consequence of this haste abundantly clear. For example, in his opening address Andrew Collins QC, counsel for the inquiry, stated the police 'while interviewing a very large number of witnesses and collating all the information [had] inevitably . . . not had [the] time or the manpower to see everyone who may have something of value to contribute to this investigation, or some piece of evidence which may help to explain material matters'. Which was something that was echoed by the QC representing the police in his opening statement, Mr Holland, reporting that 'the Inquiry is still continuing, products are still coming forwards'. Furthermore, in their report to the Popplewell Inquiry, West Yorkshire police described their approach as an 'elimination of disinformation' – quite who had been feeding them false information wasn't clear. Ultimately though, I could not understand what the inquiry was doing opening so quickly in the first place. It was Wednesday 5 June; just over three and a half weeks from the fire. Most families were still not strong enough to attend a public inquiry into the deaths of loved ones they'd barely buried.

Lord Justice Salmon had recommended an inquiry's opening statement must 'avoid any comments likely to make sensational headlines', and that 'until the evidence has been heard it would be wrong to draw any conclusions'. However, in his opening statement to the Popplewell Inquiry, Andrew Collins asserted that somebody dropped something burning beneath the floor and that this 'most obvious something was a cigarette end'. He did not comment on the unusual smell of burning plastic reported by several eyewitnesses, stating, 'All one can say at this stage is that there is no evidence of any use – I suppose the inference must be deliberate use – of a plastic cup in order to start the fire.' He also stated, 'It would seem the fire certainly started accidentally', and said of a club whose two directors – Stafford Heginbotham and Jack Tordoff – had between them served for 15 of the previous 20 years, 'I must emphasise that this was a new club . . . there was wholly new management at the top.'

These opening remarks did not fill me with confidence that the Popplewell Inquiry had been designed to provide the answers the Bradford families were looking for. I thought it seemed more like the inquiry's recommendations would simply rubber stamp what was described as the six-point cabinet war plan announced in April 1985, after a riot at Kenilworth Road between Luton and Millwall fans. The government plan called for an alcohol ban, CCTV, better policing, ID cards, new public order laws and tougher sentencing for offenders. While the inquiry did recommend a number of amendments and updates to the provisions of the Green Guide after Bradford, it seemed the only new recommendation in relation to crowd safety was a ban on new wooden stands – a redundant construction method anyway – and a ban on smoking in any existing wooden stands.

There was one area that did require urgent review. Security fencing had not been covered by Lord Justice Wheatley, as it was not in use until UEFA issued a regulation following trouble at the 1972 European Cup Winners' Cup final, a month after Wheatley's report had been published.

At Valley Parade, the Main Stand seating was surrounded, to the front and sides, by a terrace; the total capacity of the stand was 4,000, split equally between standing and sitting. The Bradford End held just 3,000 fans but, unlike the Main Stand, was fenced in. And on 11 May, fans had only escaped a 7,000-capacity Kop at the side of the terrace, through a gap in the fence where the old players' tunnel had once led out. This led to universal comments that the use of fencing be reviewed after Bradford, and Leon Brittan promised Parliament, 'There is no question of putting up a fence which would create a trap.'

But, again, nothing happened, and the fences remained in place . . . until the spring of 1989.

Mr Justice Popplewell visited Bradford on the Tuesday after the fire. He strode through the wreckage of the ground in a white mac, escorted by Heginbotham and a posse of reporters and television cameras. Popplewell assured people the inquiry was not to be about '. . . litigation. It is not a lawsuit in which one party wins and another loses. It is a factual exercise. Blame will not be apportioned,' he explained, and the issue of criminal negligence was 'not part of my remit'. He promised, 'The inquiry is not a substitution for the ordinary legal processes of criminal or civil trial. It is neither a whitewash nor a witch-hunt.' In short, it was an inquiry that was never responsible for answering the many questions raised by the fire, and was never followed up by a full investigation.

As my mum told me at the time, 'Well, it's important to get football grounds safe for next season. Blame and justice – that can wait.'

The inquiry lasted for just five and a half days. In conclusion, Popplewell stated, 'I am quite satisfied that the cause of the fire was the dropping of a lighted match, cigarette, or tobacco, in rows I or J, between seats 141 to 143 . . .' before adding, 'It is quite impossible to determine who caused the fire to start – indeed it would be grossly unfair to point the finger at any one person. The answer to how the fire started is that it was due to the accidental lighting of debris below the floorboards.'

But, reading the transcripts of the inquiry, it is impossible for me to see the basis of his satisfaction. On the day, a windy afternoon, I could not remember people smoking, so, in the transcripts, I expected – given Popplewell's conclusion – to find clear and unanimous testimony that people were indeed smoking as the first half drew to a close. Only I could find no clear evidence to confirm this.

Rufus Kolawole, who'd been sitting in seat J142, was a former smoker who now found tobacco 'very obnoxious'. He told the inquiry he smelt cigarette smoke only once, about 20 minutes before the fire started. Six seats to his left, Phillip Levitt, in seat J148, was another non-smoker who recalled the same cigarette smoke as Kolawole but, when asked if those around him smoked, told the inquiry, 'Not that I noticed.' Ahead of him, in seat I146, an off-duty detective, DC Blanchfield, was sitting with three children in I147–I149 and told the inquiry he kept 'a more particular eye' on those around him, but saw nobody smoke during the match. Certainly nobody, it seemed, was definitely smoking in the key period from 3.35 to 3.40 p.m., when smoke was first visible beneath the stand.

There was also expert evidence given by two forensic experts who said it was 'less likely' that a cigarette or pipe tobacco could have started the fire. Dr David Woolley, of the Department of the Environment's Fire Research Station, stated that a fire from a discarded cigarette end would have burnt in more intermediate steps, smouldering away for anywhere between 15 and 40 minutes before igniting timber, and would have left small 'red runs' on the paper beneath, of which both he and Ray Cooke, a local forensic expert, said there was no evidence. Indeed, Dr Woolley suggested that there was a possibility any small fire caused by either a cigarette end or glowing pipe tobacco would have gone out. I find it surprising that Popplewell's conclusion did not give more weight to this.

These findings, which made up Popplewell's interim report, were leaked on the Sunday evening of the Valley Parade memorial service, 21 July – just after the club officials and VIPs had ceremoniously marched on to the pitch; just as the bereaved families were reliving their loss once again;

just after Heginbotham's car, full of laughter, had sped away at the lights by the offices of the *Telegraph & Argus*. The inquests were free to begin the next morning.

In the summer of 1985 the consensus in Bradford was still, 'Well, it's only an "interim" report.' Responsibility, liability, accountability, some kind of deliverance of justice . . . that would all come in due course. But of course no one had really grasped the narrow remit of the Popplewell Inquiry. And once the inquests had begun it soon became clear that we would not be getting any closer to establishing liability. Contrary to popular belief, inquests cannot get fully underway until the Director of Public Prosecutions has decided if any prosecutions are likely to arise – coroners being unable to apportion blame or liability. Coroner James Turnbull, who chaired the inquests, reminded his jury, 'You are now talking about the future and not talking about the past. What you say in your recommendations must not seek to imply any particular person was responsible civilly or criminally for this event . . .' and, 'It is important to remember your conclusion or your verdict must not be couched in such a way as to imply any criticism suggesting that any particular person should be criminally liable or liable to civil proceedings . . .' and even, 'You must speak in general terms and not particular terms,' when presented with the same body of evidence as the Popplewell Inquiry. The jury returned a verdict of death by misadventure, and no criminal prosecutions would even be considered.

It's worth just pausing for a second to consider the interval between the publication of interim findings into other notable disasters and the juries of the relevant inquests reaching their verdicts: Hillsborough, 19 months; Kegworth air disaster, 13 months; Clapham Junction rail crash, 17 months. In the cases of Hillsborough and Clapham, there were 12- and 15-month periods respectively where the decision of whether to seek a prosecution was weighed up. At the Bradford inquest it took one week to reach that verdict of death by misadventure.

Reading through inquiry transcripts it also became clear to me that West Yorkshire police could never lead an impartial investigation.

By law a chief constable is required to invite an independent force to lead an investigation where a conflict of interest may arise. Four years on, after Hillsborough, South Yorkshire police, not through any act of benevolence, but to comply with Part IX of the Police and Criminal Evidence Act 1984, invited their colleagues from the West Midlands to gather evidence for the Taylor Inquiry. After Bradford, West Yorkshire police proffered no such invitation to a neighbouring or independent force despite, as the PACE Act ruled, Bradford surely being of 'sufficient gravity or exceptional circumstances' to warrant such an intervention in the absence of a public complaint. Bradford still represents the biggest loss of life in a single incident that the West Yorkshire force has ever had to deal with; I'd argue that the dozen or so police officers with whom I shared an ambulance, and those who never returned to duty after that day, were as badly let down as anybody.

In my view, the first police conflict of interest arose over the question of why the Main Stand failed to comply with any of the Green Guide safety recommendations. West Yorkshire's chief constable of operations, Michael John Domaille, told the Popplewell Inquiry that the Green Guide applied 'to people running football clubs, irrespective of whether they are designated or not' and that he would expect his officers to draw 'the attention of the club to whatever they thought was wise'. But the Manningham police division had singularly failed to draw the club's attention to anything. Rather like with the fire brigade, it wasn't the case that the police were strangers to Valley Parade – superintendent Paul Briggs made weekly liaison visits to the club and PC Paul Riley, the club's police liaison officer, spent half his week there on club duties during the season. Yet, although superintendent Briggs told the inquiry he considered ground safety part of his responsibilities and said he had read the Green Guide, he claimed he 'did not consider that it really applied'. My question is therefore: what *did* he consider applied?

A second police conflict of interest, I believe, needed investigating by an independent force, and had even more serious implications. The commanding officer on the day, Chief Inspector Mawson, told the Popplewell Inquiry, 'I have never been briefed about evacuation from sporting venues and I have never briefed anyone [either].' In fact, he'd never been anywhere where 'it had been necessary to evacuate people'. As it transpired, the evacuation from the seat of the fire was left to an unfortunate trio of constables positioned at the back of G Block. As one of them searched for a fire extinguisher, the two left in the stand initially considered the amount of smoke so minimal they were far from convinced it was actually a fire. In my view this is a serious failing of the senior management of the West Yorkshire police authority, given that Mawson and his fellow officers should have received specific training in relation to crowd evacuation.

Even though Popplewell's interim report suggested 'no serious trouble was anticipated' there was a heavy police presence on the day, and the operational priority was to prevent a pitch invasion following the wild scenes of celebration the last time Bradford had been promoted, three years previously against Bournemouth – 'There must be three or four hundred on the pitch,' John Helm had exclaimed on Yorkshire Television, after Bobby Campbell's equaliser hit the back of the net. On 11 May 1985, police were primed for more of the same. Their first move on seeing the flames was to order a localised clearance of fans back into the rear corridor until an extinguisher could be located – or until the fire brigade they'd requested as a precaution arrived. Officers trained in fire evacuation strategies would have immediately recognised the dangers of this approach, but from the way the officers behaved it's fair to assume they considered panic amongst the fans the biggest threat to an orderly evacuation – at first their actions suggested they were confident they could control the fire, clearing an area in which to tackle it. Police fully trained in fire evacuation procedure, however, would have known time was of the essence and have ordered an immediate evacuation of the stand.

The commanding officer, Chief Inspector Mawson, could have countermanded the operational priority, but he was slow to act on initial reports of a fire, suspecting it was another smoke bomb (one had gone off in the Midland Road terrace during the pre-match lap of honour) – TV footage clearly shows him walking up the touchline, with no real sense of urgency but with the gait of a man whose attention has been caught by something in the distance. He doesn't reach the halfway line until 3.44 p.m., three minutes after the first radio call of fire. Before this Mawson had been standing by the players' tunnel at the opposite end of the Main Stand, monitoring radio communications about a suspected fire, but did nothing further to investigate it for himself. It was only at the prompting of his patrolling deputy, Inspector Simpson, who walked by and asked, 'Did you hear something about a fire?' that he moved. He made it past the halfway line before player (not police) action prompted the game to be stopped, as Lincoln City's goalkeeper rushed from his area to boot a clearly distracted back pass over the stand roof above G Block. As the surprised linesman looked back he immediately started to wave his flag wildly to stop the game. At last Mawson and his fellow officers motioned people forwards out of the stand and on to the pitch. By then three minutes had been lost, and people were queuing patiently in the rear corridor.

Flames were now clearly visible in G Block, increasingly so by the second, licking up row after row of seating. Most of those in the rear half of the paddock terrace immediately to the side of G Block surged forwards, crushing everyone into the front half of the terrace. The game was stopped and, slowly, fans were allowed over the wall on to the gravel path. Mawson took charge and you can see him on the Yorkshire Television footage waving his hands, getting people to move towards the pitch, 'the obvious way to take them', as he told the inquiry. But at this point the two constables who'd had to deal with pretty much everything around G Block were left with a life-changing decision. Should they attempt to rescue the fans they had earlier instructed to go down a stairwell now full of smoke and licking with flames? Or should they go in the opposite direction over the wooden wall at the front and towards the safety of the pitch? Just 90 seconds later, over 40 people were dead along that firetrap of a corridor.

As the fire became critical, about to flashover, there had been an attempt by a few policemen to get to the back, but it had been too late. An injured PC told the *Yorkshire Post*, 'Somebody shouted that some people were trapped at the back. We went up to the back and this ball of flame just shot across the roof. It was only seconds before a small fire had become a raging inferno . . . we just turned and ran . . . the ball of flame had gone straight above us.'

Inspector Mawson was, rightly, one of four policemen awarded a Queen's Gallantry Medal for bravery, for his role in saving many lives and putting his own life at risk – he was one of 42 policemen injured on the day, every one responsible for saving lives in that blazing inferno. But had he arrived at G Block one minute or two minutes earlier, then perhaps there could have been a different outcome for those queuing at the back of the stand.

A third police issue centred around the total collapse of its control room. For a start, the police control room was not located in Valley Parade, but a mile away in the city centre, at Bradford Central police station; the inquiry was reassured by superintendent Briggs that this wasn't a problem because it was always led by an officer of superior rank, a 'chief inspector and/or a superintendent'. But still, with no CCTV cameras at Valley Parade to provide any oversight, the control room relied completely on radio messages from the ground. At 15:40:58 PC Johnson, one of the three policemen in G Block, had radioed, 'Can you get the fire brigade to the Main Stand? There is a fire under the Main Stand.' Although acknowledged by the control room 20 seconds later, the request was not confirmed, which prompted a second message from PC Johnson at 15:41:41. He reiterated, 'We are requesting the fire brigade,' before stressing for a third time, over 30 seconds later, 'We have a fire in the Main Stand, or under the Main Stand.' Yet there was still no confirmation the fire brigade were on their way.

This prompted a fourth message that can only be construed as an order. At 15:44:10 the police deputy commander thought it necessary to identify himself: 'Inspector Simpson. We need the fire brigade. *Now!*' And only then did the control room confirm, 'The fire brigade are *en route*. Over.' But even at this point the control-room operator felt compelled to ask, 'Do we have fire? Or is it a smoke bomb? Can you check, er, can you check on that please?' Inspector Simpson's response sounded more like a plea: 'Emergency. There's too much smoke for a smoke bomb . . . Will you get assistance up here. Now!'

It was already too late. Despite the fact the nearest three fire engines were less than a mile away – holding a training session at a caravan showroom on Canal Road – by the time they'd pulled away and reached the junction of Canal Road and Queens Road they could already see black smoke billowing high in the air. The fire had flashed over. Police communications from Valley Parade then became intermittent, several officers puncturing the radio silence. At 15:46:35, one sergeant pleaded, 'It's thick smoke up here, we're going to be in trouble if we don't get some assistance to clear this stand,' before declaring, at 15:47:07, 'It's going up like a torch up here.' At 15:47:27 another officer exclaimed, 'It's well alight. It's going like hell.' Incredibly, it's 3.49 p.m. – a full eight minutes after the first sight of smoke – before sirens are audible on the soundtrack of Yorkshire Television footage. 'The ambulances are beginning to arrive,' laments John Helm, 'and the stand is almost gone.'

Despite the clearly alarmed pleas from police at Valley Parade, the control room not only failed to increase their initial request for fire engines, they also failed to alert the hospitals – who only learnt of the fire as burnt football supporters started to walk into the casualty department at the nearby Bradford Royal Infirmary. It can't have helped police efforts that their radio system was unable to transmit if more than one person tried to send a message at the same time.

On arriving at the ground a fire officer on board the first three engines immediately made a 'five pump' request he knew would result in ten appliances being supplied, as well as immediately informing West Yorkshire's assistant fire chief officer, Peter Kneale. Still to learn of the scale of casualties, the fireman also asked for four ambulances (as mistakenly identified by John Helm), before pleading at 4.04 p.m., 'Send as many ambulances as possible.'

There were 3 minutes 12 seconds between the first request for the fire brigade and Inspector Simpson's request. If that is subtracted from the time the first sirens are heard on TV footage, they should have arrived just as the flashover struck. Then, the first priority, as at the City Ground fire back in 1968, should have been to break into the rear corridor with axes and breathing apparatus to rescue anyone trapped there. But by the time they did arrive the stand was completely ablaze. Inspector Simpson later told the inquiry, 'I was aware the fire brigade had been contacted. I have a lot of experience of fire brigade attendance at fires and I know that they are there very, very quickly. I foresaw the area we were clearing and continuing to clear was a sufficient safety factor for the people in the stand.' Only it was not.

It was left to the fire brigade to assume control. At 4.15 p.m., when Peter Kneale arrived at Valley Parade, believing people must be dead, he sent this information over a secure telephone line to the police control room. At 4.30 p.m., when firemen realised that what they believed to be a large amount of debris around the turnstiles in the smouldering stand was actually bodies, Kneale ordered that fire officers were not to speak to the press but to concentrate on fire-fighting duties, while he liaised with the police over the releasing of information. It was a control that once they regained, West Yorkshire police never surrendered.

The Popplewell Inquiry did not identify those in charge of the control room, nor ask them to account for their failures – neither of these things being within its remit. Yet the inquiry was told of the failures: in its submission of evidence the Fire Brigade Union clearly stated, 'There was a considerable delay between the outbreak of the fire and the reaction of the authorities,' and, 'It would be worthwhile to examine the time the fire was first noticed and the time of the first call to the fire brigade.' With fire engines stationed three minutes from Valley Parade not arriving within earshot of the ground until eight or nine minutes into the fire, we can never know for certain how many lives this delay cost.

At the end of the 1999–2000 season David Wetherall scored an early header, then Bradford resisted the onslaughts of a Liverpool side who needed to win to reach the Champions League to hold on at 1–0. Incredibly we'd stayed up. It was an emotional afternoon – we'd held a minute's silence for 'all those who set out to a football match never to return' before kick-off, and afterwards both sets of fans, united by tragedy, met in the centre circle to swap flags and scarves and sing 'You'll Never Walk Alone'.

That autumn, I wondered whether, if the detail of the collapse of Bradford's police control room had ever become common public knowledge, there would ever have been a similar scenario at Hillsborough. The more I dug, the more I found conclusions that I never imagined possible. My anger gave way to stomach-churning dread. Part of me wanted to put the shattered jigsaw I'd started to assemble back in its box. But I knew I had to continue or I would not be able to move on.

One Sunday night, after a heavy weekend's drinking, I had dinner with Ben. Over a couple of bottles of wine the conversation drifted to my time spent in the Cotswolds Fire Service library with the Popplewell Inquiry transcripts. Ben wondered what I was going to do with it all. I told him I was going to have to go back to the place where it all started.

12

City Till . . .

Mum once told me that Dad had made a sizeable pledge to save Bradford City in 1983, but refused to honour it once he realised Stafford Heginbotham had taken control of the club. I can remember him referring to our chairman as 'a crook'. I can also recall, on 11 May 1985, us all walking across the wasteland at the back of the Kop on the way to the game, and Uncle Peter joking, 'Well, even you might have to start admitting Stafford's not all bad now, John.' All of us laughed, but Dad was not won over so easily, and said, 'That may be so, just now, Peter, but I'll reserve judgment on that just a little while longer, if you don't mind?'

Dad actively disliked Stafford; in fact he was the only person I can ever remember Dad voicing such a dislike of. It was so out of character I've often wondered over the years if Dad had ever done business with him – or whether it was simply because the team of Dad's teens, the one that had won promotion from Division 4 in 1969, six years after the fanfare and bluster that heralded Stafford's arrival at the club, had proved nothing but an empty promise: Stafford had failed to invest on the back of an early promotion bid that soon petered out the following season. Two years later they were relegated back to Division 4, where they languished in 16th before Heginbotham handed the loss-making club to a consortium led by Bob Martin in November 1973. Jack Tordoff came on board a week later. However, what I do know is that when Bradford City went into receivership in 1983 and Dad had pledged money towards the rescue bid, once Stafford reappeared with Jack, Dad – always a man of his word – reneged.

Promotion had disguised the underlying financial reality at Valley Parade. Although the newly formed Bradford City made a small trading profit in its first season, that was wiped out by losses in the subsequent promotion season, as turnover increased by 24 per cent and wages by 34 per cent. Wages as a proportion of turnover increased from 62 per cent before receivership to 67 per cent on promotion. Today, Deloitte would consider a figure of 50 per cent 'healthy' when talking of wages as a proportion of turnover; and the Football League Salary Control Management Protocol places a 60 per cent cap on clubs before it imposes transfer embargoes. Bradford under Stafford had clearly lived beyond its means in order to achieve promotion. Only back then promotion to Division 2 brought with it all the attendant costs of designation – and for a club in a dump like Valley Parade there was a much bigger off-balance-sheet risk.

And Bradford City knew what was coming. In a board meeting on 30 November 1984, after topping the division, Stafford Heginbotham asked associate director and architect Geoff Lee to consider what general modifications were needed to bring Valley Parade up to scratch. Then, at a further board meeting on 12 March 1985, with promotion all but certain, Heginbotham asked Lee to draw up specific plans. Heginbotham anticipated it would cost £300,000–400,000 to improve the state of the ground for the second division. If 75 per cent of that was to be covered by the Football Grounds Improvement Trust grant, that would leave the club short in the region of £75,000–100,000.

But Stafford's estimates didn't quite tally with the experiences of similar clubs. In 1985 values Oxford United had spent £1 million on reroofing and new seats, attempting to make their cramped Manor Ground fit for Division 2, then 1. That was a quarter of a million less than it had cost Watford to upgrade Vicarage Road; itself a little under the £1.4 million shelled out at both St Mirren's Love Street north of the border and the Dell down in Southampton. The biggest outlay of all had seen Swansea City fork out £2.1 million for a new stand at the Vetch Field.

Yet club historian David Markham, writing at the time in the *Telegraph & Argus*, described Heginbotham's estimates as 'vast' and 'substantial', even with the grant offset. The sums were so substantial Stafford called a meeting with Bradford City Council to lobby them for financial help. And, as Markham warned, it wouldn't even be the case that the club's problems would end once promotion was won. 'In one sense they have only just begun,' he wrote.

It was not until the final week of the season that Geoff Lee had his plans costed. On Thursday 9 May a special board meeting was convened. Present were Heginbotham, Lee and a Bradford City Council surveyor keen to discuss plans, in the light of promotion, that called for the almost total replacement of Valley Parade. The club were keen to lobby the city council for funding; the plans included extensive improvements to meet the requirements of designation. They proposed: the ripping up of the timber floor and seats in its rear seating enclosure in order to remove and prevent the reaccumulation of litter under the Main Stand; the construction of new stairwells and gangways to meet evacuation times; the encasing of South Parade in new walls to house new turnstiles, exits, shops, tea bars, a press room and boardroom; new seating in the paddock; the underpinning of the stand with steel; newly laid terracing; and the installing of strengthened crush barriers. For a club with a £20,000 transfer budget, who'd been forced into receivership by an overdue PAYE bill of £200,000, the grand total would amount to £2 million. With only £488,000 of grants available this totalled the club's entire income for the next three seasons. The alternative – inaction – was unthinkable too. Ten months after chief engineer Andrew Shaw's letter, he would be vindicated as West Yorkshire County Council deemed the Kop and the Midland Road stand (for a third time) completely unsafe, and the Bradford End would have its capacity slashed from 3,000 to 500, now deemed to be the ground's safe capacity. Valley Parade was doomed.

Bradford City Council were more than happy to offer a solution. They owned Odsal Stadium, home to rugby league and speedway – that, at least, would ensure the club did not go homeless, and the council would have a new tenant. But the club had invested too much in Valley Parade to simply walk away. As improbable as it seems, since Heginbotham had taken control in 1983, £285,000 had been spent on the ground: £62,000 on floodlights, £48,000 on repairs to the stand roof, £10,000 on a Kop wall, £165,000 on pitch drainage, groundsman's and gym equipment, and the rest on extensive clubhouse renovations, with a new executive club and boardroom. This executive club, and ground advertising, meant Bradford City now generated only 40 per cent of its revenue from gate receipts, with a £220,000 freehold worth only £30,000 if they moved (Valley Parade was in Manningham, a notorious red-light district; it generated decent enough revenue as a football ground, but was deemed of far less value as a site alone, given its location). As Heginbotham protested in the *Telegraph & Argus*, 'What would happen to all this if City transferred to Odsal?' A club two years out of receivership would have faced a crippling £505,000 of capital write-downs, almost its entire annual revenue, of which almost half would then be lost. It would have been a busted flush once more.

Although the Popplewell Inquiry was tasked with looking into how the Safety of Sports Grounds Act 1975 operated, it never dealt in detail with how Bradford City proposed to finance its impending designation – an issue identified by Simon Inglis in *The Football Grounds of England and Wales* in 1983 – but concluded, 'Any work or improvement or alteration was wholly related to the finances that were available.' The inquiry glossed over the fact £285,000 had already been spent on the ground, stressing that to 'remedy the situation would have required greater expenditure of money and resources than was available'.

In January 1985 Heginbotham told the supporters' club at its AGM that, 'The club has gambled for far too long. That is why they went into debt and almost lost league football for this city,' before adding, 'We want second division football and we want it very much, and we shall do whatever we can to bring it here, provided it makes sound financial and commercial sense.' Only, of course, it didn't. He told the Popplewell Inquiry, 'Our first consideration was that we would never allow, financially, a situation to occur that had brought about the demise of the old company.' Except, of course, he had: in April 1985 he had told the *City Gent*, 'I am not prepared to go into multitudinous debt in order to solve what many would see as a short-term problem.'

It remains unclear, though, exactly what he *was* prepared to do. What Heginbotham did next was exploit the sentiment of a clearly shaken sports minister, Neil Macfarlane, on a 12 May visit to Valley Parade, by transforming Macfarlane's promise to see 'how the government can help in a financial sense for next season . . . to see how we can help this community' into practically a rock-solid commitment to supply a free new stadium. Within a week of the fire, Heginbotham first announced a £5-million plan, which he then increased to £7 million once the sports minister had promised to speak to local government minister Kenneth Baker in July 1985. However, with no serious evidence of any handouts forthcoming, Stafford then backtracked, announcing a £1-million plan, declaring, 'The truth is we have waited so long and we don't have the time to wait any longer.'

But wait they did. A city councillor pointed out that the club had again under-budgeted in its plans, and so as costs increased, first to £1.9 million and then to £2.3 million, a return date to Valley Parade of 1 January 1986 was pushed back to sometime in August. After further lobbying of Bradford City Council, first for £1 million, then for £1.5 million, in December 1985 two councillors on the Sports Stadia Select Committee promised to help Heginbotham lobby central government. Traction came days after the January 1986 Westland crisis that almost caused the downfall of the Thatcher government and forced the resignation of home secretary Leon Brittan. During Prime Minister's Question Time, Max Madden, Labour MP for Bradford West, demanded to know the reasons for 'the long delay' and 'difficulties in reaching a decision' over funding for Valley Parade's redevelopment, telling Margaret Thatcher, 'It is high time she honoured the promise given to the club.' Thatcher replied, 'I do not think I made a promise to do that. We are at present considering whether we should give money to Bradford City in the exceptional circumstances.' Her office would later issue a denial it had ever promised cash to Bradford City. In truth, it never had. Stafford had run with the ball, talking up the forthcoming goodwill of the government at every opportunity to the media, and by the time this fusillade had reached Prime Minister's Question Time a reeling government had enough on its hands without another crisis, this time over cash for Bradford. In February 1986, Kenneth Baker announced he would give Bradford City Council a rate-cap exemption in relation to any capital payments it wished to make towards Valley Parade.

The government had played a hospital pass, but Bradford City Council weren't playing ball, pointing out they weren't about to cut services such as education and meals on wheels to make such a payment, before, in March 1986, leaking to the media that West Yorkshire County Council would, in a series of goodwill gestures two weeks before its abolition, hand over £1.46 million of its surplus to Bradford City. The furious Conservative opposition leader of West Yorkshire County Council, Royston Moore, claimed, 'Bradford are blackmailing the County Council.' Yet, days later, county council chairman Jack Gunnel presented Stafford Heginbotham and Jack Tordoff with a £1.46-million cheque on the Valley Parade pitch. Moore publicly disputed the legality of the payment, insisting, 'Grant approval will have to be made by the secretary of state.' If that was the case, it was not withheld – an expedient political solution will always win the day.

Nine months later Oliver Popplewell would reopen Valley Parade. It had been financed by a gift from the county council of £1.46 million, fire insurance proceeds of £500,000 and FGIT grants of £488,000. The club had contributed nothing. In 2010 Jack Tordoff even told the *Guardian* this gift from West Yorkshire County Council had left them with surplus funds of £200,000. Which raises the question, if Bradford City had no funds to rebuild Valley Parade after the fire, how could they have ever found the funds to have rebuilt it but for the fire?

I couldn't believe the goverment had allowed this to be overlooked or simply ignored. I began to wonder what else about the Bradford fire wasn't public knowledge. At this point, sapped of emotional energy and beginning, again, to have nightmares about the fire, I didn't particularly want to take anything any further. But I knew I had to.

Coroner James Turnbull had put it to the inquest jury on retiring, that 'The decision you face in law is how the fire started. Was it caused by a smoke bomb being thrown into Block G or by the accidental ignition of rubbish underneath the seating?' The Popplewell Inquiry had, of course, by then, come out in favour of the latter. But the claim that a smoke bomb had been thrown into the stand had been attributed at the inquiry hearing to a *Daily Star* journalist. Ian Trueman would tell the inquiry that, although he saw no such object, he based his assertion on interviews with a series of unattributed sources he'd spoken to on the pitch after the fire. At the inquiry Trueman stood by his story, despite QC Andrew Collins telling him he had no interest in what he stood by, informing him: 'I would not normally worry about it too much, but the result of this was to waste an awful lot of police time in following up what was in fact a worthless enquiry.'

So, back at the Yorkshire television archive, I was staggered to come across the individual who seemed to have actually been responsible for this hoax. There, in front of the still blazing stand, the pitch packed with distraught supporters looking on, John Helm conducted a live interview with none other than Stafford Heginbotham, the chairman, who claimed, 'The impression in [the] directors' box was it was somebody letting off a smoke bomb, a flare, or something.' That the club chairman, 50 metres away from the outbreak of the fire, was so immediately and firmly ready to point the finger of blame at his own fans – in a stand he knew to be a fire hazard – defied belief.

The seeds of the smoke-bomb theory planted, commanding officer Chief Inspector Mawson told the inquiry he'd 'anticipated' the fire would be in G Block, as that was where most problems arose, so lending the accusation real credibility. And this dualism was allowed to define everything from that point on: first, it was mooted that a smoke bomb had been thrown, only for that to be disproved, so therefore, as the Popplewell Inquiry concluded, the fire was accidental because, 'None of the witnesses saw anything thrown from outside which could have caused the fire.' The terms of the debate were established; no one seemed prepared to think outside of this framework.

But when it came to making spurious claims live on television, Heginbotham was just getting into his stride. He was back on Yorkshire Television the night after the fire, taking part in a panel-based discussion. As West Yorkshire's fire officer made public the letters from West Yorkshire County Council the previous July, warning of the combustible materials beneath the stand, Heginbotham stated, 'No, we didn't receive the letter. I have seen a copy of the letter by the chief fire officer for the first time this evening . . . Peter Flesher, who is now one of my directors, has no recollection of the letter, nor does my vice-chairman, nor does my club secretary.' He assured viewers, 'I have brought a file here this evening with all the copy letters in, and our minute book, and there is no reference to any such letter.' His denials continued the next day, Stafford telling the media once again that he could not find a copy of the letter in the club's correspondence or minutes. 'I cannot discuss something I did not receive,' he insisted.

Except, of course, he *had* received it. On Tuesday 14 May, Football League secretary Richard Faulkner revealed Bradford had clearly referred to the 11 July letter in their Football Grounds Improvement Trust grant application. Valley Parade club secretary Terry Newman had stated, 'Repairs are urgently needed, and safety does now, according to the letters, come into it.' An uneasy silence fell over the club, before Newman released a brief written statement: 'I am under instruction to say nothing. The matter is now the subject of a public inquiry and staff have been advised not to make any comments whatsoever.' Even the usually voluble Heginbotham was uncharacteristically short of words: 'I do not want to comment because I have been advised by our solicitors not to comment.'

Such evasive wording prompted Bradford City's cult supporters' club secretary, Patsy Hollinger, into action. He released a statement on Wednesday 15 May, declaring, 'As the letters from West Yorkshire County Council have been released to the public there can be no doubt that they exist. It is not good enough now for club officials to be unavailable or refuse to comment, or simply say they have no knowledge or record of these letters . . . people have a right to know who opened the letter, who read it and why, if it is the case, it was not logged in the minute book. Too many lives have been lost for it to be ducked in this way.' He concluded with a direct challenge: 'Stafford Heginbotham should come forward with more credible facts.' For his pains, Patsy, who was injured rescuing children from the front of the burning stand, would be banned from Valley Parade by Heginbotham when it reopened.

Hollinger's challenge did, however, prompt Heginbotham into a remarkably muddled and contradictory written statement the next day. In it he claimed that Newman had received the letters – two now, not just the one – but as they'd arrived whilst he was on holiday, he'd accidentally filed them on his return without anyone reading them. It was all 'a simple mistake', Stafford claimed. But that failed to clear up how and when Newman had used them to obtain a grant.

Stafford now declared the letters were in response to a club approach to West Yorkshire County Council, conveniently disregarding the fact his earlier denials had implied there was never such an approach. He insisted the reason that his earlier search for the letters had proved fruitless had been because he was looking for letters from the fire officer. But Graham Karran, the fire officer, had presented him with only a copy of the letter –

the original's West Yorkshire County Council letterhead clearly visible – on TV. Going back over his tracks, Stafford was now tripping himself up. With the world's media camped on the Valley Parade doorstep, Heginbotham wisely chose not to permit any further questions on his frankly ludicrous statement.

He should have been eaten alive.

On releasing his mark II version of events, Heginbotham insisted, 'I have maintained from the start I never saw the letters. That is the truth.'

Weeks later he offered a mark III version to the Popplewell Inquiry. Heginbotham now revealed he'd been aware of the 11 July letter all along, and had found the 18 July letter on the afternoon of 13 May, despite the media denials that day. Club secretary Terry Newman explained these letters were not misfiled, but actually kept in the 'Football Grounds Improvement Trust' file, a file Heginbotham must have used in his dealings with club architect Geoff Lee in drawing up designation plans. Newman now said he'd shown the letters to vice-chairman Jack Tordoff during a 31 July 1984 meeting, where he'd dictated the grant application letter that mentioned 'the letters'. Tordoff would admit he may have 'caught sight' of the 18 July letter. None of the contradictions or discrepancies of this mark III version of the truth with the previous two versions would ever be addressed.

A mark IV version of the truth was then offered to the civil case eighteen months later. At that hearing in November 1986 Tordoff told his own QC the letters had been discussed at a board meeting; something Newman had also told the Popplewell Inquiry. But under cross-examination at the civil hearing, Tordoff said, 'I'm sorry. I withdraw that statement. I was mistaken.' It was a retraction that Justice Cantley had not only allowed, but actually invited. It was late on a Friday morning. Club secretary Terry Newman then reportedly 'froze' when asked by his counsel if he remembered the letters, and 'broke down' to the extent Justice Cantley gave him fifteen minutes to leave the courtroom to compose himself. On his return Newman told his own QC, 'I remember the letters,' and when asked what he did with them, sat in silence, staring at the court officials, before rambling, 'I didn't know I was coming to court today.' He then stated – as if he'd had no chance to learn his lines – 'Without looking at what I said two years ago I cannot remember a thing.'

This was the point at which the whole sorry concoction should have collapsed. But with his own disturbed witness crumbling before him, and further cross-examination to come, Bradford City's QC requested a weekend adjournment. This, despite highly charged and emotional behaviour which suggested something was seriously wrong, Justice Cantley granted – but only after placing reporting restrictions on Newman's testimony. Although he ordered Newman not to spend the weekend discussing the case, rereading inquiry transcripts, or doing anything to prompt his memory, he did not put him under court supervision to ensure it. As Mum told me twenty-five years later, 'I lost all faith in human nature at that moment when Terry Newman was allowed to leave the stand.'

That November night, as Mum returned home from Leeds High Court her phone was ringing. She picked it up to find somebody on the other end declaring, 'Nobody beats Bradford City.' A series of increasingly threatening calls continued into the early hours, when it was suggested it would be best for her and my health if the case were dropped. Mum had to take the phone off the hook to make the calls stop. The next morning Nottingham Forest chairman Maurice Roworth used his contacts to immediately change our telephone number to ex-directory. However, Mum was so shaken, she took me out of school the following week and placed me under voluntary room arrest at the Dragonara Hotel in Leeds, where with hotel security briefed, I was told a friend of Mum's who worked there was a phone call away. I remember going out of my mind watching TV all day, rereading the newspaper six times.

Despite such intimidation Mum maintained her daily court appearances, and on the Monday morning she saw a coherent and composed

Terry Newman – his memory troubles over – return to provide his rehearsed testimony, a rerun of the mark III version of the fire authority letter chronicles.

At the conclusion of the civil case a final mark V version of the truth was eventually offered. Edwin Glasgow QC, counsel for the club, now admitted in summation that the club knew all along that the stand was a fire hazard, but did not foresee the consequences of not removing litter from beneath the stand, as the county council had lulled the club into a false sense of security by doing nothing to alleviate the risks. Now off the hook, with no more questions to face, this was in complete contradiction of all previous four versions that the club knew nothing of any letters.

As far as I could see, Patsy Hollinger's intervention aside, no one had questioned the club directors over these conflicting versions of the truth. Yet the most troubling aspect of the five versions of the truth is how they stand in such stark contrast to one another. The contradictions and discrepancies were never addressed, and remain unchallenged to this day.

Stafford Heginbotham then moved to place the club above suspicion. A day after the fire he had assured Yorkshire Television viewers that the club had been planning to renovate the stand after promotion and that 'the figure which we arrived at was in the region of £400,000 [needed] to bring the ground up to the minimum requirements that were necessary, and that work was well in hand – in fact to start tomorrow morning with a brand new steel roof on the stand of £38,000, and the entire stand was to be reseated.'

It was all a lie. Heginbotham had not told Yorkshire TV the actual cost. But the media swallowed an affordable sum that was a fifth of the actual amount needed to renovate Valley Parade – the real, unaffordable estimate wasn't revealed until after the Popplewell Inquiry. Stafford meanwhile waxed lyrical about the new roof: 'We were to replace the entire stand roof and we had purchased the steel to do that, and paid for it in March.'

The following Sunday he even told Margaret Thatcher, who was visiting the ground, about the steel for the roof – in front of the world's media he assured the prime minister the steel was stored in the club's car park. But looking at an aerial shot of the wrecked stand taken a day or two after the fire – the surrounding area still sealed off, clear of traffic and all cars, white sheets on the charred rubble in the stand – the club car park is clearly empty, there's no steel for the roof.

In fact, there was to be no 'brand new steel roof'. Deputy fire prevention officer Neville Byrom told the Popplewell Inquiry the existing roof of the Main Stand was 'not one that was going to be pulled down'. Rather, it would have been simply recovered. And according to Jack Tordoff, in a David Conn interview in the *Guardian* in 2010, it would not have been covered in steel. There never was any steel.

After the fire Stafford was happy to tell the world about the building plans that were ready to roll on the Monday morning. Strange then, that the promotion supplement with that Saturday's first edition of the *Telegraph & Argus*, in an article headlined SPIT AND POLISH FOR THE PARADE GROUND, made no mention of any gleaming steel roof, nor any improvement detail, and just pointed out that the club were yet to announce their plans, before trotting out Heginbotham's £400,000-needed-to-bring-it-in-line-with-designation sum again.

A mere detail for Stafford, who had been busy elsewhere, apparently taking calls from a concerned prime minister the day after the fire, during which he moved on to the front foot and informed her that her government should have acted to ensure the disaster never happened. 'We had a good ten minutes' discussion, and I gave her my views,' he crowed to the local press on the Monday. His argument was that if the football pools tax levy had been set at the levels of horse racing, football grounds wouldn't be in such a dilapidated state (indeed, Robert Maxwell would write to Thatcher making the same point and John Major would introduce such rebates after Hillsborough). Stafford meanwhile went on to take a swipe at arts funding ('If we played in the nude we would probably get a grant from the Arts Council') and turned up the hackneyed and patronising sentiment: 'Football,' he proclaimed, was, after all, 'the opera of the people.'

All of which served to obscure the reality that the post-promotion renovation programme was a way off yet. The club had first applied for the grant to repair its roof a full 13 months before promotion. All the other purported renovations tipped over into fantasy too. Where Heginbotham told the inquiry, 'It had also been sanctioned that the entire stand was to be re-concreted, from the back of the stand down to the perimeter wall of the field, and also to the full extent of the stand area. It was to be re-concreted and the entire stand was to be re-seated . . .' the truth was these plans had not left the drawing board. No contracts had been awarded, no funds were available, no grant applications had yet been made. Nothing had been 'sanctioned'.

In fact, nothing could have been sanctioned. The ground needed to be designated first, then all sanctions would have to be issued by West Yorkshire County Council. The preliminary meeting with the council, to discuss the general designation process, was scheduled to take place on 15 May, four days after the fire. From the 9 May meeting Stafford would almost certainly have known any modifications to his plans would have to be played out over a complex twelve-month process – during which time the local authority could, in theory, have pulled the plug had they deemed the repair of any structure in the ground beyond the club's means. They'd done that twice with the Midland Road stand(s) already.

One matter could have been resolved at the Popplewell Inquiry, though. According to the club in the immediate days after the fire, there'd been no contact with the local authority other than (eventually conceding to) the 18 July letter. Despite this, Bradford had somehow managed to devise extensive improvement plans that bypassed official channels to anticipate precisely what would be required, even though the lengthy Green Guide required trained interpretation. As the 18 July letter had stated, West Yorkshire County Council would be happy to 'assist you to know what some of the Council's other considerations would be should at some time in the future the provisions of the Act apply'. As this was the only document that could have acted as the working paper for the cost contingency plan then commissioned, why was it that Heginbotham was so keen to deny all such knowledge of a letter he had surely worked from?

I began to wonder: what would it imply if any of us, when questioned on a matter where over 50 people died, changed our story five times, invented a number of other fictitious tales, and looked to shift the blame elsewhere? If you didn't know better, you'd think someone was building a smokescreen. Why would anyone ever take such a risk?

That autumn of 2001, back home from time spent in the Bradford newspaper library and film archive, I was brushing my teeth one night, when what felt like acid seemed to tear away at my left cheek. The toothpaste felt as if it were burning, peeling away my skin; my eye flickered. I knew I was about to fall, and thought I was suffocating. My legs gave way and I fell. I came to with blood on the floor beside me. Over the coming months the same thing happened four more times; my nightmares now recurring almost nightly. Still, I didn't bother going to a doctor – I knew what was causing it all.

13

Locked Doors

It was the established policy at Valley Parade that the exit doors be locked until midway through the second half. It was the same at any football ground – the policy of locking the gates was thought to date back to the Burnden Park disaster, when crowds rushed in after a father had unpicked that standard lock to get his son out. There was also a financial consideration, of course: the day after the fire, Stafford Heginbotham told Yorkshire TV, 'If the doors weren't locked everyone would be getting in for nothing.' Indeed, as Stafford himself recalled in the next day's *Yorkshire Post*, 'As a lad I always used to wait till three-quarters time to sneak in to see my local team because that was when the gates were unlocked.'

I spent days on end looking at the inquiry transcripts, and I'm still at a loss when it comes to the contradictions between different witness testimonies about the exit doors. I have to assume that everything that happened with the doors on that day was done at Heginbotham's instruction, with everyone else just following his orders as usual and unaware of what was going on, completely caught off guard by the speed with which the fire took hold. The Popplewell Inquiry wasn't responsible for questioning how or why some exits were or weren't locked on that day, but it is only by having picked through the transcripts in such detail that I can see the full extent of the inconsistences and everybody's general confusion. And one thing is clear: the transcripts make for very confusing reading.

The police requirement for the doors to be locked was discussed at reasonable length during the Popplewell Inquiry. Commanding officer Chief Inspector Mawson confirmed, 'It was the normal practice and I accepted that as the normal practice . . . We have had occasions at this football ground where people have unlocked certain gates and allowed other unruly elements into the ground.' Inquiry QC Andrew Collins actually challenged Mawson on this, asking, 'Does this really happen?' to be told, 'This really does happen and it presents a real threat.' As it had with 2,000 fans on the Kop and Bradford End ahead of the 1976 FA Cup quarter-final with Southampton.

The club's police liaison officer told the inquiry he ensured exit doors were locked before the turnstiles were opened, around 1 p.m. on a match day. Otherwise, Mawson insisted, 'If you have a crowd outside, unless you have man-to-man marking by the police, as soon as the gates open, people are in.' Popplewell asked Mawson to clarify whether he meant 'locked' or 'shut', to which Mawson replied, 'Locked shut, sir.' Mawson's assistant commanding officer, Inspector Simpson, also a fan of the club, said that in 30 years of policing Bradford City home matches, 'It has always been the case that the gates are locked until after half-time.' Just in case there was any doubt left, a West Yorkshire police report stated, 'Exit from the stand is at the rear by turnstiles and doors, which were locked during the game in accordance with normal practice.' And Andrew Collins led off with an opening statement to the inquiry that pointed out, 'It was the practice that the doors should be closed and locked until about halfway through the second half.'

There's eighteen pages of police testimony in which it's established the doors are locked until around twenty minutes before full time. So the general conclusion was that the doors were locked, and that at Valley Parade this was an accepted procedure – one the police were aware of, approved of and assisted in.

Had this procedure been followed on 11 May 1985 though, as it had been for every other game, *hundreds* would have died in that Main Stand. For some reason, on the day of the fire, this was not what happened.

Commercial manager Mike Ryan had been watching the game from the rear corridor above G Block when, on hearing the police needed a fire extinguisher, he ran the full length of the rear corridor and through a panel door, down a further corridor and through the clubhouse door to retrieve it. Standing by the clubhouse's street-level entrance was club secretary Terry Newman. Ryan alerted Newman to the fire, who then went to look out from the clubhouse balcony; when he saw flames, he ran down to the clubhouse basement, at pitch level, and told changing-room attendant Paul Keating to get the exit doors at the back of the stand open. On hearing there was a fire PA announcer Tony Thornton also went to the clubhouse balcony. He saw the flames, and it 'flashed through my mind that the gates would be locked at the back', so he ran back to the stadium microphone to advise, 'Please do not panic, make your way to the front on to the pitch.'

But it was too late. Mike Ryan made it halfway back up the rear corridor with the extinguisher before the sheer volume of spectators trying to exit the area halted his progress. Ryan and another club official tried to push through them with the extinguisher but a wall of black smoke overtook them. Nobody in the stand ever heard Tony Thornton's announcement, as the PA system, which failed if just one of the wires that ran through the stand roof to the loudspeakers became damaged, was by now disabled by the heat and flames. By the time Newman and the changing-room attendant got back up to street level in the clubhouse, they found themselves in 'seconds . . . just engulfed completely in that building with black fumes'.

There were four main exits along the back of the Main Stand; all of them double-doored, wooden-panelled affairs that opened inwards from South Parade. Following no particular logic, the doors (sometimes also referred to as 'gates' in the Popplewell Inquiry) were lettered, B, E, K and S. Moving from south-west to north-east along the back of the stand, the first door, marked exit B on the map supplied with the Popplewell interim report (see the illustration p. 180), was the one closest to the clubhouse. Here, straight away, things become confusing. The plan of the stand included in the Popplewell interim report shows this exit is at the very end of the Main Stand's rear corridor, at the far end of the A Block seats; whereas the plan obtainable from the National Archive in

Kew shows a panel door dividing the exit from the rear corridor – the door through which Ryan had run through looking for the clubhouse fire extinguisher. To confuse matters even further, maps of the stand reprinted in the *Yorkshire Post* just after the fire don't show this exit at all.

Either way, fans leaving the paddock terrace in front of the clubhouse would head up the stairs and out of these gates on to South Parade; whereas most people seated in A Block and B Block, the other side of these stairs, would leave by exit E (on the Popplewell plan), some 30 feet along from the clubhouse exit. Police dog handlers would hang around by this exit, gate E. The third exit, gate K, was right on the halfway line. The fourth exit, gate S, was definitely behind a mirroring panel door at the other end of the stand. Gate S allowed standing fans from the other end of the paddock terrace, which ran down the side and in front of G Block, to spill out on to South Parade. You couldn't reach gate S from the rear corridor of the stand during the game – you couldn't have the terrace hardcore wandering into the more expensive seats, after all! – but it would be unlocked at full time. For similar reasons, the panelled door down the other end of the stand had a steward by it.

All along the back of the stand, directly above the stairwells which fed down into the various blocks of seats, were the single exits, but these had been boarded up 'Wild West' style at some point since the clubhouse had been built in 1962, effectively truncating the end of the stand – more than likely by the time the two new turnstile blocks had been built in the 1970s. The turnstiles were always chained, with the outer doors locked, once the game kicked off. There was a small gap in the amber wall above the plastic seats, between E and F blocks, but, should the crowd have had to leave in a hurry, the whole north-eastern half of the rear seats – from the directors' box, the press box, and up through E, F and G blocks – seating potentially 600 to 800 people, had only one exit to reach South Parade, out the back of the stand, everyone slowly filing down the narrow rear corridor, which was no more than four or five feet wide, to the halfway line exit, gate K.

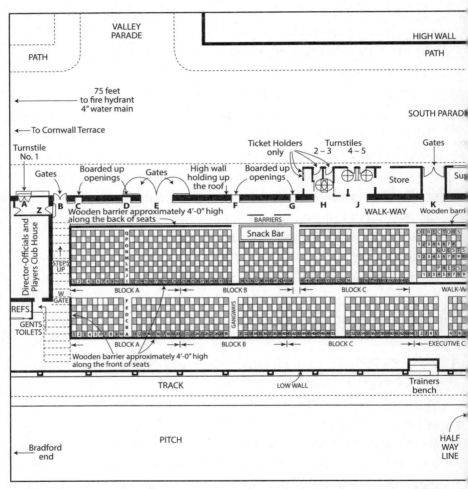

Main Stand at Valley Parade, 1985, as shown in the Popplewell Interim Report. (See also Author's Note on page 24)

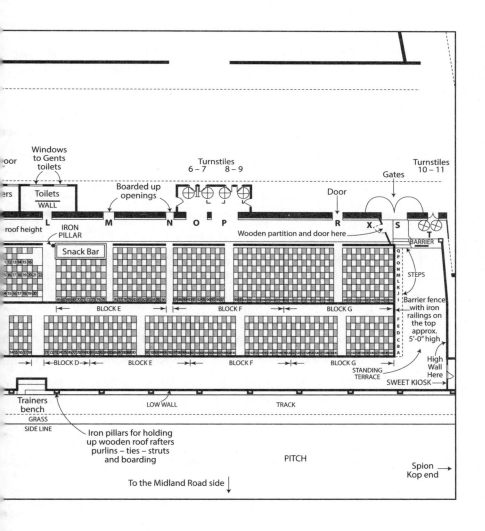

The police didn't have keys for any of the four main exit doors/gates, nor for either of the panel doors at each end of the rear corridor.

Two other Keating brothers, Peter and Anthony (the brothers of changing-room attendant Paul), were the keyholders: Peter Keating was responsible for the doors in the Main Stand; Anthony, for those elsewhere in the ground. In his testimony, Peter Keating explained that normal procedure on arriving at the ground was to collect the six keys for the Main Stand exits from a board in the gateman's room. When he was asked, 'When is it that you, generally speaking, have to unlock the gates?' he told the inquiry, 'About twenty minutes before full-time.' The normal match-day policy was that both Peter and Anthony 'remained in physical contact with the senior officer on the ground' in case he needed them to unlock any exit doors. As the club's police liaison officer told the inquiry, 'When they were not unlocking the gates, [the Keating brothers] were always to be found in the players' tunnel leading off the pitch. I always knew that one could go to that area, if you were having any problems, and ask them to come and deal with the problem.' Chief Inspector Mawson told the inquiry, 'They were always at that end of the ground where we stood.' It was not a question of locating them, but simply, 'Stretching out my arm and saying, "Go and open a gate."' The brothers had worked at Valley Parade for over a decade. Edwin Glasgow QC, for the club, asked them, 'You ever had any trouble with anybody saying to you, "We didn't know where you were", or "We could not find you"?' Anthony Keating replied, 'No . . . if there were any trouble, or owt like that, the police would come to see us, radio somebody near where we are and they would tell us to open the gate if they need them open, and we would open them.'

But once the fire had broken out the brothers could not be found. At 15:41:41, PC Thompson, one of the officers in the rear corridor looking for a fire extinguisher, radioed, 'Can we get someone to open the doors at the back of the stand?' On receiving no confirmation this would happen – all police in the ground with radios should have heard him – he repeated his request thirty seconds later: 'Can you get the doors from the back of the stand open in case we require it to evacuate the stand?' He was told, 'We can't find a steward with keys to open up.' The control room requested, 'Can an officer go to the main part, to the offices, and get it put over the microphone?'

Within two minutes the rear corridor was gridlocked. There was no way forwards, no way back, no way out. It was not surprising that off-duty detective Stephen Mayfield, who escaped through an unlocked storeroom, felt, 'In view of the situation I was envisaging hundreds dead.' Yet, seconds before the smoke fell – and I can recall it like it was yesterday – the gridlock in that corridor somehow inexplicably cleared.

Andrew Collins QC had told the inquiry, 'The fire spread with such rapidity that the man who was in charge of the key . . . simply did not have time to get to open them [the rear exit doors].' But when I examined what went on at the individual main gates along that corridor, and studied the inquiry transcripts, I came to the view that things may not have been quite that simple.

Having already informed the inquiry that each of the stand's exit doors was locked until midway through the second half, counsel then claimed that the exit Sergeant Hendrick opened '. . . was a door which could not be padlocked. It could only be bolted, and it was bolted, but that, of course, meant it was easy enough to open in an emergency.' So 'bolted' didn't exactly mean 'locked'.

Club counsel Edwin Glasgow then suggested that door E 'had been unlocked' in order for the dog handlers to have easy access to the dogs if needed, and Sergeant Hendrick agreed with this suggestion. But dogs had been used in the ground only twice in the previous decade and Chief Inspector Mawson appeared not be aware of this practice, claiming 'It was not as far as I am aware left open for that specific purpose.'

If the dog handlers knew this door was always left unlocked, why did it take Sergeant Hendrick so long to open it? The first radio call to open the exits was made two minutes before Hendrick actually unbolted gate E – 90 seconds before PC Thompson's second call. But the suggestion of the inquiry seems to be that Hendrick and his fellow dog handlers did not hear PC Thompson's earlier messages and were not aware of the fire or the pressure that was building up in the gridlocked corridor at the other end of the stand. This seems odd to me as the match had been abandoned at this point, with an evacuation already underway for over a minute, and the smoke was clearly visible to all in the ground and people watching on TV at home. But frustratingly, Hendrick (and his fellow officers who he asked to open the other doors at the far end of the stand) were not asked to clarify the timing of their actions and so I didn't find a satisfactory answer from reading the testimonies.

Whatever the reason for the delay or the confusion around the unheard radio messages, it is at least clear that gate E was opened by Sergeant Hendrick. That was one door open.

Meanwhile, just along the corridor, by the clubhouse, was exit door B. In his opening statement Andrew Collins stated, 'It was the normal practice [for gate B to] be opened at about half-past three . . . in order to enable guests of players and club officials who were seated in the stand to leave the stand and get access to the clubhouse from South Parade.' The guests and VIPs could have gone out that way . . . but it would have been much quicker, once through the partition door, to walk down a short corridor and through another door, one which led directly into the clubhouse bar. This second door was referred to by commercial manager Mike Ryan as the 'porchway to the executive club', and was acknowledged by both stadium manager Allan Gilliver and Heginbotham in their testimony. But according to Andrew Collins, in his opening statement, that executive club door was to play 'no material part in our consideration' – he claimed, 'That door, I think, was solely for the use of the directors and their guests.' But that door also meant there was no need to turn right once out of the stand, out of exit door B, round the front of the clubhouse and into the main executive club entrance. Why walk outside and round the corner when you could just walk along the corridor, giving you an extra couple of minutes to finish your half-time pint and get back to your seat?

Certainly there was no standing on ceremony just before half-time on 11 May as toxic black smoke began to billow down the stand. Captain that day was Peter Jackson, and his wife Alison wrote, in *Living With Jacko*, of fans piling into the clubhouse bar from the stand, and heading for the exit at the far side of a room, which soon became terrifyingly overcrowded. If 'normal practice' had applied, Alison Jackson would have witnessed fans charging in from outside, to immediately charge back out of the door they'd just come through. That would have been a scrum; or a Monty Python sketch – people trying to get back into a blazing building they'd just escaped from. It seems more likely fans would have flooded down the connecting corridor, through the door that played 'no material part' in the inquiry. (As it happened, things became so desperate in the clubhouse bar that Alison Jackson ended up throwing her daughter ten feet from the balcony, before following her over – both were caught by the club captain.)

It was also this same executive club door that changing-room attendant Paul Keating and club secretary Terry Newman burst through on their way to open the exit doors at the back of the stand. From my reading of the transcripts, I found it strange then, that at 3.43 or 3.44 p.m. they were not only rushing to open a door that should have been opened nearly 15 minutes earlier (according to Collins), but that the first people they bumped into, wrestling with one side of exit door B, were the key-holding brothers, Peter and Anthony – whom nobody else could find. As Paul opened one double door, his brothers opened the other. Paul recalled, 'There were a load of people going out.'

Collins told the inquiry several times that it was normal practice for gate B to be opened at 3.30 – for those VIPs, reporters and clubhouse members who'd paid for the privilege to walk out through the snow and pouring rain, around to the front entrance of the clubhouse, rather than take the warm connecting corridor straight to the bar.

But then there were also the two off-duty firemen, one of whom told the inquiry that before going to the police charge room he looked at a stadium clock, which 'said twenty-five to four' and accessed the charge room through the clubhouse executive door rather than exit B, which in contradiction with his earlier open-at-3.30 assertion, Collins now suggested to the fireman was 'not open', after all – something the fireman confirmed. Which, again, all rather suggests it wasn't open as 'normal practice' would dictate, at 3.30 p.m.

Gate B wasn't open at 3.30 either, according to Sergeant Iles, who was on foot patrol outside on South Parade, and told the inquiry the first exit to open was the dog-handlers' door (E), followed by exit S up at the far paddock.

That second door to open, the far paddock exit door – exit S – had been opened by PC Steven Hirst, who was clearing people forwards from the back of the steep paddock terrace when black smoke suddenly rose up separating the crowd ahead of him. Instinctively, he ushered those around him away, towards the back of the terrace, where seconds later they were engulfed in smoke and intense heat funnelling out the end of the roof. When asked how he had planned to get the fans on the upper paddock out, he told the inquiry, 'It hadn't occurred to me, but had I thought at that time, I would have realised that the gates are normally locked throughout the game.' Except they weren't: on reaching the exit gate S all PC Hirst had to do to open it was to simply lift a wooden beam.

This, on the one hand, tallies with what Andrew Collins said in the latter part of his opening statement specifically about the paddock exit doors – which he claimed, 'were shut, but they were kept shut by means of a wooden beam on the inside, so all that was necessary was to move the beam and the gates would open'. On the other, it doesn't tally with the general position set out near the beginning of Collins' opening statement claim that, 'It was the practice that the doors should be closed and locked until about halfway through the second half.' So that was now two sets of doors open that were supposedly 'locked' – doors which the police (with no keys) had managed to open in under two minutes, by sliding bolts or lifting a wooden beam once the fire became critical.

The top of the paddock, by gate S, was where the club's troublemakers gathered. This was the spot where a likely smoke bomb would have been thrown from (and very possibly the spot where someone had been cautioned, before the fire, according to the interim Popplewell report, for chucking a meat pie). Given the police and club concerns over fans gaining unpaid entry, it defies belief that the heavy mob had hung around this gate for years, unaware it was actually unlocked.

As people spilled out of three exits – gates E and S, and now down at the clubhouse gate B too – on to South Parade it was clear those behind the fourth exit, gate K by the halfway line, could not get out. Sergeant Hendrick was now out of the dog handlers' gate and ran round the back of the stand; he told the inquiry that, as the smoke turned thick and black, desperate pleas came from those banging on the now bulging exit doors. But the bangs began to subside, and fans beside him declared 'the gate had got to come off', so they grabbed the bottom of the two inward opening doors of gate K – which were by now bulging out six inches as the weight of those trapped behind multiplied – and the whole thing quickly flew off its hinges as 'a lot of people' followed through. But sadly not the 15 people who died behind this door.

Back in the stand, many had yet to even reach an exit, especially those in G Block, seat of the fire, and half a pitch length away from gate K. Having initially been shepherded by the police into the narrow rear corridor, most fans were thinking, 'We'll be back in our seats in a minute, once the police have dealt with this.' No one was panicking yet, and so no one thought to try the panel door behind them, on to the terrace, which they knew to ordinarily be locked.

At 3.41 p.m., on hearing the first police radio call for the exits to be opened, Sergeant Emmel had left the clubhouse main entrance at the far corner of the ground, and begun to walk up South Parade, along the back of the stand, heading at an increasing pace to G Block, where he'd heard the smoke was rising fast. He told the inquiry that as he reached the second turnstile block, directly opposite F Block, and just by where those fans were queuing patiently the other side of the wall, the white smoke that was seeping from beneath the roof suddenly turned black. As it did so people started to desperately bang on the locked turnstile doors. He kicked one of the outer doors of the turnstile block three times, but it refused to give way, until a rally of successive blows from fans (who'd by now spilt out on to South Parade) and other police shattered it. Others followed suit on the other doors. Yet all that met them was a thick black wall of blinding, choking smoke spuming out of the turnstile entrances. PC Hirst, who had now made it down from the paddock exit, also tried to enter the turnstile block but was forced back. For those on the other side, other than me, it was too late.

Forty-three people died in that rear corridor: 19 bodies were found by the locked turnstiles above F Block; three were in the recessed toilet block just beyond. Then there were the 15 found further along by the halfway line exit, gate K, and four in a recessed turnstile block beyond that; two others short of the dog handlers' exit above B Block. Nobody died beyond that easily opened gate (nor around the other unlocked exit gate S). Nor, of course, by the clubhouse exit the Keating brothers had opened.

How the gridlock had so suddenly cleared – while we were in the corridor, trying to get away from G Block – was now very clear to me.

I was much less clear about the testimony of the Main Stand keyholder, Peter Keating. In cross-examination, Andrew Collins QC led him up the stand, taking him door by door along the corridor, asking him about the nature of the 'locked' doors. Collins reminded him he was the person responsible for opening the clubhouse exit (gate B) at 3.30 (despite testimony that rather pointed to the fact he hadn't on this occasion – and the account of the two Keating brothers wrestling with it closer to 3.45 p.m.). It seemed to me that even though there was a padlock on gate B by the clubhouse, you could open it by just 'unbolting' it. The dog handlers' door (gate E) had turned out to be openable by bolts alone too, of course, even though there was also, according to Keating, a padlock on there. This was how Sergeant Hendrick opened it, though he didn't mention any padlock. Then there was gate K, by the halfway line. Keating confirmed that that door also had a padlock on it, one that worked. But, once again, he could actually open the door without a key: 'I just used to undo the bolts and pull them both together.'

'If anyone saw that with the padlock on would they have realised you could have got it undone without the need for undoing the padlock?' asked Collins.

'Yes,' replied Keating.

'They could?' Collins asked again.

'Yes.'

'If they could have seen it?'

'Yes.'

'That is K,' concluded Collins. Given that gate K is where 15 bodies were found, I could not understand why he had not questioned Keating further on this issue.

Collins then moved along the corridor. So far, all three exits could be opened without the keys for a padlock – if you knew what you were doing with some combination of drawer bolts and plunge bolts and the simultaneous moving of doors together. In my view Keating should have been cross-examined further about whether any one of these gates was actually padlocked or not, and Collins should have looked deeper into the discrepancies between his own opening statement (all doors locked) and the reality (they weren't, they were just held shut with bolts or a beam). Trying to ascertain whether these doors were locked or not, I found, was about as clear in the Popplewell Inquiry transcripts as it would have been in a smoke-filled corridor. At door S on the paddock, the same again – and where Keating again talked of a padlock, PC Hirst talked of lifting a beam.

There was even talk at the inquiry of a recently unboarded single exit, which was apparently kicked down by a PC Chadwick, but Keating became confused as to where this recently unboarded door was. Collins suggested it was door R, just opposite the G Block entrance. Chadwick later believed it to be door F, down near B Block, which is testimony that makes sense because the people who didn't get through that door were pushed by Chadwick in the direction of the neighbouring dog handlers' door. Sergeant Hendrick also corroborated this in his testimony. If the unboarded single door had been door R, as Collins suggested to Keating, right opposite the G Block stairwell, then I must have been as blind as everyone else leaving that section, moving straight past this exit and heading towards gate K, where everyone knew the nearest exit was, on the halfway line.

Things became even more confusing when stadium manager Allan Gilliver, on being asked to point to where he believed the single unboarded exit was, pointed at door N, just beyond the turnstiles, before his assistant Rodney Lawn, who'd actually unboarded the door in question, suggested it was door M, a bit further down, opposite the E Block stairwell. I thought this was getting ridiculous: there were only three boarded exits to choose from between G Block and gate K on the halfway line, and each of the three men picked a different door. Add in PC Chadwick's and Sergeant Hendrick's accounts of kicking down door F, and that's four possibilities. Even allowing for human error in recall, I don't think it would be unfair to refer to this as 'the phantom door'.

Furthermore, all this single unboarded door testimony came before we got to the turnstile operator who apparently also had a key for the panelled door opening out on to the paddock terrace, which it seemed Peter Keating, the key man, didn't know about. The panelled door was another one that should have been locked but was apparently now open. Not that any witness was ever called who had actually used this door.

Peter Keating wasn't the only Keating brother to become confused when being questioned about the doors. Changing-room attendant Paul Keating was asked at the inquiry, 'What made you first aware there was any problem, any fire?' He replied, 'At half-past-three when Mr Terry Newman came down and asked me to go and open the doors at the back of the stand.' It seems there was confusion amongst the witnesses as to the exact timings and order of events as well as which gates were locked or simply bolted.

Locked Doors

'*At half-past three . . .*' Nobody in the clubhouse should have known of a fire until fifteen minutes later. Newman himself didn't know about it until commercial director Mike Ryan saw him by the clubhouse entrance, at what must have been 3.43 or 3.44 p.m., which is back where we started. In his testimony Newman doesn't seem to be asked what time he first became aware of the fire, but he does confirm that he was talking to a doorman in the clubhouse when Mike Ryan came in looking for a fire extinguisher. So is it possible that Paul Keating had simply got the time wrong? It's not clear, so it made me wonder why Collins had not questioned Keating or Newman further over this discrepancy. It was clear to me, however, that when the fire did break out the keyholders were not in their usual posts, and could not be located by the police. In fact, on examining inquiry transcripts it was very clear to me that the keyholding Keating brothers were in the corridor before the fire began. Anthony Keating told the inquiry he was 'concerned that if those [exits] were going to be opened that there should not be trespassers strolling into the ground' – which was an odd concern to be troubled by if the stand was actually alight, but more understandable if the first request to open the doors came when it was not. Then, when asked to clarify if he realised 'it was possible that a lot of people were going to want to get out quickly', he insisted, 'No I did not know about that,' which suggested he was in an empty corridor before the fire started, and not a gridlocked corridor full of fans trying to get out, as both brothers had clearly implied in a radio interview with a startled Tony Delahunty.

This might explain why doors that were ordinarily locked could be opened with a bit of quick thinking, bolt-manoeuvring and brute force on behalf of the police and some of the fans – unengaged padlocks notwithstanding. What seems more plausible from my reading of the transcripts is that, once the smoke started to descend, people tried the doors in desperation and found, contrary to a normal Saturday afternoon, that they opened. Unfortunately door K took that bit longer to force from the outside; and for the fans in G Block, well, they were at the back of a long queue, half a pitch length away from the only door they could reach, their nearest exit – but sadly, they were closest to the seat of the blaze. As the black smoke descended and the fire flashed over, they didn't stand a chance, and I found it hard to read suggestions that there was an available exit there when there wasn't.

In 2001, as I put all this together my alarmed friends watched my weight balloon to 18 stone. Ben and Will told me that there were still rare places available to run the New York marathon that autumn – they had both signed up, and I agreed to give it a go. That summer it became clear life had changed. My friends started settling down. Ben took a job in Dubai. I had the choice of law school in London or an independent financial advice job in Birmingham, and opted for the former, to relive a youth free of my past, to hang out with students a decade younger than me, many of whom would have only been dimly aware of some fire in Bradford.

I was staying with one of our gang from law college, Don McLean, and one Sunday night I collapsed in the bathroom again. As it was the fifth time in a year, I'd put myself in the recovery position before Don broke into his own bathroom to find me having a seizure. I came to with a lovely looking paramedic holding my hand. She seemed to be wearing what looked like a green jumpsuit. I was so high on oxygen I thought we were at a party, and she shook her head in disbelief as I tried to chat her up before telling her I was flying to New York to run the marathon that Wednesday. Once out of hospital, I knew the risks of still running the marathon but, having trained for 6 months and lost 5 stones, I knew I'd probably not get another chance to run the New York race – and almost certainly not with my university friends all around me. And so I went.

It would be our last big overseas trip together. Over 20 of us landed in New York the night before Halloween. We drank in Mid-Town Manhattan till 2 a.m., then in the Meatpackers District until 6. I passed out over breakfast in a diner, and Ben carried me back to my room, reassuring the sceptical diner owner that yes, this pair of crazy Englishmen would be running the marathon 53 hours later. A hangover, a Knicks game and another couple more nights in bars, and I ran the marathon in five hours, losing 40 minutes having walked three of the last four miles, so as not to overdo it. That night we drank till 2 a.m. and I ended up with a beautiful American girl on each arm.

A few weeks later I had another seizure whilst brushing my teeth – the usual trigger. Another ambulance, oxygen mask and the concerned face of flatmate John, and this time I finally sought medical help – a consultation with Dr Kennedy, a neurologist at Lister Hospital in Chelsea. As I described my symptoms Dr Kennedy looked at me gravely.

'At what time in the morning do you find you need your first drink, Mr Fletcher?'

I laughed. I was no alcoholic.

'Mr Fletcher, this is no joking matter,' he chided me.

The friend who had accompanied me assured him not only was I only a social drinker, I'd actually run the New York marathon a few weeks earlier.

'*You did what?!*' he replied, before admitting me for observation in the private ward at the Chelsea & Westminster Hospital and administering a dozen or more blood tests.

'If you find you want to leave the hospital, do feel free, but please tell the receptionist before you go,' he assured me, no doubt convinced I'd end up in the bars on Fulham Broadway till the early hours, at which point he could demonstrate to me I was indeed an alcoholic 'in denial'.

I did break out, but only to fetch my law books for some revision in the canteen. And the blood tests, when they came back, showed no sign of alcohol, while the EEG and ECG tests for epilepsy were negative too. Dr Kennedy had diligently worked through the options for a patient suffering potentially life-threatening seizures. Which left just one test outstanding – an MRI brain scan. With all the other tests negative, but something clearly having caused half a dozen seizures in a year, I was now convinced I had a brain tumour. Having ignored my symptoms for over a year, I presumed if it were a tumour, it would likely be inoperable and I'd not have long left to live. Not that it scared me – I'd been on borrowed time for seventeen years.

Dr Kennedy was about to finish for the night when he came into my room with a smile, holding an A3 orange file under his arm. 'Good news, Mr Fletcher, surprisingly everything's all right,' he told me in an upbeat tone, as he showed me my scans and where he'd expected to find issues.

Although keen to put me on epilepsy drugs to prevent any future potentially fatal convulsions, I told him I'd prefer to initially try to moderate my drinking. Although alcohol withdrawal seizures were typically a sign of chronic alcoholism, I knew what had led me to drink. I knew it was time to temper my reckless behaviour. Waking up in a hospital bed on the morning of my 30th birthday had made me realise I'd been given yet another chance. I vowed now was the time to concentrate on my studies and to build that normal, happy and successful life I'd always promised myself and my (very concerned) mum. Post-traumatic stress disorder – who needs it?

14

'I have just been unlucky'

Three years later, having completed law school, I was halfway through a tax training contract with PricewaterhouseCoopers LLP, living a happy, single life in a cheery flat-share in Clapham. I was a regular at Twickenham, and Wimbledon every June, and flew to Dubai several times a year to party with Ben, who was living out there. A young partner at work had taken me under his wing and earmarked me for the firm's fast track. Then, in early 2006, my mobile rang and although it was a number I didn't recognise, I answered it.

It was a freelance journalist, Mark Metcalf, who'd been given my number by Simon Hattenstone of the *Guardian* (for whom I'd written the first critical article about Bradford, on the twentieth anniversary of the fire the previous year). He was keen to talk to me about the fire. We met in a pub in an alley off Borough High Street near London Bridge, the following Sunday. There was such a clandestine feel to it all that I had a couple of friends – one a rugby lock, the other a basketball player – sitting in the corner of the pub incognito. But I spoke with Mark for a good half hour, and he told me he'd been in touch with a West Yorkshire fire prevention officer who was also the source behind a Paul Foot *Daily Mirror* column, written in 1985.

'I'm surprised they've admitted to that story existing,' I told Mark, having requested a copy myself only for an employee of the Mirror Group Newspapers to tell me it was not in their archives. Mark had had the same problem, but told them he knew it had been published, because he knew the source.

The original Paul Foot article had appeared in the *Mirror* on Friday 31 May 1985, just a day after the world was getting to grips with the enormity of Heysel – the ultimate morning to bury bad news.

Under the headline FIRE JINX IN BRADFORD Foot revealed that 'at least five fires have damaged premises owned by or connected with Mr Heginbotham or his companies' and mentioned that a huge blaze at Stafford's Tebro Toys company, housed in Douglas Mills, Bowling Old Lane, Bradford, in November 1977 had resulted in an insurance payout of £174,663 for 'fire damage and loss of profits'. Foot went on, 'In the fifteen years between 1965 and 1980 there were four other fires at premises connected with Mr Heginbotham or his companies – two at Cutler Heights, Bradford; one at Aked Street, Bradford; and one at the Foster Warehouse, Castle Mill, New Street, Idle.' Foot had tackled Heginbotham over these fires, but the Bradford chairman had refused to be drawn, stating, 'I don't even want to hear what information you've been given or who has given it to you. Anything personal to do with myself or my family or my business, I regard as being my business.' But twice in the article Heginbotham felt the need to stress that the 'incident[s]' to which Foot was referring had 'absolutely nothing' to do with Valley Parade. From the article, however, it seems Foot was merely pointing out to Heginbotham that a man with his experience of fires should perhaps have been 'more on his guard than in normal circumstances' when it came to fire prevention and the identification of safety hazards. A week later in his column, Foot repeated this sentiment – also alerting *Mirror* readers to the fact that Heginbotham had complained in the Bradford *Telegraph & Argus* of the *Mirror* journalist's 'muck-raking' and warned that he was 'consulting his solicitors'. 'Bring it on,' Foot seemed to be saying.

The *Mirror* had been pursuing Bradford's dog's breakfast of an attempt to cover their tracks regarding the West Yorkshire fire authority letters, and Robert Maxwell was in town at a function with the mayor of Bradford when – according to Stafford Heginbotham himself in the *Telegraph & Argus* – the rotund newspaper magnate bundled the Bradford City chairman into a hotel room for a frank exchange. Stafford told Maxwell 'his assumption was totally different to the truth'; Maxwell implored his hostage to be truthful about the letters. Thereafter it seems the air was cleared.

Paul Foot wrote of Maxwell after his death, that 'he demeaned everyone who worked for him, myself included, but I was able, by sheltering behind my editor, to protect myself from his monstrous excesses.' Although on this occasion, possibly not. The *Mirror* went on to issue a few sympathetic stories on Bradford and Heginbotham. And Paul Foot never wrote a word on the story again.

A few days after meeting Mark Metcalf, I spoke on the telephone with Paul Foot's fire prevention expert source, who explained, 'I was working in Warwickshire at the time [May 1985] and when I saw Stafford Heginbotham was involved with Bradford City I contacted Paul Foot to tell him about the fires I knew he'd had.'

Reading Foot's article it seemed light on detail concerning the times and places of the fires. His source didn't disagree, saying it had been 'just what I knew at that time – I hoped he [Paul Foot] would follow it up.'

'And he didn't?'

'I don't believe so, no. But I know there were more [fires].'

I expressed surprise, but put it to him that if I went digging, I'd perhaps find more . . .

'For sure. Let's put it this way: when we [the fire brigade] went on strike in 1977 we ran a book on who'd be the first man to have a fire in Bradford. Stafford was the favourite – then, guess what . . .?'

I knew the scale of this task. If I headed to the old British newspaper library in Colindale, north London, full time it would take three or four months, but to do so every Saturday, even without my studies, would probably take three or four years. I should have sat down with PricewaterhouseCoopers and told them I needed a sabbatical, but I'd not been there long enough. I had one out, though: if I failed a resit, my training contract would be terminated. I thought that was too daft to even contemplate, but it's funny the tricks your subconscious plays.

I spent the weekend before my two final ACA professional stage papers at Twickenham, watching England v Ireland. As I headed through the concourse between the stand and its steel boundary fence I saw a tightly packed crowd, 30–40 metres from the staircase we were heading towards. I told my flatmate, John, to hang back. Then we climbed the concourse fence to our right and watched a serious crush develop. As the crowd tightened eventually around us, police and stewards shouted and wildly waved their arms; women and children were in tears, large rugby playing men, powerless. It was only relieved by opening an exit gate to let people out on the concourse on to Rugby Road.

I'd hung back as it was not the first such incident I'd witnessed at Twickenham. The previous November, as I headed to the North Stand to watch England v New Zealand, I tried to pass the staircase at the foot of the North and East stands and was met by severe congestion. Again, it hadn't cleared, just tightened uncomfortably – and as the stewards and police on the staircase started yelling at the crowd, it was clear they'd lost control. At the front of the crowd, I scrummed my way past the staircase before it worsened, telling my friend Dan to get a move on. But he hung back, and this 16-stone, 6-foot-4-inch bodybuilder was shaken by the pressure of the crowd all around him, and the sight of screaming women and tearful children. It took him ten minutes to reach his seat – a gentle man, he was visibly angered by his powerlessness. Afterwards I asked the head steward outside the main East Stand entrance why they'd allowed a situation similar to Hillsborough to occur. Apologetic, he agreed there were similarities, although he assured me it was a one-off and was under control because it was being monitored on CCTV. 'Yeah, so was Hillsborough,' I told him.

A year before that I'd been at Wycombe's Adams Park to support Northampton Saints at London Wasps. Sat in the end block of the full Dreams stand, I headed to the nearest exit at the end of the game. It was locked, so I asked the steward to open it. He refused. Instead, he told me to use an exit at the opposite end of the stand, 75 metres away, claiming the locked exit was not for the use of people in our stand. So I asked him to show me an alternative exit within 30 metres of my seat, which I informed him would be in the ground's safety certificate. He said he couldn't do that. So I asked what would happen if this were an emergency, and he told me he'd contact someone to unlock the door. Although the law should allow fans to exit a ground within eight minutes, I was now stuck in a slow, congested queue, with Mum, for 15 minutes, furious at a system I'd last encountered 20 years before, at Valley Parade.

As I climbed the external stairwell at the north-east corner of Twickenham, just ahead of the England v Ireland game, I looked down at the dropped pint glasses and puddles of beer which marked out where the crush had been minutes before. It dawned on me then that not only had complacency returned but that, one day, disaster could well revisit a British sports ground. I thought of the Working Group report to the Popplewell Inquiry I'd found in the Public Records Office that stated it was the 'strong opinion of the Fire Inspectorate Service that 8 minutes is too long a period to allow for the evacuation of any stand under the conditions of emergency'. Yet over two decades on from Popplewell's report here I was, in an 'age of terror', climbing to an upper tier I knew I'd be unable to exit from in eight minutes.

'All that is necessary for the triumph of evil is that good men do nothing,' was the Edmund Burke quote that kept ringing in my mind as I drank the night away. So I contacted the *Guardian* and, a month later, on 21 April 2006, Paul Kelso wrote that the RFU would call to stagger Six Nations kick-off times to avoid a repeat of such crushing. Stadium director Richard Knight believed the congestion was due to Wales v France having finished 17 minutes before the England v Ireland clash began, resulting in a mass exodus from nearby pubs, everyone heading into Twickenham at exactly the same moment. He stated, 'We are aware of the incidents and we are looking at how to avoid them in the future. One of the issues is when games kick off, and I don't think it's for fixtures to be scheduled in the same way again.' Happily, they were not.

In the week after Twickenham I narrowly failed both my business finance and audit exams. I wouldn't go as far as to say it was preordained, but I do wonder why I chose to revise for my resits by the pool at Dubai's Grand Hyatt. That period of intense study was followed by a week or two sunbathing on Clapham Common – in between World Cup games from Germany. My books were beside me all the time, just largely unopened. Still, I was the healthiest I had been in a decade – the 44-inch suits now replaced by 38-inch ones – and I was a year from becoming ACA qualified with a 'big four' firm. The future looked bright. What could go wrong? Then, at 5 p.m. on the Friday of that year's British Open at Royal Liverpool Golf Club, slumped in front of the TV, I learnt I'd spectacularly failed my audit resit, with a 42 per cent score so bad that if I'd achieved that originally I'd have been immediately dismissed for a 'bad fail'.

I had to wait until the following Monday before I was formally dismissed. There was no soul-searching, and no job search. But I knew I'd now make a daily journey from Clapham Common to the British Newspaper Library at the opposite end of the Northern Line, where I vowed once and for all to get to the bottom of the business history of Stafford Heginbotham. As there were no local newspaper index books in Colindale, I'd have to get there for 9 a.m. each morning, fill in the slips for the maximum number of items I could order – usually four bound volumes of the Bradford *Telegraph & Argus*, dating from January 1965 onwards, the year Stafford Heginbotham became involved with Bradford City – and would sit at a desk, scanning each article by article, page by page, day by day, until I'd covered 20 years' worth of newspapers. The whole process took two months, during which time I discovered there was a pattern to Stafford Heginbotham's fires. In a nutshell, they all spread incredibly quickly, produced an unbelievable amount of toxic smoke and devastation, and they all caught the fire-fighters unawares. But even more staggering was the sheer number of them.

'I have just been unlucky'

I read how on a Sunday afternoon, 21 May 1967, fire engulfed a three-storey factory and its two-storey loading bay, as a 200-foot pall of toxic smoke temporarily overcame two firemen in Cutler Heights Lane, near Bradford city centre. Fifty firemen in all, deploying 14 jets, 8 pumps and a turntable, were needed to bring it under control. No staff were in the factory – Sundays in the 1960s being very much the day when Britain went into a weekly slumber – but, despite apparently having sold his interests in the foam-cushion manufacturer he'd set up five years previously, Stafford Heginbotham wasn't at home in the village of Tong – three or so miles away – that afternoon, but was standing in the crowd watching the blaze engulf the Matgoods premises. A man with a likely 'earn-out' from his deal would, of course, have a legitimate reason to be concerned. The young Bradford City chairman was surrounded by scores of boys watching the inferno, and the police, mystified as to how – with no employees at work and no sign of a forced entry – a fire might have started in the factory, announced their inquiries would continue with the children who were playing outside at the time the blaze broke out. At a time when the average national UK house price was £3,700, the fire caused £25,000 of damage, with a stock loss of £10,000 (the equivalent, in terms of house-price inflation today, of £1.6 million, and £600,000 respectively).

Then, on Good Friday 1968, overtime staff at Tebro Toys looked out of their windows as an 'awfully black' pall of smoke drifted towards their premises from a three-storey factory at the opposite end of the industrial estate. When the managing director went to investigate he found what he described as a 'fire going like a bomb' in the neighbouring building, also occupied by Tebro Toys and, the *Argus* stated, 'Genefoam (Bradford Ltd) rubber manufacturers whose managing director is Mr Stafford Heginbotham, the Bradford City chairman'. By the time the fire brigade arrived a 500-gallon fuel tank had exploded, bringing down the factory's 40-foot walls and roof. Again, 50 firemen and 11 appliances were needed to bring the blaze – visible for miles around – under control. The photo on the front page of the *Telegraph & Argus* resembled a scene of bomb damage from the war – a crater, smoking wreckage and a huge gap where once stood a factory wall. It had caused £80,000 of devastation (or some £4.75 million in today's adjusted terms), and arson charges were immediately brought. A young witness had seen two brothers, aged 10 and 13, light a small bonfire by the factory wall. Although he said they'd tried to put it out, it was too fierce, so they ran away. In court the defence would claim that although the brothers lit the bonfire they did so unaware a fuel tank – filled only that morning – was placed on the other side of the factory door. In the end both boys were held to be below the age of criminal responsibility, but as I read the reports I couldn't help think that was a strange place to have a bonfire, right by a door that opened on to a fuel tank. And who'd fill a fuel tank on the morning of Good Friday?

I thumbed through another decade's worth of newspaper archives before I found another fire involving a firm owned by Stafford Heginbotham. On Tuesday 8 November 1977 the front page of the *Telegraph & Argus* reported that Heginbotham was still at his desk around six the previous evening when he heard the sound of breaking glass. Thinking his car was being vandalised he ran out, presumably to confront the vandals, only to find glass falling from the top two floors of the three-storey Douglas Mills, when he reportedly raised the alarm and called the fire brigade. The fumes breathed in by the first four firemen to arrive at his blazing toy firm were so toxic they were violently sick and required hospital treatment. As did one of the employees: it was noted that '18-year-old John Disley of Spooner House, Killinghall, Bradford', was also hospitalised suffering from the effects of smoke. In the end, 40 firemen were needed to control the blaze. In 1971 Stafford had formed a new Tebro Toys company – six years later his extensive stock of soft toys for Christmas was destroyed. Later the same night, around midnight, a neighbouring mill was also ablaze. In fact, Bradford was in the grip of what the *Telegraph & Argus* called 'a fire blitz'. A two-storey section of a mill on Huddersfield Road had been destroyed, and there had been the 'John Street Market inferno'. With a fire brigade strike having started that November (it would last until

January 1978), there was no thorough fire investigation, and a discarded cigarette was considered the most likely cause of the Douglas Mills fire.

Indeed it had been a most unfortunate year for Douglas Mills. Three months earlier, in August 1977, two boys had been arrested for arson after pouring oil over, then setting light to 150 paper rolls stored at Yorkshire Knitting Mills, which had occupied the ground floor of the Douglas Mills building owned by Stafford Heginbotham. A Tebro Toys employee who noticed smoke rising through the floorboards raised the alarm, and four fire engines took over 20 minutes to control the blaze. The police explained, 'The fire brigade were able to deal with it promptly, or it could have got out of hand.'

Four weeks to the day after the Tebro Toys fire a 100-foot pillar of flame threatened to devastate the industrial heart of Bradford city centre. Monday 5 December was a month into the firemen's strike, and two army fire crews arrived at the Coronet Marketing factory in Leeds Road, confident they could control the flames, only to pull back after a series of explosions saw the four-storey building completely alight within two minutes. It was the most serious fire of the strike and took 50 soldiers and a dozen army appliances to bring the blaze under control. Coronet Marketing rented the premises from the council. They were an outdoor lighting manufacturer, and a subsidiary of Tebro Toys, owned, needless to say, by Stafford Heginbotham. The factory supervisor, a Miss Edna Normanton, was locking up for the night when she saw smoke seep through second-storey floorboards. As she did so, a labourer, Cyril Oliver, ran into the room to throw her down the stairs before both ran to safety. Somehow, a ground-floor gas pipe, normally the sort of thing that would have been designed to withstand a fire's heat, had fractured and in seconds the building became an inferno – all stock and machinery was destroyed. Although Heginbotham talked of moving production to Douglas Mills, he simply collected the fire insurance and wound the company up. His two big fires of 1977 saw him collect a striking total of £174,663 (£3.165 million in today's terms) in insurance pay-outs. But again, with the fire service strike ongoing there would be no explanation of how that ground-floor gas pipe came to break. These were the blazes that had piqued Paul Foot's attention.

A headline on the front page of the next day's *Telegraph & Argus* had announced FIRM IS DOGGED BY BIG FIRES. 'I need fires like I need a hole in the head,' claimed Stafford Heginbotham, after the latest in a series of fires to hit his businesses. He told the newspaper, 'It makes you wonder what is happening,' before adding, 'I have just been unlucky.'

As it happened it wasn't all the doing of Yorkshire urchins with a pyromaniacal bent. In August 1978 John Disley, the hospitalised 18-year-old from the Spooner House hostel, overcome with fumes in the November Douglas Mills fire, pleaded guilty to arson and vandalism in setting fire to a packet of plastic foam granules at Tebro Toys. Strangely, Disley had been taken on by Tebro Toys a month after the Yorkshine Knitting Mills fire, only to be let go again a month after the Tebro Toys fire, from where he went on to torch the Globe Mills building he worked at in the spring of 1978.

After the December 1977 fire at Coronet Marketing, 'unlucky' Heginbotham had conceded in the *Telegraph & Argus*, 'The fires I have had seem something of a joke to some people.' The printing and stationery firm where Mum worked in Leeds had Stafford as a client at one point. That was before her time, but she remembers the standing joke in the office being: 'If Stafford had a problem, it got torched.'

The real joke was that his next fire, which killed 56 people, resulted in Bradford City receiving insurance proceeds and associated grants of £988,000. In today's adjusted terms (based on a 1985 average UK house price of £34,000), that's £7 million. It's also a bit of a joke that, back in 1985, nobody picked up on the fact that Heginbotham – seemingly a one-man walking nightmare for insurance companies – had already recouped nearly a million pounds (£10 million in today's terms) before his club was rewarded with the further gift of £1.46 million (worth £10.25 million in today's money) by the local authority, to take his total fire proceeds from his Bradford firms to £2.74 million – or £27 million in today's adjusted terms. A simply staggering sum.

Before I embarked on my own research I'd looked closely at the definition used by Paul Foot to identify 'at least five fires' he said had occurred at 'premises owned by or connected with Stafford Heginbotham'. I decided to extend the search into companies and premises Stafford had had some link with – often at one remove from the more concrete link of the five fires mentioned above. Ploughing back through 20 years of each page of the *Telegraph & Argus*, I applied this wider, if looser, definition.

It wasn't long before I discovered that Matgoods, a firm Heginbotham had founded, also had a fire in 1970, which started with an explosion in a storeroom that destroyed another £10,000-worth of foam rubber (£500,000 in today's terms).

Then Castle Mills, which Heginbotham also owned, had a tenant fire in December 1971. Although Stafford's tenants, Frionor Packing, a frozen food company, had an operable automatic fire alarm system – one which, the local fire chief said, once fitted, was responsible for keeping all fire-damage claims below £5,000 over a 20-year period – the blaze saw £15,000 damage (£650,000 in today's terms) to packaging equipment used for frozen fish.

Heginbotham-owned Douglas Mills, once over their fire-ravaged year of 1977, fell victim to another tenant fire in June 1981. This time a hundred workers had to be evacuated from a ground-floor plastics factory, with industrial quantities of plastic melting, running and resetting to form a waist-high barrier that, while keeping the flames in, did nothing to alleviate the toxic fumes.

And I found the only reference – in twenty years' issues of the *Telegraph & Argus* – to a fire in Aked Street, Little Germany, back in the January of 1981. Paul Foot had identified an Aked Street fire in his original article, and had presumably discovered a property-owning link between the gutted city-centre office complex and Heginbotham. The fire had started in the nightclub basement of the old wool warehouse (which now housed several offices and business premises) – luckily, just an hour after the club had closed for the night.

But could any man really be as unlucky as Heginbotham had been? From standing around with a bunch of kids and onlookers on a Sunday afternoon in May 1967, as his former foam cushion business went up in flames, to standing on the pitch at Valley Parade 18 years later, making noises about smoke bombs while 56 people perished behind him . . . that made a total of ten fires at business premises connected to Stafford Heginbotham. Even if Paul Foot had erroneously linked the Aked Street nightclub fire with Heginbotham's properties – we'll never know, Foot died in July 2004 – the total would be nine. After the fire at Valley Parade, any police officer or journalist worth their salt would start looking into Stafford Heginbotham's business interests and premises *before* he became associated with Bradford City in 1965 . . .

Rereading Heginbotham's profile from the 'Up with City!' promotion supplement, first published on the day of his tenth fire, it sent a shiver down my spine. The piece opened with the line, 'There's a sign in Stafford Heginbotham's office which says "there are three types of people – those who make things happen, those who watch things happen and those who wonder what happened". Stafford certainly falls into the first category.'

What I hadn't realised at that point, though, was that Stafford Heginbotham was indeed a man who needed to make something happen – and not just because there was a huge shortfall in Valley Parade's designation costs. He was on the brink in more ways than one. He was about to lose everything he had.

Stafford Heginbotham had come from nothing. A grammar school scholarship boy, he grew up in a two-up-two-down in the mill town of Oldham. Although bright enough to win a scholarship, he left school at 15, where it seems he spent most of his time concentrating on selling the wealthier children the toy soldiers he painted and the rationed sweets he hoarded. During two years of national service, he saved and borrowed from relatives to open a sandwich shop, but after six weeks his initial brisk trade suddenly disappeared – all three mills around his Oldham shop closed and, lacking the funds to compete with larger businesses, Stafford had no plan B. On the face of it, this sounded familiar – a thriving football club at Valley Parade, but one that, behind the scenes, lacked the funds needed to develop, compete or even consolidate in Division 2? Stafford had been there before.

So, back in the mid-fifties, in a move that would hurt any entrepreneur, he took a job as a foam-cushion salesman. It transformed his life. As the *Telegraph & Argus* said of him in 1995, in a rather darkly apt metaphor, 'Ideas flew from his lips like [sparks from] a Catherine wheel. Many of them were immediately consigned to the rubbish bin, but some were inspirational.' It made him well suited to his new role and he became his firm's best salesman. When the company expanded into Yorkshire, Stafford was appointed, at 24, to head its sales team. Life flourished after he met his wife, Lorna, and he renovated an old house in Harrogate, with the profit from that sale allowing him to set up his own foam-cushion firm, Matgoods.

As I now knew, he would sell out there to establish Tebro Toys in 1971. But Stafford's timing for this move from soft furnishings into toys wasn't great – the seventies was the decade that saw most of Britain's fifty or so toy firms close, or be threatened with closure, due to competition from cheap Asian imports. Tebro suffered like everyone else, but closure was forestalled by a series of fire insurance payouts, and Stafford channelled proceeds for a move into character licensing. At a time when no major international toy maker had any interest in soft toys, Heginbotham acquired successful licences to produce Britain's 1980 Moscow Olympics mascot, Rupert the Bear and ventriloquist Keith Harris's Orville and Cuddles characters. It seemed to work: Tebro's turnover increased by 50 per cent in 1980, then a further 40 per cent in 1981, peaking at £1.8 million.

But by 1983 the major international toy companies were playing catch-up and entering the soft toy market. Inspired by the huge success of Kenner's Care Bears and Hasbro's My Little Pony, multinational marketing teams were now creating advertising-led, storyline-based characters. Before long, bidding wars broke out for the licences, all funded by companies diversifying licensing activity into bedspreads, curtains, wallpaper, clothing, stationery and household accessories. To offset costs licensee lists were closed by the multinationals, with production brought back in-house, then outsourced to developing nations, which practically did away with the rest of the UK's soft toy makers in one sweep of Cinderella's plastic broom.

The blow came hardest to Tebro Toys, who had used their insurance proceeds to specialise in media-generated toys. January, the month of the Harrogate Toy Fair, had always been Tebro Toys' most important month. But in 1985 it was the month they lost a key licence that made up for over half their turnover. Fifty-two-year-old Stafford Heginbotham then suffered a heart attack. Much as he was unable to compete with the larger wholesalers from his little sandwich shop in Oldham, he was now struggling to keep up with the multinational corporations from a little factory in an old mill in Bradford. A replica fur Dusty Bin, and pale green Orville the Duck may be sought-after retro items on eBay today; and, indeed, for a time back in the early eighties they were all the rage – I remember Andrew getting a cuddly Orville duck in Blackpool. But in the new, shiny world of Hasbro Transformers and Fisher-Price airport terminals, they came to look a little tired and wan, and didn't have quite the longevity of their competition.

Any company that loses over half its turnover starts to haemorrhage cash. A more prudent man, with no public profile to keep up, would have immediately laid off over half his workforce. Instead, Stafford continued to pay his 65 staff in the naive hope he might somehow replace this lost business. By May 1985 he knew he'd be unable to pay his workforce beyond the end of that month. Just then he learnt of the costs promotion would bring to Valley Parade. Back at work after his heart attack, he would have no doubt looked up from his desk at a sign that told him, 'There are three types of people . . .'

Stafford knew promotion would bring no riches. The previous season, 1983–84, after the best finish in 26 years – seventh in Division 3 – that summer's increased prices had seen season-ticket sales fall by 40 per cent come the opening day of the 1984–85 season. He told the *Telegraph & Argus* on the morning of the fire, 'I just couldn't believe that after we had been through hell and fire in the summer so few people could turn up. I asked myself, what the hell was all the effort for?'

By the time of the Popplewell Inquiry the Tebro Toys' workforce were on a two-day working week. All the while in Parliament Margaret Thatcher was being implored, in Prime Minister's Question Time, to conclude the Popplewell Inquiry with 'the utmost urgency'. A month after Popplewell's interim report was published, and the inquest concluded with such speed, Stafford Heginbotham met with his creditors. A month after that Tebro Toys called in the receiver. In January 1986 the official receiver wound up the company, saying it had 'a chequered history' and was sustained by non-trading income in the late 1970s. Tebro had racked up debts of £752,204 (or £5 million in today's adjusted terms).

Stafford Heginbotham would sell his shares in Bradford City a year after Popplewell reopened Valley Parade. Having suffered a second heart attack in May 1987, Heginbotham was looking for around £1 million to reflect the club's £3 million net asset value on their return to a stadium rebuilt with public money. Yet despite the club being debt-free and mounting a nascent promotion bid, there were no takers. So he accepted £450,000 from vice-chairman Jack Tordoff in January 1988. Tordoff then received largely the same amount per share as he sold up when the club headed back to Division 3 in 1990, relegated after squandering £2 million from the sale of its three best players, Stuart McCall, John Hendrie and Ian Ormondroyd.

Stafford may have sold up at a distressed price, but he didn't hang about with the proceeds. After Tebro Toys had gone into receivership, the only other notable asset that Heginbotham owned – other than Bradford City – was Pastures, his large nineteenth-century vicarage home, out in Tong, a picturesque village equidistant between Bradford and Leeds and close to the M62 and M621, offering easy access to Wakefield, Huddersfield and Halifax. Ever the networker, Stafford somehow obtained change-of-use planning permission to turn this luxury green-belt home with extensive grounds into a conference-based hotel. As soon as the planning permission was granted Heginbotham received several offers. Yet, despite having reportedly left Valley Parade on health grounds, it seems he was well enough to turn down all parties and take on the conversion of his home into a hotel himself, which he began in late 1987. Two years later the Tong Village Hotel opened.

Having maximised his return potential, months later Heginbotham sold up again. In 1990, in a share transaction deal, he received a million Whitbread shares for his hotel, and moved to Jersey as a tax exile.

So the next time you're having breakfast at the Leeds–Bradford Holiday Inn Express – a 53-room conference hotel, with eight meeting rooms capable of holding 700 guests (220 overnight) – pause for a second to ponder your surroundings. The luxurious 'ivy clad former vicarage . . . with extensive gardens where you can hold your meeting or event on sunny days' was originally built with the £450,000 Stafford Heginbotham received from his sale of Bradford City, which in turn resulted from the windfall of a free new stadium erected after a fire that killed 56 people, providing the lifeline that turned a £20,000 investment in a struggling football club into Whitbread shares that today would be worth £50 million. Not a bad outcome for a man whose two businesses stood on the brink of financial ruin until fire – as Mum told me it so often did – came to his rescue.

In the end Stafford took one risk too many. Keen to improve his quality of life, in April 1995 he was informed a suitable heart had been found, and he flew to London where a transplant was performed at St George's Hospital in Tooting. But his body rejected the drugs needed to support the new heart, and he died two days later, on Friday 21 April, aged 61. His funeral was held in Bradford Cathedral in early May, and he was interred at Undercliffe Cemetery, overlooking Valley Parade where, ten years earlier, 56 others had died.

15

The Popplewell Inquiry Revisited

All this new information led me to re-examine the Popplewell Inquiry transcripts with a fresh eye. We were in row O, three or four rows back from where the flames first broke out, and I had been at the snack bar, of course – but, still, there were only nine rows of seats in total, and it troubled me more and more over the years that I just couldn't remember anyone smoking around us. Mr Justice Popplewell had identified six seats in the front two rows of G Block, where the fire could have started. The first witness called before the inquiry, Leslie Brownlie, had sat in seat I142, and stated he'd not smoked, nor seen anyone else smoking during the game. But then Steven Alcock, who'd sat in I141, admitted that he had smoked that day, before and during the game and that Brownlie had had one too, but he only remembered him smoking before the game. Then there was Brownlie's uncle, Samuel Bennett, who'd been sitting in seat I143, who claimed, after explaining he'd had a recent triple-heart bypass, 'My family still don't think I smoke.' Then Bennett's nephew, who'd sat beside him, stated he had 'had one during the match because I haven't smoked a packet of cigarettes for a week, for months. I know I had one in there. I had two.' But Collins didn't press him very hard on exactly when he might have had them. He thought, possibly early on. On Bennett's left, Phillip Tempest had sat with his father, Alan, in seats I145 and I144. Phillip told the inquiry that although they'd seen Bennett smoke during the match it was not a cigarette, but a pipe. Bennett's uncle, confirmed his nephew, was a pipe smoker. The row behind Bennett corroborated this, but in a way that should have prompted concern not satisfaction. In seat J146 Stephen Wilkinson told the inquiry he noticed an unusual smell of burning plastic, so he'd asked 'if anybody was smoking burning plastic in their pipe', before a man replied, 'Oh, it's not me, but it's under me,' but 'was sort of looking round, to see, you know, as if it was him'. Keith Levitt, who had sat in seat J148, told the inquiry he 'noticed one man in particular looking down earlier', and William Cleworth in seat J145 described how that same man 'seemed to be looking up and down'. Several others reported a burning plastic smell.

Only one man ever publicly stated he saw the cigarette that might have started the fire. On 15 May it was reported in the *Telegraph & Argus* that Czes Pachella saw three men stub their cigarettes out in the same polystyrene cup, which he said they then dropped under the floorboards, where it ignited. Only later, at the inquiry, Czes Pachella, sitting in I149, six seats to Bennett's left, claimed of the reports attributed to him that they were 'jumbled' and insisted, 'I never said that. I never saw anybody ducking cigarettes in any plastic cup.' Not that Popplewell's inquiry probed or cross-examined this – but neither did anybody else. Some people could remember others smoking; some had no memories of people smoking.

Rereading the testimony, it seemed about half the occupants of the seats identified by Popplewell were not regular Bradford fans, but normal people who had just decided to come to the game to celebrate Bradford's promotion. Both Bennett and Brownlie had emigrated to Australia 20 years earlier and were now visiting relatives in Bradford. Although neither had followed the club when they lived locally, they told the inquiry they were keen to see the presentation they'd read about, and they had got tickets to a sold-out stand on the morning of the match, but took none of their relatives with them. Rufus Kolawole, in seat J142, testified aisle seat J141 was empty – the very aisle seat under which flames were first clearly photographed (and featured in the Popplewell interim report). Then, after all other supporter testimony was heard on the opening day of the inquiry, on its penultimate day a Robert Whetherhill was called. He'd bought a ticket the week before, and he too arrived late, and for some reason he was directed by a steward, through a sold-out stand, not to his seat in C Block, but to an empty seat, J141, in the supposedly sold-out G Block. There, a fire started beneath him just minutes later. However, nobody has ever asked questions about these unusual circumstances, and it seems to me that this is exactly the kind of issue a full inquiry should have cleared up.

My re-examination of the forensic testimony also left me with more questions. Dr Woolley of the Fire Research Station agreed he had been 'cautious' about some of his assessments as to what might have caused such ignition, but stated it was only possible to ignite rubbish beneath the stand if there was 'a line of access from the match to that material and the material is not unduly distant from where the match is held'. But it is not quite clear what constitutes a 'line of access'; nowhere is a full definition of 'line of access' given – and here the combustible material would have been a few feet away, beneath wooden floorboards. By the time Popplewell produced his interim report, Dr Woolley was concluding that 'it was perfectly possible that a lighted match dropped through a gap in the floor, could have ignited rubbish and that a lighted cigarette might have done so, although he thought the latter was less likely, on balance.' It made me wonder what had happened to the 'line of access' theory.

At another point Woolley stressed there had to be a significant amount of compressed rubbish for the fire to take in sufficient intensity, but the other forensic expert, Ray Cooke, calculated that the sloping space under the stand where the fire took hold was probably only half-full of litter, which doesn't particularly suggest compressed or highly compacted rubbish. (Groundsman Allan Gilliver also told the inquiry 'there wasn't as much [rubbish] as everyone makes out there was' and that it had been removed during pre-season repairs.) Then there was Woolley finding no evidence of long-term smouldering.

Nothing here definitively ruled one way or the other. On the one hand you could see from the testimony how the rubbish could theoretically have taken light and worked up to an intensity to set fire to the timbers; on the other, nobody could be conclusive on how long this would take, or even whether anyone was actually smoking or not. Dr Woolley's reconstruction seemed to involve dropping a lit match a few feet on to some paper – although that didn't really replicate the conditions of the day. And no one followed up on the handful of mentions of a burning plastic smell, in one case reported as early as 3.20 p.m. Indeed, after the inquiry, but before the release of its findings, Popplewell wrote to Dr Woolley, stating, 'It would be wise at this stage to emphasise not all the questions could be given answers.'

What alarmed me most from my research was a *Telegraph & Argus* article from August 1984. In it West Yorkshire fire commander Ron Phillips had told the paper he was 'very concerned about the high number of commercial and industrial fires' in Bradford and described many of them as being 'of doubtful origin'. His deputy divisional fire officer, Ken Fabian, explained, 'We know for a fact that between 60 and 65 per cent are caused deliberately and it may be as high as 85 per cent.' Often, he believed, the fires resulted from 'the firm setting them off or getting someone else to do it' in order to recover insurance proceeds. Where suspects could not be prosecuted Fabian mentioned that they were logged in West Yorkshire records as 'incendiarism by unknown persons'. The conclusion of the Popplewell interim report was, 'It is quite impossible to determine who caused the fire to start; indeed it would be grossly unfair to point the finger at any one person.' Incendiarism by unknown persons, in other words.

The more I looked at the Popplewell Inquiry the more unanswered questions I had. I looked into how fire investigations today would normally seek to explain fires by mapping scientific explanations on to specific structural layouts and how it was usually done back in the 1980s. Today, computer models are used, but in 1981, after 48 people died in a Dublin nightclub blaze, a full-scale replica of the nightclub was rebuilt in the UK Fire Research Centre hangar in Boreham Wood in Hertfordshire. In the same hangar, barely three years after Bradford, and following the deaths of 31 people in the King's Cross tube station fire, a third-scale replica of the King's Cross escalator was built. Both reconstructions, involving models of foam seating or the trench of an escalator, overturned initial preconceptions of the speed at which fire could spread. But after Bradford, where 56 died in the UK's deadliest land fire in living memory, forensic experts called to the inquiry spoke of the fire in general rather than specific terms, and simply performed an open-air test of dropping matches on to a mound of accessible rubbish. The interim report of the Department of the Environment's Fire Research Station report clearly states, 'It is not entirely clear how exactly the fire started.' And its final report noted, 'Some features of the Bradford fire required a detail of understanding greater than that presented to the formal Inquiry.' The Popplewell Inquiry findings, the Fire Research Station report pointed out, were based on 'video recordings' that did not begin until three minutes into the fire – and so therefore could never have explained its ignition – and on 'a limited study of still photographs'. It stressed that, 'Without the results of a wind-tunnel test it is very difficult to predict the detailed effects [of fire] . . .' There simply wasn't enough time in the Popplewell Inquiry to investigate more fully.

It wasn't long before I came across a document at the Public Records Office in Kew, which stated what the likely outcome of such a test might be. In December 1983, TRADA, the Timber Research & Development Association, had inspected the Main Stand in support of the club's first roof-grant application. TRADA was the one independent body to carry out such an inspection before the fire. It submitted its evidence to the Popplewell Inquiry and concluded, '*It is extremely unlikely that a small source of ignition on its own, say a cigarette in a plastic cup, could have been the primary cause of the ignition of the timber structure* [their emphasis].'

Another issue I thought the Popplewell Inquiry failed to investigate fully because of its remit was the fact that people had been smoking in that stand since 1908. The subsequent report into the King's Cross fire of 1987 noted there'd been 46 fires on London Underground between 1956 and 1958, and 32 of those had been attributed to smokers – one of them being a serious fire at Oxford Circus, which led to an experimental smoking ban in February 1985. But it wasn't quite the same story at football grounds. A week after the fire the *Sunday Telegraph* calculated, bearing in mind there'd been no previous fire at Valley Parade and there were, they anticipated, up to 500 smokers at any time in that stand, odds of 1 in 1,250,000 of a fire being caused by a smoker. The *Sunday Telegraph* were wrong to base their calculations on 50 games a season, but if you amend that to a more realistic average of 26 home games per season, and, working on the assumption that half the population smoked back then, a third of whom would be in the rear seats, that would result in odds of 1 in 2–300,000 over a 17-year period (i.e., the oldest piece of rubbish found in the debris being a newspaper from 1968). Dr Woolley, in a video produced for the Building Research Establishment in November 1987, pointed out it took five attempts to set a pile of rubbish blazing from a spent match head; if those odds of 5 to 1 were applied to smokers in wooden stands over a century of watching football there'd have been a blaze every week before a game even kicked off.

There was also yet another loose thread hanging from the inquiry that I felt had not been adequately explained. PC Leesing, who was standing on the paddock terrace, over 10 metres from the seat of the fire, told the inquiry of an inexplicable 'burning smell in the air, of plastic or rubber' about 'a matter of a minute, two minutes' before anything appeared wrong in G Block. Even at this distance he found this smell was so overpowering and immediate that he 'turned round to one of the youths that was stood by me. I just said, "You're not stubbing your fag out on my coat?"' and explained that PC Knapperley beside him, who was not called to give evidence, 'said the same as I did about the burning plastic. He went a little further down the paddock to speak to a couple of youths [also not called] who were on the floor. They were like us, looking for where this burning plastic [smell] was coming from. It was then that we looked into G Block and noticed smoke.' It was clear to me that such a smell could not have been explained by one plastic cup this distance away. I felt PC Leesing's observations, at the very least, should have prompted alarm, raised suspicion and have been worthy of a more thorough investigation. But this never took place.

Reading the Popplewell Inquiry transcripts, I couldn't help but question whether the basic rules of fire investigation were followed during the Bradford inquiry. Everything I have read over the years suggests that it is standard practice to prove or disprove arson by a detailed reconstruction of events (including, for example, testing scale models). But there was no such reconstruction at Bradford. I also strongly believe that the police interviews should have explored in more detail inconsistencies in eyewitnesses accounts, interviews and statements to develop the lines of inquiry. As far as I am concerned, that did not happen. I think the police should have confronted potential suspects with anomalies, contrasting what they said with what was possible, from inconsistent information. It doesn't seem to me that any such cross-examination took place. And this is all before any line of inquiry moves on to examine possible motives. To quote a Los Angeles Police Department fire investigator in *Blaze, the Forensics of Fire* by Nicholas Faith: 'It's rare to have a coincidence. If we start having multiple coincidences then it's not a coincidence.' It is clear to me that at Bradford, with Stafford Heginbotham in charge, there was a mountain of coincidence.

I began to wonder, bar the Widgery report into Bloody Sunday, had there ever been an inquiry so premature and rushed? One where the terms of reference were so narrow? One where the investigative work was undertaken so quickly and so less thoroughly than a reasonable man would have expected? It was hard to fathom.

Discounting disasters on boats and planes, Bradford had been by far Britain's largest fire in living memory. There had been more fatalities in the Bradford fire than in any other blaze in recent memory – but only just. Bradford had several similarities with the Summerland leisure centre fire of August 1973, on the Isle of Man, in which 50 holidaymakers had died. Superficially, the rickety old wooden stand at Valley Parade and the futuristic, climate-controlled indoor pleasure gardens and amusement arcade on the seafront at Douglas couldn't be more different. One was cramped and dilapidated; the other was spacious and only four years old. But both structures were housing upwards of three thousand people when they burnt to the ground; and both conflagrations took off in no time, following a blaze that got out of hand. At Summerland, kids had been smoking in a disused crazy golf kiosk, and it took the organist, midway through his evening set, to alert holidaymakers to the flames. But no one thought to call the fire brigade for around 15, 20 or possibly even 25 minutes – reports vary as to the precise length of time. And as in the Main Stand at Valley Parade, people had a matter of minutes to get out.

Both fires are termed, now and again, 'forgotten disasters'. Perhaps life is cheap for football fans, or working-class holidaymakers in an all-in camp. At least the public inquiry into the Summerland fire lasted six months; Bradford, as we know, lasted less than six days. The Summerland inquiry also ruled death by misadventure – even though there was a crush and fire exits were found to have been locked – and, again, as with Bradford, no one was prosecuted.

The Isle of Man is a UK dependency, with its own civil service and government in Douglas, and having chosen not to implement Westminster's Fire Precautions Act of 1971, the local fire chief publicly warned of the hazardous conditions of Summerland a matter of days before the blaze. Parliament was rightly critical of the Manx government, but the needless deaths of so many British holidaymakers should have rung alarm bells and spelled out the obvious: any failure to implement safety legislation, or to take heed of the warnings of local authority inspectors, would likely result in disaster. The Safety of Sports Grounds Act was still dragging its way through Parliament at this point; more than a decade later, in West Yorkshire, it was obvious that exactly the same lessons had failed to be learnt.

For me, a *Sunday Times* editorial written the day after Hillsborough best exposed the attitude of the ruling classes in Britain. It spoke of a 'slum sport, watched in slum stadiums by slum people'. That one sentence indicated how out of touch the powers-that-be were. I've watched football with public school boys and council estate lads alike, and all our dads, regardless of their backgrounds, unwittingly and unknowingly entered a world of Jim Crow-style apartheid to allow us simply to watch a couple of hours of football with them every other Saturday.

As the Summerland blaze demonstrated, this institutional neglect wasn't just a problem where football was concerned. Although Bradford saw the biggest loss of life in the UK for a decade, its aftermath coincided with a flurry of disasters in which over a thousand people died. The eighties in Britain became known as the 'disaster decade': there was Bradford and Hillsborough; the Manchester runway, King's Cross and Piper Alpha fires; the Zeebrugge/*Herald of Free Enterprise* and *Marchioness* sinkings; the Kegworth air crash; the Clapham Junction rail crash . . . all are imprinted on the minds of my generation – a series of disasters that had no place in a civilised country; in one governed by the rule of law rather than in the name of Thatcherite deregulation, cost-cutting efficiency and profit. Valley Parade was the first in this line of disasters, and I have little doubt that had more of the truth of the fire come out 30 years ago a different political culture, one which had learnt the lessons of the past, would now be in place.

The Popplewell Inquiry Revisited

The echo of similar sentiment in present-day Conservative party circles has finally prompted me to write this story. Those who fail to learn the lessons of history are doomed to repeat them. My story is simply the story of thousands of innocents who went about their daily business in the expectation they'd be safe and looked after – and if not, then those responsible would be brought to book. That TV lottery finger which claims 'it could be you' has a hidden hand; disaster could touch you as suddenly and unexpectedly as it touched me. Unless, that is, we make clear our safety is not up for sale at any price again.

Just as this book was going to press, the 30-year rule saw the release of government papers covering both the Bradford and Heysel disasters. Unsurprisingly, while the latter document runs to a thousand pages, the Bradford file is a somewhat slimmer affair, coming in at 40 pages, half of which, on closer examination, are made up of letters of condolence received from a variety of world leaders, from as far afield as Ghana, Portugal and various Arab nations. There's also Oxford United chairman Robert Maxwell's letter to Margaret Thatcher, strangely echoing much of what Stafford Heginbotham said he told the prime minister in his phone call the morning after the fire; and a two-page statement prepared for the prime minister on her return to Downing Street from Chequers which, it transpires, she declined to read out. She had made a statement on the Saturday night, talking of her grief and expressing sympathy to families affected, and then elaborated upon that on the Sunday evening, but it's curious that the largest loss of life from a single disaster in living memory would warrant no official statement from the prime minister in Parliament.

Further notes in the file ask, 'How far were Bradford City football club warned about the fire risk of their stand?' and, while 50 bodies lay unidentified in a mortuary on that Saturday night, wondered, 'Should all professional football clubs be required to bring their facilities up to the "designated" standards?' Someone hadn't been listening to Lord Justice Wheatley 13 years earlier.

The released file also appears to include a direct violation of the democratic principle of the separation of power between the executive, legislature and judiciary. There's a memo to the prime minister, written by her private secretary, Charles Powell, which advises, 'The Lord Chancellor be urged ("told") to find a suitable judge.'

The final letter of condolence was added to the collection on the Monday, two days after the fire; and the file doesn't appear to have been accessed again following the inclusion of a thank-you letter from the chief constable of West Yorkshire received on 22 May 1985. It seems crystal clear Margaret Thatcher had chosen to wash her hands of the entire affair . . .

Back in 1974, as a result of the inquiry into the Summerland fire, building regulations concerning flammable materials were radically redrawn. After Bradford, Mr Justice Popplewell, although proposing significant amendments to the existing crowd control regulations, only made one new crowd safety recommendation directly as a result of the Bradford fire: that no further wooden stands would be constructed. However, no one had constructed new wooden stands at sports grounds for decades. In my view this was an apposite outcome for an inquiry that devoted just 27 pages of its interim report to the specifics of the Bradford fire and a mere two pages of it to summarising the likely causes. It seems clear to me that, although such a significant loss of life deserved a lengthy investigation, the institutional neglect of the government meant Popplewell wasn't tasked with such an inquiry nor given sufficient time to undertake any kind of detailed inquiry.

Instead, we had an inquiry that in my view started way too soon after the date of the fire . . . an inquiry that relied too heavily on limited expert evidence and video footage that started to roll three minutes after smoke was first seen rising up from beneath the seats where the fire started . . . an inquiry that was not responsible for cross-examining conflicting accounts of basic issues like time and place in more detail . . . an inquiry that was only able to deal with very detailed matters in general rather than specific terms . . . an inquiry that considered at the same time both the deaths of 56 people in a fire in an unsafe football stand and the death of one individual at another stadium where football hooliganism caused a wall to collapse . . . an inquiry with such a limited timeframe and remit that it was never going to deal with the forensic causes of the fire in a way that they had been dealt with in public inquires in similar incidents such as the King's Cross fire . . . an inquiry that, given the extent of the conflicting testimony, for me raised as many questions as it answered.

After all this it proved impossible to regain any momentum in my life. Although I resat my audit exam in March 2007 and emerged with a distinction, I was so far through my ACA qualification that many firms shut their doors to me. Then, on April 18 that year, as I was working with the *Telegraph & Argus* on a front-page story to get a video of the fire withdrawn from the All4Humor.com website, I suddenly remembered it was Andrew's birthday. Mum told me how upset and disappointed she was with me for forgetting. I spent the night in a bar on Lavender Hill, knocking back after-hours tequila shots till 3 a.m. Brushing my teeth that Saturday morning, the inevitable happened. I had another seizure, my first since 2002. This time my face turned blue before the paramedics arrived with oxygen. My flatmate John saved my life by making that call. A week later, I joined a small firm in Islington to finish my ACA, a world away from the high-flying PricewaterhouseCoopers fast track. Then, within a year, the 'Great Recession' started and all the career doors began to shut.

That summer, I was at the second day of England v India at Trent Bridge with friends from Warwick. Sitting at the back of the open Hound Road Stand, a man in the seats used his lighter to try to ignite candles on his girlfriend's My Little Pony birthday cake. I watched his frustrations grow, as the wind blowing into the stand, much as it did on 11 May 1985, left him unable to ignite his candles. After a couple of minutes he gave up. His girlfriend told him he couldn't 'help the weather'. Indeed, he could not, and I told Ben we'd just seen an excellent example of why we should ask more questions about the ignition of the Bradford fire. I'd seen my own wind tunnel test in action, and its results were clear. Because football fans understandably believed a disaster in their ramshackle ground was an accident waiting to happen, nobody saw fit to question it properly when it did happen.

16

Fletcher 56

Over the years I've sometimes reflected on how sad it was that Stuart McCall's father, Andy, a former professional footballer himself, never saw his son play again after 11 May 1985. McCall Snr had been in the burning stand, but was dragged out before spending time in the Pinderfields burns unit. He survived, but could never bring himself to step inside a football ground again. McCall was only 20 at the time of the fire, and he went on to have a lengthy league career that took in Everton, Rangers and Scotland, a career bookended by nearly 400 appearances at Valley Parade. One of his teammates that day was former Leeds United hard man and future Bradford boss, Terry Yorath. I recall him in tears, at the charity match a fortnight after the fire, telling my mum how his children were seated near us in G Block. As it was such a time of raw emotion we didn't twig back then just how literally Terry meant. But 20 years later, reading his daughter Gabby Logan's account in *The Times* of her and her sister wearing pastel suits – their 'best togs because there was to be a bit of a "do" afterwards in the players' lounge' – the penny dropped, and I realised who'd been sitting near me and Andrew. Well, I still couldn't quite believe that was the BBC's Gabby Logan I'd seen in the corridor, but it would have made sense – she'd got out ahead a minute or so before the fire, keen to beat the crush and pick up some crisps and sport mixtures on the way to the clubhouse – and when I saw a photo of her with her sister Louise in the *Daily Mail* from 1985 I immediately recognised her sister, now a dancer, even 25 years on. Daniel Yorath, who was zigzagging down that corridor, died tragically young, seven years after the fire, aged just 15, playing football in the garden with his dad.

Fifty-Six

Talking of the 56 who went out that day to watch a football match but never came home again, Gabby Logan concluded, 'I feel their story was forgotten too quickly by the world of football, with the disasters that would follow.'

A few days after the fire, once my personal news blackout had ended, Mum let me sift back through a week's papers. I pulled up short on seeing one story in a local paper: it was of the lovely bubbly blonde girl from the B Block snack bar, who would always give me a smile and who had told me to have a good summer. Moira Hodgson would have been 16 the day after the fire. For years, I kind of kidded myself that it couldn't be so, until practically three decades later a chance conversation with another boyhood admirer confirmed that yes, she'd gone.

It never leaves you, the kaleidoscope of scenes, memories, images from the day: the blazing stand, the panic to get out, the scenes from that corridor, just prior to and just after the smoke came down – they're seared into my consciousness; literally the stuff of nightmares to this day. But there are other memories too: our players – including striker John Hawley, centre-back Dave Evans, Greg Abbott and captain Peter Jackson – staying on the pitch to drag people from the burning stand; the immense bravery of fans who just went to a game and ended up pulling people out and running for their lives from a burning stand; the gallery of burnt policemen sitting in a row in the ambulance; the kindness of those who helped, like Margaret; and then there were people like Mr Hudson – Eric – whom I'd lain next to on the pitch, and who had been so calm and dignified, and no trouble to anyone. And there was Mum, who took on the club and the local authority and won, which resulted in the multimillion-pound settlement for 110 people and 44 police and fire officers – at the time, the largest civil action in history. And following that she somehow managed to rebuild a new life for herself too.

My grandma was hit incredibly hard as well, of course. She lost her two sons, her husband and one grandchild. She said afterwards that she knew Dad and Uncle Peter, and Granddad and Andrew too, were all dead '. . . three or four hours after the fire, as I knew how they were, how I'd raised them. If they were in danger they'd have found some way of getting a message home . . . if they could.' Cousin Chris later told me she'd broken down on that dreadful Monday lunchtime, and there were dark days in later years. But I try to remember the strong woman she was, and the good times.

Two thousand people stood in Centenary Square on 11 May 2010 for the 25th annual memorial service. The memorial itself was gated off, and red carpets led to two temporary stands of leather-backed chairs, tickets for which were sent out in advance. The Archbishop of York, Dr John Sentamu, looked out over a sea of claret and amber and said, 'Every community that forgets its memories becomes senile, so you, the city of Bradford, do well to remember the Bradford City fire disaster.'

Personally, I felt this city had been treated like a senile patient, unable to handle the truth. After the service, seeing I was uncomfortable with religious sermons, the Archbishop took me aside. 'It's good that it hurts . . . it should hurt, there,' he said, gently prodding my heart. 'If it didn't hurt there it would mean they no longer mattered to you as they'd no longer be in your heart. So hope that it never stops hurting, as that hurt means they're with you. Always!'

Later that afternoon, at 3 p.m., Bradford City club chaplain Paul Deo held a memorial service at Valley Parade. He told us we were not just talking of a number, or a list of names, like the national or local media were, but of people who carried meaning to us all – before reading through the names and pausing by each one, staying silent to let us absorb the moment, the person, and then moving on, and then repeating this process 56 times. He informed us that the club had opened all areas to us so that we could be alone with our thoughts. Mum left me alone in the stand. Having taken four of the 56 small budding claret flowers the club provided, I perched one on the upright back of the plastic seat on my left and three on the seats to my right. As I looked out on the pitch

I remembered our final half-hour together – the jokes we'd played, the promises we'd made, and the dire football we'd watched. It had been my final half hour of childhood.

Then a few minutes before 3.40 p.m., I went to the back of the stand, this time to meet Mum. I remembered how, 25 years earlier, we'd watched the smoke grow as the block ahead emptied. Then, after two minutes I left, turning back to smile at Mum from the end of the row, before heading to the street-level row where the corridor once was. I briefly paused where I'd been trapped, then walked briskly to where the turnstiles had been, paused for a few seconds more, before quickly walking to where I believed the E Block stairwell was once located. Climbing down, over and along each row, I retraced my jagged dash to the halfway line, until I reached a small pitch-side wall, then jumped over it, paused on the running track to look left, and briskly walked across the pitch.

That evening Paul Deo held a further service in Bradford Cathedral. This time, as he read the 56 names out from the cathedral's dais, he invited those present to lay 56 candles on the altar floor. As we were in the front row, Paul invited us to lay the first candles but, as shyness saw a lack of volunteers, I kept going back until a queue of half a dozen had formed. Paul said, 'Andrew John Fletcher, aged 11 of East Bridgford, Nottinghamshire,' as I walked up with my final candle, then, as I bent down to place it on the altar floor, 'John Fletcher, aged 34 of East Bridgford, Nottinghamshire,' and I blew that candle a kiss. Sitting back down, looking at each of the tiny 56 candles flickering, I realised they took up little more space than the bodies in that corridor, where 43 had died. Staring at them, in such a confined space, it was hard to understand how I'd not been a 57th candle.

The sculptor of the Centenary Square memorial, Joachim Reisner, and his wife had sat behind us. At the end of the service she asked for a hug, telling me how brave I was and how moving it was to see me lay the candles. I told Joachim that he should be very proud of his work, and his eyes filled with tears. The sculpture is a thing of great beauty; it's intricate but simple, with three figures and 56 names inlaid into bronze. Like with all great art, I appreciate it more each time I see it. Placed as it is, in the heart of Bradford, it's nice to think it will be there for all time.

The autumn following the 25th anniversary I ran the Bradford half-marathon and raised £4,000 for the burns unit, on the weekend after what should have been Dad's sixtieth birthday. That spring I had also met David Conn of the *Guardian*, as we worked on a 25th anniversary feature. He told me that such was the accepted, established view of the fire that'd I'd only be able to take one step at a time. Which was fair enough, and I was pleased from the resulting piece to see that where coroner James Turnbull in the summer of 1985 had instructed the inquest jury to not 'imply criticism suggesting that any particular person should be criminally liable or liable to civil proceedings' in this article he also told David Conn, 'It crossed my mind to consider manslaughter . . . it is difficult to make a corporate body liable, but with the warnings they had it was very close. Ultimately I thought misadventure was more appropriate, and the jury came to that conclusion.' But even if the coroner had privately considered other options, to me it seemed just one small step. I was still disappointed and frustrated at the slow pace of overturning the established view of the fire. Although I later saw that David was right; a bird can fly only so far each day, and I thanked him for his powerful and moving piece.

A year later I picked up Ian Ridley's history of how two decades of the Premiership had transformed football, *There's a Golden Sky*. At the beginning of chapter 7, 'The Unforgettable Fire', Ridley talked of how the Bradford fire marked 'the beginning of the end of probably the most brutal decade in English football'. He also mentioned how, as news filtered through to the press box he was in that afternoon, '. . . we even joked, shamefully, in hindsight, that the chairman had probably torched the grandstand on the last day of the season to claim the insurance money for a new one'. That was before the reporters had realised there were casualties, though I never really understood why, on the contrary, the human cost didn't spur writers on to really dig that bit deeper.

That October I watched a parliamentary debate on the release of cabinet papers surrounding the Hillsborough disaster. The debate in turn prompted Oliver Popplewell to write a letter to *The Times*, in which he regurgitated his sentiment that had so angered me on the 20th anniversary of Bradford: 'The citizens of Bradford behaved with quiet dignity and great courage,' he believed. 'They did not harbour conspiracy theories. They did not seek endless further inquiries. They buried their dead, comforted the bereaved and succoured the injured. They organised a sensible compensation scheme and moved on. Is there a lesson there for the Hillsborough campaigners?' he wondered.

Unsurprisingly it provoked outrage on Merseyside. Local MP Steve Rotheram described it as a 'load of drivel' and 'unbelievable'. 'To mention other tragedies simply because they are football related, as if there is some common denominator because they happened in football stadiums, it beggars belief,' he concluded. But there were similarities, of course.

Steve Rotheram made contact via Linked-In, then over the phone apologised, explaining how he'd now read my 2005 *Guardian* article – raising the notion of institutional neglect, and wondering how the Popplewell Inquiry reached its conclusion in just five days – saying he'd had no idea. I told him not to worry, stressed we were on the same side and that I had unfinished business with Popplewell, whose attack I wouldn't let stand. That night I texted David Conn at the *Guardian*, and the following lunchtime David filed a lead story that provoked a Twitter storm, but I was not a little boy any more, happy to stand around while people threw misinformed opinions about.

Weeks later, after prime minister David Cameron claimed Hillsborough campaigners were 'like a blind man, in a dark room, looking for a black cat that isn't there', I met with Steve Rotheram in Parliament. Sitting on the terrace outside the House of Commons I suggested a likely candidate for Bradford's black cat, showing him newspaper articles of Stafford Heginbotham's fires. If Bradford had been investigated properly, perhaps the issue of fencing, the one issue in clear need of review, might not have been ignored – then there might never have been a Hillsborough. Steve later fixed me up with my local MP, shadow justice secretary Sadiq Khan, who was so startled by what I told him he missed the State Opening of Parliament.

Sadiq finally asked, 'What do you want?'

What I was arguing for, I told him, was almost certainly not included in any official documentation, so it wasn't a case of disclosure – just that a competent police force would, given the financial circumstances of Stafford Heginbotham and his past, surely have conducted a criminal investigation. Yet there is no evidence to say they did, and I wanted to know why.

Sadiq put his hand on my shoulder and said, 'Can I just say I'm very sorry for your loss . . . You're one of mine, but I don't have the sufficient locus. We need someone from Bradford.'

I immediately grimaced, telling him, 'The people of Bradford don't want to know – they never have.'

'You need to speak to Gerry Sutcliffe,' said Sadiq. 'He's been around for years, he's a guy we all look up to, a former sports minister, whose Bradford through and through.'

'He won't want to know,' I assured him.

'He will, trust me.'

I knew he wouldn't, but agreed to Sadiq's suggestion that I put forward the questions I wanted answers to in a document for Sutcliffe. Although I had no belief he'd act on them, the mere fact that Sadiq had given me his time meant the least I could do was bow to his knowledge and experience. So over the weekend of my 39th birthday I wrote a series of questions I knew most of the answers to, totalling 5,000 words. After returning from a holiday over Christmas and New Year, there was no response from Gerry Sutcliffe. I chased Steve Rotheram and twice emailed Sutcliffe, but he did not even reply to my emails, let alone meet me. I'd always believed he'd do nothing, but the extent of that nothing surprised even me.

In mid-September 2012 the Hillsborough Independent Panel released its final report. As I watched Steve Rotheram declare on LFC TV that the document was the closest to the truth we were ever likely to get over Hillsborough (at that stage), I texted him: 'The people of Merseyside are blessed to have the MPs they do. Congratulations on all your efforts in universally establishing what some of us always knew or suspected.'

At midnight I received a reply, 'Thanks, Martin. I wish you every success in your continued fight for justice. I never thought the day would come. Never give up. Best wishes, Steve.'

I never would.

Among the 450,000 Hillsborough panel documents was a two-page South Yorkshire Police memo written by a Superintendent Nettleship to a chief superintendent Wain, dated 5 May 1989. It followed Nettleship's meeting with the Humberside Assistant Chief Constable Charlesworth, formerly of West Yorkshire Police. They'd been in touch because, after Bradford, Charlesworth had prepared 'proof of evidence on behalf of the chief constable' in the initial West Yorkshire police investigation into the fire. This was essentially the role Wain was about to perform at Hillsborough.

Nettleship noted that the Popplewell Inquiry 'despite the circumstances' only lasted for seven days and was described very much as a '"seat of the pants" affair'. He also observed that 'the manner in which tribunals deal with evidence is entirely different to a Court of Law. Once a witness is able to verify a particular point, the enquiry then moves on to the next subject . . . with a result that there is a "severe pruning" of witnesses.' He stressed using the 'minimum number of witnesses' to 'verify a specific point', emphasising how 'It would be clearly impossible for us to examine ALL the documents available in the time available.' He suggested that 'good liaison between the police and the solicitors acting for the tribunal is probably one of the most important aspects to be considered' before concluding that, as far as Bradford had been concerned, 'It was considered that by "pre-empting" the criticism which was likely to be made by the tribunal, this would effectively "defuse" the situation.'

As he compared the two inquiries, Superintendent Nettleship added the seemingly regretful rider that although his points confirmed 'what we have already learned ourselves in recent days . . . obviously there are differences, the main one being that West Yorkshire conducted their own investigation into the cause of the disaster, without the involvement of an outside force.' However, this document revealed the root of such an approach lay in Bradford.

A new inquiry? I wouldn't go back to a casino that had cheated me – similarly, why engage with a system that has done the same? Thirty years on, I think the only thing a new inquiry could achieve would be to, as Lord Salmon indicated, restore a sense of public confidence. A sense that maybe the world has moved on, that no future public inquiry would last just a working week, that just maybe the political climate might possibly have changed – although, as I've mentioned, with the current government we could be sleepwalking complacently towards another disaster.

I was 12 when this story began; 27 when I seriously started researching it. I'm 42 now, and have had 30 years of this. I can't see justice being seriously delivered; I've no wish to be dragged into an attritional fight. I wouldn't mind having my life back.

'And finally . . .'
  'Number 3 . . .'
  'Bradford City . . .'
  'Will play . . .'
  'Number 1 . . .'
  'Arsenal . . .'

The tie was to be played on 11 December 2012.

'Well, trust your dad to find a way to spend your birthday with you,' was Mum's line.

A week or two later, a taxi dropped me and Ben off on the Midland Road. As I jumped out I was struck by how the tall, slim floodlights of my childhood pierced the mist of the wintry night, but where they once dwarfed the stands, they now seemed small next to them. As we queued at the Midland Road turnstiles I turned my back on its scrum to look out on the lit valley and up to Hanson Grammar School, where I imagined Dad looking down as a child, and hoping he now looked down on my return.

'The foreigners don't fancy it,' Ben said, as we looked out on a white, frosted skating rink of a pitch, Arsenal clearly wary of conditions underfoot as Bradford pressed them like men possessed.

''Course they don't, and that's what this place was always built on,' I told him with relish. 'You're at the bottom of the valley now, lad, and cold air sinks.'

A quarter of an hour in, Bradford City won a free kick in a similar position to where David Wetherall had headed home to beat Liverpool 12 years earlier. 'This is the Arsenal position to concede, mate, this is not good,' I told Ben, just before Garry Thompson powered in a header from a cross to put Bradford 1–0 up.

A policeman then walked along the platform behind the back row and asked, 'You an Arsenal fan?' He was clearly confused, as if he recognised me from somewhere.

'Am now,' I laughed. I explained I had been a City fan, that they were my family's club, but then the fire happened.

There was a faint smile of recognition. '"Then the fire happened",' the officer repeated, ruefully shaking his head, before walking away.

Arsenal, for all their territorial and possession domination, did not, until the final 20 minutes when superior fitness showed, look worthy of an equaliser. They hadn't had a shot on target, but then with a certain inevitability Thomas Vermaelen headed in in the 88th minute and it seemed Arsenal would go on to win, but for a string of excellent saves from Matt Duke and steadfast Bradford defending to take the game to penalties, which Bradford City ultimately won 4–2 to reach their first semi-final in 102 years.

As the team went on its lap of honour I sat on the back of my seat, exhausted. As the fans in the other stands happily twirled their claret and amber scarves, I laughed at how Dad had got me back to witness the rebirth of his football club. Looking out over the stand opposite, to our old C Block seats, I'd have given anything to be there celebrating my 40th with my 62-year-old dad, 60-year-old uncle and 38-year-old brother, but then I looked right over to G Block, to where my ghosts were.

Ben had gone, and the Arsenal fans too, but I lingered a while after the final whistle, breathing in the smell of the fresh, wet grass. No one moved me out of the stadium; a friendly steward smiled.

The next morning I headed to the Centenary Square for 9.25 a.m., the moment I was born 40 years earlier. It was deserted. There were three wreaths around the memorial to mark birthdays not celebrated for some 28 years. I clutched on to one of the memorial's three frost-covered figurines and glanced up at City Hall. I accepted that this was not my city, not my life – that had all been robbed from me. I wasn't sure if I'd be coming up again, and a part of me thought it would be nice for the last memory to be a happy one. Then it suddenly dawned on me that, despite it all, Dad had engineered Bradford City into my DNA. I saw how, only last night, they'd taken on incredible odds to beat the establishment in Arsenal by believing in their cause, pressing and battling, never giving up, despite the stature of those before them. I turned 40 and ran my finger over each Fletcher and wiped the frost away.

It had never occurred to me to go to the semi-final against Aston Villa, but come the final whistle of the first leg I was as delirious and disbelieving in front of the TV as anyone inside Valley Parade. I told Mum on the phone that part of me realised that night that I would always be a Bradford City fan. It was my home, it was where I came from.

Two days later, convinced Bradford would reach Wembley, Ben confirmed he could get us a free pair of Gold Club Wembley seats from his brother-in-law. A bit like with Dad's promise of season tickets for 1981–82, the only hitch was, whatever happened, we'd have to go. Even if that meant watching Aston Villa in the Capital One Cup final.

During the first half of the second leg, I defiantly hollered, 'C'mon City,' as Villa seemed like they'd sweep all before them with Christian Benteke's 24th-minute opener. Then, ten minutes into the second half, James Hanson headed home from a corner to put Bradford City 4–2 up on aggregate. With the away goal nullified and the Villa storm over I felt we were safe.

This truly was English football's most remarkable tale. Bradford City, the first ever fourth division team to reach a major Wembley Cup final, and only the third fourth-tier European team to ever reach a major domestic final. It would gain the club global recognition, with articles in both the *Miami Herald* and *USA Today*. And one thing made it all the more remarkable still. As I watched BBC's *Look North*, live from Valley Parade, one jubilant fan shouted, 'I said we'd do it – we'd do it for the 56 – and we did.' Another on a coach to Villa Park said, 'We'll do it for them who went to a celebration never to return.' I ordered my Cup final shirt that day – an original claret-and-amber hooped 1903 Toffs replica shirt with FLETCHER 56 on the back. If they could not be there in person they would be so in spirit. Mine was not an isolated view, as Bradford City later announced they'd walk out with '56 Always With Us' on the fronts of their black Nike track jackets. This so moved Mum she ordered one to wear as she watched the final on TV at home.

In the week before the final the spotlight fell on both the club and its tragic fire. I gave Daniel Taylor, the *Guardian*'s chief football writer and an old Junior Reds school friend, match-report quotes; then, just three days before the final, the *Observer* called to request an interview, telling me how sympathetic their news editor was to my views. After that, club chaplain and stadium announcer Paul Deo asked on Facebook if the media had been in touch, as he'd had calls in York: 'I've had the *Daily Mirror* on at me asking for your number . . . I do wonder what their angle is sometimes.'

I called him and told him about the critical nature of my *Guardian* pieces but reassured him this wasn't the time, that anything I had to say could wait for another day. The last thing I wanted to do was to be responsible for spoiling Bradford City's biggest occasion in 102 years.

'Great, that's how we all feel,' he said.

'I know. It's how all Bradford City fans feel.'

Determined to spend Cup final day with the fans, I met Ben at the Globe on Baker Street at midday. I arrived early, layered up, a black jumper under my new 1903 jersey, a Bradford City '56 Always With Us' track jacket on proud display, wearing a black cap on which a giant eagle soared. I took my jacket off, to display my FLETCHER 56 shirt. I could sense eyes on me. 'Everyone thinks you look like a total maverick!' said Ben. As I edged my way through the pub to the toilets, some other fans recognised me, and nodded respect. It was the same in the Green Man, the main staging post for Bradford City fans that day, which was packed. In the ground, I nodded to John Helm, further along our row, and then turned round to see a man in the disabled section looking directly at me, who winked. I could get used to this; it felt great – part of a community. Perhaps this was what making peace with the club, with aspects of the past, felt like.

The only problem was Swansea City hadn't read the script, and started fluidly zipping the ball around on the vast Wembley turf. As Nathan Dyer shot Swansea into a 16th-minute lead, Michu added a second and suddenly the game was up. We headed to Club Wembley's Gold Bar to drown our sorrows on bar stools overlooking the distant City of London. As we watched Dyer put Swansea 3–0 up in the 48th minute we decided to finish our second beers. I went to the toilet a few minutes later, and a Bradford fan asked, 'All right, Fletch?'

'It's like everyone knows me but no one wants to say anything to me,' I confided to Ben back in the bar.

'Well, what can they say, Fletch?'

Then, in the 56th minute (of all minutes), Matt Duke conceded a penalty and was sent off. I paced the Gold Bar, and put my head in my hands.

But back in our seats the 31,000 Bradford fans were waving their sea of claret and amber flags and they never stopped. Chairman Mark Lawn stood up in the Royal Box to applaud them. In the face of adversity the fans stood tall to a man, strong, defiant and proud, knowing we'd get to fight another day. They celebrated the moment like they were 4–0 up not 4–0 down – this was in the moment, for the moment. It must have transmitted to our ten men as Swansea were kept at bay until scoring a fifth in injury time, then gave our players a guard of honour at full time. As our players collected their medals I shouted at how proud they'd done us and the 56. Two blonde women, sat with their mum and two children, hugged me as they left, one telling me, 'Love you, Fletch,' and another, 'We think you're great,' but as I turned for a chat they were gone.

The night ended with me talking to a 20-year-old called Rosie, a lovely blonde student from York University, dressed in a smart claret overcoat. We agreed our fans had done the 56 proud. I looked into her eyes and told her, 'We're going to wake up tomorrow and we'll see that the whole world knows we've got the best fans in the world.'

In the 90 seconds it took for a flashover to become a total conflagration, 50 fans were publicly documented as having saved a life, and received police commendations for bravery. Many of them went on to save several lives, and some, having escaped, kept going back into the stand to save others, quite a few ending up hospitalised as a result. Like ten-year-old Joanne Hill, for instance, who somehow managed to help an old man over the pitch wall, despite being seriously burned herself; or Phil Shaw,

Mick Bland and their mate Martin, who repeatedly went back in to the inferno to help people out. Yet none of them ever claimed to have done anything extraordinary or different; 'anyone would have done the same' was the overriding message. It was the same for Dad's friend Colin Butterworth, who didn't receive any commendation, but managed to get an old man over two walls on his way out of the stand. On the pitch the man's son thanked Colin for having saved his dad's life. But Colin, like so many others, simply told him he did what had to be done. That hundreds did not die was testament to the bravery of many like Colin.

I arrived in Bradford again on the morning of 11 May 2013 proudly wearing my '56 Always With Us' track jacket. Colin, now in his early seventies, was there, as usual, with his wife Mavis. They had been my pillars of support, and later told me how happy it would have made Dad to have seen me reconciled with the club. In a moving service Rev. Jimmy Hinton spoke of a total darkness he could only compare to being in a coal shaft that fell on the city 28 years earlier and that still hung over it like a pall. He spoke of both the 'darkness of betrayal' and the 'darkness of injustice'. However, he assured us, a light would find a way to penetrate this darkness, and that this light would be the truth.

After laying our wreaths I defiantly sang 'Abide With Me' with a senior West Yorkshire police officer, who patted me on my back and later shook my hand in the Lord Mayor's Chambers. There, I talked with Bradford City manager Phil Parkinson and, after explaining how I'd come back for my 40th, joked that of all the miracles he'd performed that year, making a Bradford City fan of my mum had topped the lot!

Bradford had only been to Wembley once in 90 seasons, yet the following Saturday we were back there for the second time in three months, this time for the League Two play-off final, which saw Bradford City take a 3–0 lead over Northampton to end the contest a third of the way in. In the 56th minute 24,000 City fans stood to proudly applaud the 56 they'd never forget. Captain that day, Gary Jones, would later tell the *Yorkshire Post*, 'The memorial service was something special and by winning promotion I think we have made 56 people very proud. Maybe they were looking down on us. One thing I am sure about is that there will have been relatives in the crowd who lost loved ones in the fire. That is why I want to dedicate this promotion to them.' Even the *New York Times* championed the occasion, and Rob Hughes opened with, 'If ever something in sports could be a metaphor for life and the human spirit it would be named Bradford City A.F.C.'

That spirit can never die and it's why I resolve that my love of life and belief in tomorrow will overpower those who've dragged me back into the orbit of an unresolved past for three decades now. Life will forever be lived in the moment, for the moment, just as my Dad would have wanted. I, of all people, know just how suddenly such moments can end. In the final analysis I see that the only thing in life we don't have in passing is our love, as that's ours to keep for ever. So wherever life takes me, I'll always cheer Bradford City on, just as Dad always wanted: for the 56. May they rest in peace.

Acknowledgements

It's impossible when writing the story of your life to thank everyone individually who has had an influence on such a very personal journey, especially when you've been lucky enough to have as many great friends as I have over the years. However, if you're not named I can assure you that you do know who you are, as you were there when it mattered most.

As I look back on my life I realise how blessed I was to be raised in Birstall, a community a mile closer to Bradford than Leeds. I'd like to thank all those we knew at Birstall County school on Chapel Lane, Birstall Youth Club and Howden Clough JFC for such happy memories that I'll always look back on with such great fondness – you'll always know the real me best.

I'd also like to thank my many friends in Nottinghamshire and Nottingham Forest FC for their support. In the end I loved my time at Toot Hill, which is rightly considered an outstanding Ofsted school today, and the very many friends I made there who, in the end, by never mentioning the fire, made my teenage years as close to normal as I could have ever hoped for.

Great thanks to the University of Warwick, where I rediscovered myself. It's hard to imagine what life would have been like without my best friend Ben Livermore, but it would have been a hell of a lot less fun, that's for sure. Twenty years on, we're still in touch with Andy Lodge, William Battle, Steve Newberry, Adam Cullen, Sudipta Sarkar and Paul Hurst. Through them I truly found a life free of my past. Who says you can't find answers at the bottom of a glass? We found plenty!

Then life moved to London. John Arthey's been the best friend and housemate over that time anyone could have hoped for – a rock. Duncan

Ironmonger, Simon Gillies, Dan Balmforth, Hamish and Rita Allan, and Carl Allen: thanks for such great times and for suffering with me as I put this all together.

At Bloomsbury I'd like to thank Charlotte Atyeo and David Daley for their unstinting support in ensuring we had the platform on which to write this book. Many thanks too to my agent David Luxton for his sage advice in making it all happen, and to the man without whose support over many years none of it could have ever proved possible: my very own Quincy Jones and editor, Ian Preece. Also many thanks to Simon Inglis for both his time and valuable counsel and to Nathan at the North Street Deli in Clapham for providing a Saturday retreat to write in. If he'd opened on Sundays the entire book would have been written there!

In Miami I'd like to thank Stefanie Huber for inspiring me to want to be the best person I could possibly be and, in doing so, finally be free of all this. You truly did prove my angel.

Of course the greatest thanks must go to the woman without whom none of this journey could have proved possible, and her steadfast refusal to let one day in my childhood define or limit my entire life – my mum. God knows how, but we did it, together. Also great thanks to Richard for all his help and support of us both since 1990.

Finally, this book is in no way a criticism of Bradford City today or its wonderful fans. Indeed, I'd like to thank its current owners, Mark Lawn and Julian Rhodes – like all of us childhood fans of the club (and just 24 and 16 at the time of the fire) – for being such great custodians in remembering 11 May 1985 and for how they are currently rebuilding a true club. I've had the pleasure of experiencing the unique bond they've built at a club currently vying for a League 1 play-off spot on its current FA Cup run, being warmly embraced by old school-friends Anton Edwards and Nigel Ward and new friends like Kathryn Hey and Les Hall as we beat Chelsea 4-2 at Stamford Bridge, and then Sunderland 2-0 at a full and bouncing Valley Parade to reach the quarter-finals for the second

Acknowledgements

time in 95 years. I just hope we soon have more Wembley appearances to enjoy together.

I had previously stopped coming as I felt my discoveries were inconsistent with being a fan; I now know that was wrong. May the truth set you free, they say, and it's in that search for personal freedom I wrote. Oh, and OK, Dad, you win – one last word: CTID.

Author's Note

A question I've often been asked – and undoubtedly will be again many more times in the future now – is, 'Where did you find all this information?' The true surprise lies in how accessible it all is from the public record. As they say, the devil is often in the detail . . .

As regards the fire itself, I primarily relied upon the testimonies provided in the Popplewell Inquiry transcripts, which are stored at the Fire Service College in Moreton-in-Marsh in the Cotswolds. These made up a substantial part of the raw material for Part Two of the book, but I also drew on the evidence and reports submitted to that inquiry by the Fire Brigades Union, West Yorkshire Police, the Fire Research Station, TRADA, and from the Royal Commission Report on Tribunals of Inquiry by Lord Justice Salmon, also stored there. *Hansard* from 13 May 1985 also proved useful, as did the 1999 book *Aberfan: Government and Disasters* by Iain McLean and Martin Johnes.

The British Newspaper Library in Colindale, now transferred to Boston Spa, and the News Room at the British Library in St Pancras, proved a treasure trove. I read all the contemporary local and national newspaper articles covering the days, weeks and months after the fire, and have relied on articles from *The Times* and *Guardian*, and occasional *Daily Mail, Sun* and, of course, *Daily Mirror* pieces. Perhaps unsurprisingly, the source of numerous articles was both Bradford's *Telegraph & Argus* and the Leeds-based *Yorkshire Post*. I also drew on documentary, panel discussion and live footage and news bulletins produced by Yorkshire Television, which were stored at the old West Yorkshire Archives in Bradford.

As regards the history of ground safety I drew on 1983's *The Football Grounds of England & Wales* by Simon Inglis, and Inglis's 1987's post-Bradford updated edition of *The Football Grounds of Great Britain,* as well as Phil Scraton's 1999 book *Hillsborough, The Truth*. Primarily, though, I sourced articles from contemporary copies of *The Times*, with a reliance on the *Nottingham Evening Post* for the 1968 City Ground fire, and articles from the *Guardian, Daily Telegraph, Daily Express, Daily Mirror* and even the *Financial Times* following the 1971 Ibrox disaster.

For information on Bradford City and Valley Parade, 1988's *A Game that Would Pay: A Business History of Professional Football in Bradford*, by the University of Essex's A. J. Arnold, and *Of Boars and Bantams: a Pictorial History and Club Record of Bradford City AFC* by D. R. Gillan, John Dewhirst, Tim Clapham and Keith Mellor, also from 1988, proved invaluable. As did, again, articles from contemporary copies of the *Telegraph & Argus*.

Regarding Stafford Heginbotham I also drew primarily on articles about this very public man from contemporary copies of Bradford's *Telegraph & Argus* over a thirty-year period, as well as from 1984–85 interviews featured in *The City Gent, the Book of Bantam Progressivism, an alternative view of Bradford City 1984–99* compiled by John Dewhirst and Richard Halfpenny.

For fire forensics I drew heavily from the very accessible (to a layman) *Blaze, the Forensics of Fire*, by Nicholas Faith, whose 1999 book was also a Channel 4 documentary. I also relied on professional trade magazines *Fire* and the *British Medical Journal*, and *Toy Trader* and *Soft Toys* with reference to the state of the British toy industry in 1985.

Finally, I must give personal thanks to the Politics and International Studies department at the University of Warwick who, through my undergraduate and postgraduate studies, provided me with the ability and confidence to take on a task of this magnitude.

A note on the diagram of the Main Stand: In addition to the inconsistencies mentioned in the text regarding the various layouts of Valley Parade's Main Stand and the existence of 'door R', it's worth noting the 'low wall' at the front of the stand was actually five feet high; the clubhouse was not exclusively the preserve of 'directors, officials and players' but also primarily welcomed Executive Club members; the wooden barrier at the back of the stand was closer to five feet high than four; and the width of the corridor at the rear of the stand is certainly not to scale – the diagram suggests it was comparable to three or four rows of seating; in reality it was no more than four feet wide, as is clearly visible in photographs of the smouldering ruins.